8 SPIRITUAL
HEROES

THEIR SEARCH FOR
GOD

BRENNAN R. HILL

ST. ANTHONY MESSENGER PRESS

Cincinnati, Ohio

Library of Congress Cataloging-in-Publication Data

Hill, Brennan.
 Eight spiritual heroes : their search for God / Brennan R. Hill.
      p. cm.
Includes bibliographical references and index.
 ISBN 0-86716-421-2 (pbk.)
 1. Spiritual life—Catholic Church. 2. Catholic Church—Biography.
I. Title.
 BX2350.65 .H55 2002
 200'.92'2—dc21

                    2002008492

PHOTO CREDITS

Mohandas Gandhi, *cover, p. 5:* AP/Wide World Photos.

Dorothy Day, *cover, p. 41:* Used with permission of Catholic News
 Service (CNS), courtesy of *Milwaukee Journal.*

Martin Luther King, Jr., *cover, p. 83:* Michael Evans/Getty Images.

Pierre Teilhard de Chardin, *cover, p. 119:* Copyright photo used with
 permission of Fondation Teilhard de Chardin, Paris, France.

Oscar Romero, *cover, p. 153;* Edith Stein, *cover, p. 191;* Daniel Berrigan,
 cover, p. 223; Mother Teresa, *cover, p. 255:* Used with permission of
 Catholic News Service (CNS).

Cover design by Mary Alfieri
Book design by Sandy L. Digman

ISBN 0-86716-421-2

Published by St. Anthony Messenger Press
www.AmericanCatholic.org

Printed in the U.S.A.

To a true hero,
MICHAEL LYNCH,
*a fireman who gave his life for others
in the World Trade Center,
September 11, 2001.*

*Blessings and courage for
the loved ones he left behind:
Denise,
Michael and Jack,
his parents,
sisters and brother.*

Contents

INTRODUCTION

When I started this book, my purpose was to explore the God experience and at the same time make some effort to restore the notion of hero. I have found that many of my students are familiar with celebrities, but few with heroes, especially religious heroes. They know sports figures, movie stars and rock singers. But they rarely know people who inspire their deeper longings or serve as godly role models.

Then came the catastrophe of September 11, 2001, and suddenly the news was filled with stories of true heroes: the hundreds of firefighters and police who rushed into the World Trade Center, only to be burned and pulverized by the implosion and collapse of the buildings; the man who stood by his wheelchair-bound buddy to the very end; the two men who carried a disabled woman—and her wheelchair—down eighty flights of steps to safety. And how could any of us forget the group on United flight 93, who courageously overpowered the terrorists and gave their lives to save many others. That horrible day brought with it countless stories of people who put the lives of others before their own. Throughout the nation, there was much talk of ultimate questions: God's presence and power, death, suffering, sin, forgiveness, the afterlife. The mysteries of God's providence were before us like never before.

Godly Heroes

The heroes we will meet in this book are of a different sort. Their heroism is not defined by a moment of super-human effort, but by a lifetime of deeply human faith. This kind of hero, the religious hero, lives out his or her faith in an outstanding manner. Each of these people experienced God so powerfully that their lives, and those of countless others, were forever changed. Each experienced God so uniquely that they expressed their faith unlike anyone else. We will examine the words and works of these heroes in order to trace the evolution of that God experience in their lives and witness its trans-forming effect.

We will become acquainted with a diverse group of people: an Indian Hindu, a German Jewish woman who converted to Christianity, an African American Baptist minister, an American woman who came to religion only after years of atheism, a Salvadoran archbishop, two Jesuit priests—one French, one American—and an Albanian nun. Not only are these selected people out-standing for the lives they led, but also they have written enough to give us some insight into their understanding and experience of God.

Biographical Theology

A novel kind of theology seems to emerge from this approach. It is a lived theology, a theology that comes out of experience and events. Like liberation theology, this is a "theology from below," a theology which comes from the heart and from action. As Mohandas Gandhi, one of the heroes in this book, would say, it is a theology that moves from truth to truth as we live our everyday lives.

We are indeed "religious critters." Theologian Karl Rahner, S.J., was right when he said that each of us has been created with a unique openness to God, a "supernatural existential," whereby we can search for and experience the divine. As noted theologian David Tracy pointed out, experience, events and culture revise our beliefs, and our faith can serve to revise our cultures.

We will see within this "biographical theology" new and exciting interpretations of religious traditions about the sacramental presence of a God within. We will learn from Gandhi as he prayerfully spins cotton thread on his wheel, and from Dorothy Day as she sits by the sea in wonder.

In the experiences of these people we will observe God's providence as the lives of such extraordinary people as Mother Teresa and Edith Stein are shaped by events. We will see the false gods of our society exposed by Daniel Berrigan and Oscar Romero. We will learn a new Christology from Teilhard de Chardin as he meets Jesus Christ in the cosmos. The title "child of God" will never be the same for us after we study Mother Teresa and Martin Luther King, Jr. We will learn a new ecclesiology from Dorothy Day and Oscar Romero, and we will rediscover the enormous treasure of prayer as it was lived and breathed by Mother Teresa and Edith Stein. Most importantly, we will discover a fresh new God of peace and justice as we watch nonviolence lived out so heroically by Gandhi, Day and Berrigan. We will not simply hear the Christian tradition on social justice, we will see how people like Romero and King have lived it and died for it.

—*Brennan R. Hill, Ph.D.*

CHAPTER ONE

The God of Truth

MOHANDAS GANDHI

In 1893 a young, well-groomed lawyer from India, dressed in a new suit, sat comfortably in the first-class car of a train bound for Pretoria, South Africa. He was en route to a client, hoping to establish himself in this country to which he had just immigrated. As the train reached the high mountain town of Maritzburg in the evening, a European entered the compartment, took one look at its dark-complexioned occupant, and left to inform the railway officials.

The lawyer was told that he would have to leave his seat and go to the third-class car where he "belonged."

Insisting that he had a ticket and, therefore, a right to be there, he refused to leave. The police were brought in; they tossed him off the train like a mailbag, his briefcase tumbling behind him. It was cold in the station that night, and his coat was being held along with the rest of his luggage, so all night he shivered and brooded in the waiting room. He was infuriated, but not so much by his personal experience, as with the notion that people could be persecuted because of the color of their skin or their social status. Now he knew what the "untouchables" back home in India must have felt!

Without realizing it, those railroad officials had lit a fire that night in the heart of Mohandas Gandhi, who would become one of the twentieth century's key figures in the struggle against prejudice and oppression. Gandhi had just felt the bitter lash of prejudice personally and, from that moment, he decided to be a force for the recovery of this religious truth: "We are all children of the same Creator.... We are one brotherhood and sisterhood...."[1] This was the beginning of intense struggle for recognition of human dignity, a tenacious resistance to prejudice and violence. Gandhi would gradually renounce his ambitions and search for God by working for human dignity.

Slow Starter

Gandhi got off to a slow start. Born in 1869, he was a poor student with a stutter and little interest in his family's religion. Though somewhat spoiled as the youngest child in a comfortable home supported by the chief minister for a maharajah, Gandhi was often teased and scorned by his classmates. Early on, he became quite shy and withdrawn—hardly the right stuff for a leader who would liberate his country from the British Empire!

Talk of God always seemed like fairy tales for the young man. His mother, a follower of the ancient Indian religion of Jainism, was saintly and deeply religious, always praying before meals and daily attending temple services. She taught Gandhi the value of fasting, making difficult religious vows and, most importantly, nonviolence (*ahimsa*). Later, these values would deeply mark Gandhi, but in his youth, none of them interested him. By his own testimony, young Gandhi was inclined "somewhat toward atheism." He generally avoided the Hindu temples, finding them to be places of "glitter and pomp." He resisted the dietary restrictions of his religion and did not take seriously Hindu rules forbidding the killing of snakes and bugs. At fifteen he experimented radically by eating meat and seemed to enjoy shocking his elders with his agnostic views.

In spite of his youthful resistance to religion, Gandhi liked to discuss different religions on an intellectual level, especially Jainism and Buddhism. From his religious training, he derived a strict morality from the start. He refused to cheat in school—even on one occasion when he was given permission by his teacher to do so in order to impress a school inspector. His flirtations with temptation were humorous. Once persuaded by an older friend to eat meat, he became nauseous and had a nightmare that a live goat was in his stomach. On another occasion, he was persuaded to go to a brothel only to sit dumbstruck on the bed and then be shown the door by the prostitute!

After high school, Gandhi was told by friends that

the best path to success would be to study law in England. His family resisted this, however, thinking that he would be corrupted by living in another culture, far from his family. He had been married by arrangement at thirteen to a child bride named Kasturbai, and his mother believed that if Gandhi were separated from his wife, it would destroy his marriage and ruin his life. Only when he vowed not to touch wine, women or meat did his mother consent to his travel to England. But, despite those vows, Gandhi still incurred the wrath of his religious elders. He was told that, should he go to England, he would be cursed by God and be viewed as an outcast among Hindus. Undeterred, Gandhi bought a steamer ticket, necktie, short jacket and enough sweets and fruits for the three-week journey, and departed for England. Though not yet eighteen, he had decided that the only way to be a respectable man was to walk away from Hinduism—with all its gods, goddesses and super-stitions—and become an English-speaking, cultured man of the world.

In the course of his law studies in England, Gandhi occasionally picked up religious texts. He began to read the *Bhagavad-Gita* (an important Hindu scripture) and was impressed with lessons that would mean much more to him later on. He was curious about the teaching that without God's grace, human effort was useless. He was moved by the readings on renunciation and self-lessness in action. The *Gita*'s lessons on the delusion of happiness attached to wealth and the need to control all his human drives impressed him. At the same time, he did not agree with the *Gita*'s approval of violence, and concluded that the stories that encouraged violence had to be allegorical and were not applicable to real life.

Also during this period, Gandhi began to read the Bible. Like many others before him, he took it up as a book to read from cover to cover, and lost interest somewhere between Leviticus and Numbers. He said that the Old Testament put him to sleep. Only later did he come to realize that the Scriptures are a whole library including books about the prophets, Psalms and writings on wisdom. He found the New Testament more interesting, and was fascinated by Jesus. Gandhi said that the Sermon on the Mount went straight to his heart. Jesus' advice to "turn the other cheek" delighted him, as did the Beatitudes.

Gandhi was beginning to believe that there is really one religion and that all people worship the same Creator under different names. He wrote: "But He is invisible and indefinable and, one might literally say that He has as many names as there are human beings on earth."[2] He believed that people choose to belong to some "branch" of the one religion but, no matter their choice, they all stand before God as equals.

Gandhi returned to India in his early twenties, and by that time he said that he had passed through the "Sahara of atheism." Though he was still quite worldly, Gandhi wanted to find out more about God and the religion in which he was raised, especially now that life was presenting him with more serious challenges. Upon his return to India, he learned that his mother had died. His wife was no longer a child, and he now had a four-year-old son.

It soon became clear that Mohandas was failing as a lawyer in India. He was timid, soft-spoken and often lost cases without uttering a word. On one occasion, he was sent by his brother, who had financed his studies in

England, to settle matters with a British agent. Gandhi made a firm effort to stand up to the agent, but ended up being physically thrown out the door. Gandhi said that this event changed the course of his life. He decided that he was not willing to pay the price of being a servile flatterer to get ahead. He rejected the petty intrigue and snobbery that surrounded his profession in India, and jumped at an opportunity to start over in South Africa. He set off dressed in a fashionable frock coat, pressed trousers, new shoes and a handsome turban.

A Turning Point

We have already seen how being thrown off a train into the cold night affected Gandhi's life. He would later describe it as the most "creative" experience of his life. He had discovered the hard way that his people, no matter how educated or well dressed, were still seen by the English as "coolies." He would no longer attempt to ape English respectability.

Soon after the train event, Gandhi was beaten and nearly pushed off a stagecoach for refusing to ride outside at the driver's feet. He continued to ask for rooms at hotels where he was not welcome. And he even bought more first-class train tickets! On some occasions he found people who were not prejudiced and gave him what he asked for. More often, though, he was abused and ejected.

Gandhi now renewed his religious reading in earnest. He returned to the *Gita* and meditated on giving his mind and soul to God. In his own words, Gandhi here describes the ideal that he was setting for himself:

...[A] devotee who is jealous of none, who is a fount of mercy, who is without egotism, who is selfless, who treats alike cold and heat, happiness and misery, who is ever forgiving, who is always contented, whose resolutions are firm, who has dedicated mind and soul to God, who causes no dread, who is not afraid of others, who is free of exultation, sorrow and fear, who is pure, who is versed in action yet remains unaffected by it, who renounces all fruit, good or bad, who treats friend and foe alike, who is untouched by respect or disrespect, who is not puffed up by praise, who does not go under when people speak ill of him, who loves silence and solitude, who has a disciplined reason.[3]

Just a little over a year after he had been thrown from the train, Gandhi was beginning to organize resistance to the discrimination against his people in South Africa. In 1894 he established the Indian National Congress, made appeals to the government against discriminatory laws, gave numerous speeches, called for reform on tax legislation and lobbied the Indian Congress to help his people in South Africa. He was kicked off footpaths and sidewalks, attacked by mobs and beaten, but steadfastly refused to return violence and did not even prosecute his assailants.

Gandhi continued his voracious reading and was deeply influenced by authors such as Russian novelist and historian Leo Tolstoy and British essayist and reformer John Ruskin. Gandhi was fascinated by Ruskin's ideas on how riches are at the heart of inequality and power over others. He was moved deeply by the author's call for simplicity, his praise of the life of physical labor, especially farm work and crafts. And he was profoundly moved by Ruskin's call for the rich to follow Jesus and abstain from luxuries until all have enough. Gandhi said that this reading was a turning point in his life and brought him to decide to move to a farm with his family and followers.

Gandhi said that he most vividly experienced God in his heroes, whether they were famous people or the untouchables in the gutter. Gandhi's admiration for such people convinced him that he had to live more simply. The detachment recommended by Ruskin, however, was elusive. Gandhi's law practice in Johannesburg had become quite lucrative, and he was living a comfortable life in an English villa at the beach. He had forced his family to wear Western clothes and even to use knives and forks at meals. At the same time, he was beginning to practice constraint. He established a notable simplicity for himself and his family: a strict diet, natural cures of ailments, no running water and no untouchable servants to carry out the chamber pots. On one occasion, when his family was presented with expensive gifts, he insisted that the items be returned.

In 1904 he bought a farm and established the Phoenix Settlement, a hundred acres outside of Durban, where he put up corrugated iron huts and set up shop. Here he could live a much simpler life, close to the soil. In 1906 he took a vow of lifelong celibacy in an effort to discipline his desires and dedicate all his energies to the service of God and God's children. He continued to support himself by doing legal work for his fellow Indians from his law office in Johannesburg.

The Search for Truth

Gandhi began to study the Bible in more depth, and searched the Koran for religious truth. He loved Jesus, and kept in his hut a print of him with the words, "He is our peace." It is said that in later years during a visit to Rome, Gandhi saw Michelangelo's painting of the crucifixion and was moved to tears. When asked about his religion, Gandhi would say: "I am a Christian, and a Hindu, a Moslem and a Jew."[4]

Gandhi held that there was only one religion in essence, but that there were many branches. Just as all branches take their sap from one source in the tree, all religions derive their essence from one source. Historically, many different religions and sects have emerged because no tradition and "no individual can be the exclusive receptacle of boundless Truth."[5] Gandhi studied other religions in order to grasp the "unity of religions and find the universal and absolute truth that lies beneath the 'dust of creeds.'"[6]

Gandhi believed that each religion articulated a unique vision of God and emphasized different attributes of the divine. He felt that Christianity uniquely presented God as a loving parent and emphasized universal love, forgiveness and uncomplaining suffering. Islam presented a rigorous monotheism, rejected intermediaries between God and humans and emphasized equality. Hinduism made clear distinctions between the personal and impersonal conceptions of God, uniquely emphasized detachment from the world while being active in it. Its contribution was teaching the unity of all life and the importance of nonviolence.

For Gandhi, religion was more than worshipping God. In the larger sense, religion should lead us to self-realization, to the discovery of truth in the self, and there to meet "the all pervading Spirit of truth that is in all."[7] The very purpose of life, according to Gandhi, was to know oneself. Gandhi's search for truth would be a ceaseless effort to understand himself and his destiny and to become perfect. He was fully aware, however, that he would never find this truth perfectly. Gandhi always humbly admitted: "I am painfully conscious of my imperfections."[8] To find the truth, Gandhi believed, we must identify ourselves with everything that lives. He wrote: "To see the universal and all-pervading Spirit of Truth face to face one must love the meanest of creation as oneself. And a man who aspires after that cannot afford to keep out of any field of life."[9] For him, God was the sum total of all life.

Lived Truth

Gandhi was much more concerned with how a person lived than with what a person believed. He much preferred an active and lived faith to what he described as the "dead bones of dogmas."[10] Thus, morality—not theology—was the core of religion. He once mentioned his admiration of two friends who gave up theology to live the gospel.[11]

The truth was always vitally important in Gandhi's life. As we saw earlier, his personal experience with prejudice moved him to be firmly committed to the cause of equality. Following that humiliation, he called meetings of Indians so that he could give them a clear picture of their unjust condition. By this time, it was his belief that God was in everyone, and that an offense against people was a sin against God. He reminded his audience that they were "children of God," and that no one had a right to treat them unjustly. Here was a shy lawyer of twenty-four, reminding his people to live up to their God-given dignity, advising them to tell the truth in business, adopt sanitary living habits, dress properly and give up caste and religious divisions.

Gandhi was deeply concerned about justice for his people. The Indians had come to South Africa in the mid–nineteenth century as indentured serfs. Many of them were untouchables who came to avoid starvation in India. Many other Indians followed this immigration and acquired riches and property living off their own fellow Indians. During Gandhi's time in South Africa there were serious controversies about the right to vote, heavy taxes on the serfs, the right to own property, the need to carry passes on the street, and even the right to walk on footpaths and sidewalks. Gandhi's interventions resulted in much opposition and even hatred from many whites. He was kicked, stoned, beaten and nearly lynched. In the face of all this abuse, he cheerfully carried on and refused to return in kind. He even refused to prosecute his assailants, saying: "This is a religious question with me."

Those around Gandhi were increasingly amazed at how easily he forgave those who abused him. A certain greatness was becoming more apparent in this little man, yet he remained humble. He believed that he was an ordinary man with extraordinary goals given to him by God. Gandhi began to use powerful imagery about his call. He said that he was but a spark from the divine fire, a drop from the divine ocean, a ray of light from the divine sun. It was from this God that he received his energy and power. No matter what the setbacks or dangers, Gandhi felt that God was always with him:

> If I am journeying Godward, as I feel I am, it is safe with me. For I feel the warmth of the sunshine of His presence. My austerities, fastings and prayers are, I know, of no value, if I rely upon them for reforming me. But they have an inestimable value, if they represent, as I hope they do, the yearnings of a soul striving to lay his weary head in the lap of his Maker.[12]

Inner Voices

Gandhi continued his pressure on the railway authorities and made them promise that Indians could travel first- or second-class. He worked for his people for a year and then prepared to return to his family in India. At his farewell party, he was asked to stay one more month to help the Indian people to fight to keep their vote. As always, Gandhi listened to his "inner voices from God" for direction. He wrote: "For me the Voice was more real than my own existence. It has never failed me, and for that matter, anyone else."[13] It had become clear to him that he was called to stay in the struggle to regain his peoples' God-given dignity and rights. His fellow Indians, like all humans, were children of God. This was the truth, plain and simple, and Gandhi was willing to suffer a great deal to see to it that the truth be told. He somehow knew that the hand of God was on him in a special way. He was determined to "follow His will and no other," and give his all, and "leave the result to God."[14] After a short stay in India, he returned to South Africa and remained there for twenty more years.

Desirelessness

Gandhi was an ardent seeker of "desirelessness," which he believed to be the path to union with "the Supreme," the way to see God in all things and all things in God. An American journalist once asked Gandhi if he could reveal the secret of his life in three words. Gandhi, always the gracious respondent, smiled and said: "Renounce and enjoy!" His goal was to simplify his desires, for he was convinced that desires kept us from God. He was determined to follow other religious leaders like Buddha and Christ in a life of self-sacrifice and renunciation in order to gain true happiness, which he could in turn share with the world. Along with Buddha, he believed that our desires are at the root of the suffering that we bring upon ourselves and inflict on others. In his autobiography, he points out the importance of spiritual discipline: "To develop the spirit is to build character and to enable one to work towards a knowledge of God and self-realization."[15] Gandhi disciplined his desires, even to the extent that he gave up sexual pleasure in his own marriage. He found that the less he possessed, the less he wanted and the better he was. But he did not see this as being better for enjoying life, but rather being better able to serve his fellow beings with his whole body, soul and mind.

Gandhi used to quote Krishna from the *Gita* on sacrifice: "He lives in wisdom who sees himself in all and all in him, whose love for the Lord of Love has consumed every selfish desire and sense craving tormenting the heart."[16] Renunciation meant not being selfishly attached to anything— family, money, power or possessions. His experience in giving up as much as he could was that he never wanted for basic needs like food, shelter or financial support. On the other hand, he said that this opened the way for God to make new demands on him. Gandhi said that God never let him down amidst these challenges. He wrote:

> God is the hardest task-master I have known on this earth, and He tries you through and through. And when you find that your faith is failing or your body is failing you and you are sinking, He comes to your assistance somehow or other.... He is always at your beck and call, but on His terms, not on your terms. So I have found, I cannot recall a single instance when, at the eleventh hour, He has forsaken me.[17]

Gandhi taught his followers to rely on God's goodness. He often said "there is plenty for our need, but not enough for our greed."[18]

Renunciation also meant not worrying about the desired result of our actions. Gandhi held that all one can do is act rightly with pure motive and then leave the rest to God. He taught that such detachment prevents the frustration, insecurity or even despair that so often envelops us when we fail.[19]

Soul Force

The tension between the Indians and the government of South Africa grew stronger, as General Jan Smuts enforced compulsory registration and strict immigration laws. Gandhi now had a large following, not only of Indians, but also of Europeans who shared his indignation over racial prejudice and who were willing to support his movement with money.

Gandhi now developed passive resistance into

satyagraha, also referred to as "soul force." He organized a mass movement of civil disobedience, which included deliberately breaking laws, general strikes, mass meetings where registration cards were burned and overcrowding of the jails. Repeatedly, Gandhi himself was arrested and put in prison. Each time he was released, he would return to his ashram (a place where he could detach himself from worldly pleasures and pursue his deep desire to be more godly) and continue to organize his movement, at times making trips to England to rally support for his cause.

In all this, Gandhi taught his followers to never return violence or give anyone power over their spirits. Eventually, General Smuts found himself fighting to defend laws that had no public support, and he was forced to sign the "Magna Carta" of South African Indians. It was said, "Victory came to Gandhi not when Smuts had no more strength to fight him, but when he had no more heart to fight him."[20] Smuts later unwittingly summed up the spirit of *satyagraha*:

> It was my fate to be the antagonist of a man for whom even then I had the highest respect.... He never forgot the human background of the situation, never lost his temper or succumbed to hate, and preserved his gentle humor even in the most trying situations. His manner and spirit even then, as well as later, contrasted markedly with the ruthless and brutal forcefulness which is the vogue in our day.[21]

The victory for people of color in South Africa would be short-lived, but Gandhi had shown the power of passive resistance. Gandhi would move on to India in 1914 and work there for the next thirty-four years.

It was soon after his arrival home in India that

Gandhi established a rural ashram. This did not mean, though, that Gandhi was going to isolate himself. Instead, life in the ashram represented a deeper commitment to simplicity, identification in dress and lifestyle with the untouchables, and renewed search for the truth about himself, his world and his God, so that he could vigorously and actively bring truth to the world. Here he would have time to open himself to the God force and energize himself for the struggle for freedom for his people.

Gandhi said that God was a mystery beyond the power of reason. He wrote: "The Reality we call God is a mysterious, indescribable and unique power. If we cannot comprehend Him with our mind, how can our poor speech describe Him?"[22] For Gandhi, reason was incapable of grasping the reality of God:

> He is smaller than an atom and bigger than the Himalayas: he is contained even in a drop of the ocean, and yet not even the seven seas can compass Him. ...[God] is beyond the reach or grasp of reason.[23]

Gandhi was deeply aware of human limitations, and that humans cannot solve the mysteries of the universe because they are not God. He wrote: "If we could solve all the mysteries of the Universe we would be equal with God. Every drop of ocean shares its glory but is not the ocean."[24] Human beings partake of the nature of God but they not God.

If asked the perennial question "Who is God?" Gandhi would answer that God was not some person outside ourselves and away from the universe. Rather, God pervades everything and is omnipresent as well as omnipotent. For Gandhi, God was a being immanent in all being—one who hears everything and reads our innermost thoughts. He once said that God "abides in our heart and is nearer to us than the nails are to our fingers."[25]

Generally, Gandhi did not ascribe personal images to God. He was uncomfortable with images like "ruler" or "king" for God because such images often engender fear, which he held could negate the practice of authentic virtue. He once said, "God is not a person.... God is eternal principle. That is why I say that Truth is God...."[26] For Gandhi, the law of life was a living law of nonviolence, compassion and love, the law of Truth. The living law and the Lawgiver were the same reality.

At times, however, Gandhi was not always consistent in resisting personal images of God. He was known to refer to God as the parent of the whole creation, as friend, mother and father. As mentioned earlier, he once made the touching remark that in troubled times he would put his head in God's lap. He wryly observed that for those who need God to be personal, God will indeed be personal. Gandhi was always open to new insights and could change his mind. He said he agreed with American essayist Ralph Waldo Emerson that foolish consistency is the hobgoblin of little minds.

God Is Truth

As we said earlier, Gandhi's central image for God was truth. Early in his search for God, he identified the goal of life with truth itself. Eventually, as he moved deeper into the truth of himself and his world, he changed the formulation and said "Truth is God." He wrote,

"But that has been my pole star all along during life's journey—the conviction that Truth is God and untruth is a denial of him."[27] For him, truth was the very essence of God, and every relative truth was somehow a reflection of the ever-present God. Lies and distortions of the truth were thus comparable to atheism.

Gandhi's word for truth was *satya*, which is derived from the word *sat* ("to be"). Gandhi in turn saw God as "that which is," as opposed to everything else we sense that will not last. He saw God to be the only "true" reality, the only reality that pervades everything, the one being that will endure. God is the reality that cannot be seen, reasoned toward, or defined. God is the basis of all order, the unalterable law governing everything that exists. The divinity is the reality which pervades all, and which will never change or die. Gandhi wrote:

> I do dimly perceive that whilst everything around me is ever changing, ever dying, there is underlying all that change a living Power that is changeless, that holds all together, that creates, dissolves and recreates. That informing Power or Spirit is God. In the midst of death, life persists; in the midst of untruth, truth persists; in midst of darkness light persists. Hence I gather that God is Life, Truth, and love. He is the supreme Good.[28]

Gandhi said the truth always comes to us "on the feet of doves," unannounced and in stillness. To discover it, one must live with the facts and events of everyday life and be ready for its sudden coming.[29] His life was a vigorous search to discover the truth about himself as well as the truth of the world around him. As he uncovered the truth about prejudice, violence, injustice, greed and dishonesty, Gandhi's mission was to be a truth teller, to shout the truth from the rooftops and to then take action to regain honesty and goodness for the world around him.

As mentioned earlier, Gandhi always began with himself in his search for truth. He worked constantly to root out egotism, which he believed puts a barrier between God and ourselves. He was known for his humility, and though determined in his views, he never laid claim to infallibility or superiority. He held strong beliefs, but not dogmas. He was firmly committed to being honest in his speech and his actions, believing that to be the path to the God of Truth. He often disarmed his listeners with his candor about past blunders, including how he had mistreated his own wife, Kasturbai. He once pointed out that her patience with his abuse had helped him greatly in his understanding of the power of nonviolence.

People began to call him Mahatma, meaning "Great Soul," a title with which he was never comfortable. There are many stories that demonstrate that Gandhi never took himself too seriously. At the height of his fame, when visiting London to discuss Indian independence, he insisted on living in the East End with the poor. In the morning he would walk in the neighborhoods chatting with the people and visiting their simple houses. The children would run up to him, hold his hand and call him "Uncle Gandhi." On one occasion, a young lad yelled out, "Hey Gandhi, where's your trousers?" Gandhi roared with laughter. Neither was he ever embarrassed, even in court, by his simple attire. He once said: "You people wear plus-fours, mine are minus fours," and when asked if he thought he had enough on when he went before royalty in his loincloth, he answered, "The King had enough on for both of us."[30]

The use of "cover-ups" and "damage control" so prevalent today had no place in Gandhi's career. He openly admitted his limitations, mistakes and failures. He said that some of his errors in judgment in dealing with the British were so huge they could be called "Himalayan." At his trial for sedition in India, he totally disarmed the judge by declaring that he was guilty on all charges and he should be given the maximum penalty for his actions. Gandhi relentlessly followed what he felt to be the true dictates of his conscience in all matters. He was wary of religious and political dogmas, always wanting to maintain a detached and flexible individuality and the freedom to go through life "without a map." His own open and free search for the truth of self would be the only way to discover God. He said: "Everyone has faith in himself and that multiplied to the nth degree is God."[31]

Gandhi believed that God was the divine essence, the living force that pervaded the entire universe. His views sound like those of Native American Chief Seattle who said, "All the earth belongs to God.... Like the earth we, of it, also belong to God."[32] Gandhi discovered truth not only in himself but also in others. He held that a living faith in God meant acceptance of a brotherly and sisterly relationship with every human being. Truth, for him, was identified with discovering God as uniquely appearing in each individual. This, as we shall see later was his basis of nonviolence. To harm another was to harm God.

Gandhi, much like another saint of India, Mother Teresa, was uniquely gifted to recognize God in the poorest of the poor. He believed that God comes to us in the form of the poor and has a special preference for them. He once said: "The poor have their savior in God."[33] Gandhi could see the truth of God shining through the eyes of outcasts when they smiled in gratitude for his kindness to them. He recognized God in the fellow prisoners crowded around him in the interminable prison sentences given to him in South Africa and India. In South Africa, he found the truth in quiet hope in his listeners in rallies for human rights. He had seen the truth in the suffering victims of the Boer War and the Zulu Rebellion. God came to him in the intense peacefulness of Kasturbai, who was always by his side, saying little but in solidarity with his mission. The truth of God glistened in the eyes of the many villagers who came out to him with hope in their hearts as he walked on his famous Salt March to the Indian Ocean in 1930. Nehru once said that the picture of Gandhi on the march was the most dominant in his memory. "Here was the pilgrim on his quest for Truth, quiet, peaceful, determined, and fearless, who would continue that quest and that pilgrimage, regardless of the consequences."[34] God was to be experienced in the broken bodies of his people as they were beaten for their march on the Dharasana Salt Works.

Gandhi also tried to see God even in his opponents, and was often able to bring the best out of them. As we have seen, General Smuts, who was persistently resisted by Gandhi for his brutal treatment of the Indians in South Africa grew to admire Gandhi. Years after Gandhi left that area, Smuts movingly returned a pair of sandals that Gandhi had made for him, saying that he was not worthy to wear them. Louis Mountbatten, the last British viceroy of India grew to have deep respect for Gandhi, and after Gandhi's death said: "Mahatma

Gandhi will go down in history on a par with Buddha and Jesus Christ."[35]

The Untouchables

One of the first issues Gandhi addressed in India was that of "untouchability." This doctrine arose not from the tyranny of colonialism, but from his own Hindu religion. The untouchables were the lowest caste or social class—those thought to be punished for sins of their past lives. They were thought to be cursed outcasts and were not permitted to enter the temple, or the homes or shops of other castes. They were forced to live in the lowest outskirts and slums and were completely shunned by other castes for fear of being polluted or cursed themselves.

Gandhi had never agreed with this doctrine. As a child, he rebelled against his mother's commands and played with untouchables. Gandhi came to believe that untouchables shared in divine energy, and much to the dismay of many of his fellow Hindus, he affectionately called these outcasts *harijans* (children of God). In South Africa he took up their cause, and in India he organized meetings to discuss untouchability and invited the outcasts to come. On one occasion, when he was about to deliver his address he said: "Is there an untouchable here?" When he saw that none had been allowed to enter, Gandhi displayed his characteristic obstinacy—he sat down and refused to speak! There was a principle—a truth—here on which he had to insist. Indians could not hope to struggle for freedom from the oppression of the British if their own religion was depriving their own people of their rights. How could they resist the British belief that all Indians were untouchables, if the Indians themselves were rejecting some of their own? How could Hindus accuse the British of being unfaithful to the commandments of God if they were just as hypocritical?

Gandhi's life demonstrated that the path to the truth led up a steep slope, and the march was not for the faint of heart. Only the brave—those willing to undergo suffering and even death—could achieve truth. There would be little room for self-interest here. His followers would be expected to accept brutal beatings, deprivation, imprisonment and even death to expose the lie of oppression and bring to bear the truth of freedom. Such suffering, he held, was "therapeutic" when accepted for the sake of the truth, for it helped us gain valuable knowledge about ourselves and our own capacities. Gandhi also saw a redemptive power to suffering, in that it somehow has the power to provide "healing" for ourselves and those around us. Courageous suffering and truthful action was the only way to God.

For Gandhi himself, such action would bring humiliation, beatings and countless days in overcrowded and smelly jail cells. The time spent in his many jail visits was the equivalent of nearly seven years of his life. He passed these endless days with just his thoughts, books and prayers, never ceasing his search for truth. Often he suffered hunger during the long days of his fasting, to do penance for those inflicting pain and to persuade violent people to stop their brutality. Such brave and long-suffering actions were integral in his search for the truth. He wrote: "I have grown from truth to truth."[36]

For Gandhi truth and love were inseparable. Truth

was the very essence of God and was reflected in all things, and the only way to truth was through the love of all things. "And when you want to find Truth as God, the only evitable means is love.... God is love,"[37] and this would be Gandhi's basis for having intense compassion and love for all things and all people, and for abhorring violence in any form. It was the reason why he embraced all of creation, dedicated himself to the freedom and dignity of his people, and sacrificed everything, including his life, for the poor. They were where he found his God:

> I know I cannot find Him apart from humanity...I claim I know my millions. All the hours of the day I am with them. They are my first care and last because I recognize no God except the God that is found in the hearts of the dumb millions.[38]

All forms of prejudice, hatred and violence were seen by Gandhi to be negations of love and denials of truth. They denied the existence of God in life—the equivalent of atheism—and killed hope, which Gandhi believed was the inevitable result of atheism.

Gandhi was not only a truth seeker, he was a truth teller. Once he found the truth, he would shout it from the rooftops no matter how much it angered those caught up in lies and oppression. He was relentless in his struggle to speak out for the have-nots. He spoke his truth in the courts, at countless meetings, in speeches, in numerous letters and articles, in personal consultations with people from all over the world who sought him out, and he tirelessly protested the injustices done to his people and proposed a new way of freedom.

Some of the most memorable images of Gandhi are from his visit to London for the Round Table Conference to consider his proposals for Indian independence. Members of Parliament and other British notables came to the meeting armed with boxes of materials and teams of advisors. Gandhi showed up with a wrinkled manila folder. The truth was in his head and his heart, and it had come to him after years of study, experience and prayer. He knew the real truth, and he believed that this truth would make his people free because it had its source in God.

At one point, the English were becoming frustrated with this little man from India, and decided to catch him off-guard by having a huge birthday party for him, with a cake and many presents. At the height of the party, the guests asked Gandhi to say a few words. In one of his finest speeches, Gandhi began to list the atrocities the English had perpetrated against his people over several centuries, and pointed out that their occupation of his country had been a curse. As the room grew ever more silent, he stated that clearly the only solution was for the British to leave his country forever. The party ended rather abruptly that night, and no doubt, there were some whisperings about the proverbial "skunk at the garden party."

Gandhi was a man of action and often said that action was more important than doctrine. He could never comprehend the idea of salvation through faith alone. Only genuine action for the poor could reveal the true and loving God. God comes to us only in action: "To a people famishing and idle, the only acceptable form in which God can dare appear is work and promise of food and wages."[39] His God was constantly in action in the world, and service to the deity meant joining in this tireless endeavor. Gandhi often used the ocean as an image for God, and saw our activity as being part of the great movement of God's endeavor. Erik Erikson observed, in his psychological study of Gandhi, that in spite of living in an ashram, Gandhi never believed in withdrawal from the world. He ardently believed that the measure of a person is her or his creative action.[40] Toward the end of his life, some friends told Gandhi that he should think of retiring. He laughed as he said:

> There can be no rest for me so long as there is a single person in India whether man or woman, young or old, lacking the necessaries of life, by which I mean a sense of security, a lifestyle worthy of human beings.[41]

Nonviolence

Gandhi lived through two World Wars, the Boer War, the Zulu Rebellion and many bloody conflicts between the Moslems and Hindus of his country. As we have seen, he himself suffered physical abuse. Yet, never did Gandhi return in kind or act out of revenge or hatred. Nonviolence was central to Gandhi's way of life, as well as to his protests for justice. Throughout his life he perfected nonviolence as a powerful tool for gaining justice. His insight and example have deeply influenced other leaders, including Martin Luther King, Jr., Cesar Chavez, Dorothy Day and many other advocates for social justice. It is rather ironic that Gandhi, a Hindu, was in part influenced in nonviolence by Jesus, and then passed on his lessons to a Baptist minister (King), a Catholic migrant worker (Chavez) and a Catholic advocate for the poor (Day). This circle of great leaders certainly endorses the validity of the nonviolent perspective.

For Gandhi, God could only be envisioned and reached through truth. Gandhi believed that truth and nonviolence were inseparable. For him, all existence mirrored the divine, so any violence was a blasphemous repudiation of the deity. "If all souls are sparks of the divine, rooted in transcendental Truth, all violence is a species of deicide."[42] The God of truth could only be reached through nonviolent action carried out in compassion, love and forgiveness.

Gandhi was consistent in his demand for *ahimsa* throughout his life, although there was a decided progression in his understanding and techniques. Gandhi in his younger years somehow believed that if he played the English game, things would change. He had tried that with his education, dress and lifestyle. The train incident was a traumatic setback, but Gandhi still believed in the "system" and remained loyal to it. During the Boer War, he remained loyal to the British Crown, and in 1899 led an ambulance corps of three hundred Indians, who carried the wounded under enemy fire and sometimes walked twenty-five miles a day. For this, he won a medal.

After the Boer War, Gandhi continued his efforts to oppose the South African government's efforts to either take away Indian rights or drive the "coolie Asian cancer" out of the country. But still he remained loyal to the British, and when the Zulus rebelled in 1906 he organized stretcher-bearers. In the ensuing slaughter, Gandhi saw what the British did to rebels. He and his men ended up helping the sick and dying Zulus, many of whom had been flogged until their skin hung in strips. Gandhi won another medal for his service, but he was never proud to wear it.

After the horrible massacre at Amritsar in 1919, Gandhi's loyalty to the Crown collapsed. On this occasion, the infamous General Dyer marched on a large group of Indians who had gathered for a peaceful meeting, and opened fire on them in what has been called a turkey shoot. Over a thousand Indians were killed and wounded. Gandhi realized that the British would sink to any depth of brutality to maintain control over India. He returned the medals he had received in the past wars for serving the wounded.

This massacre strengthened Gandhi's resolve, and he began a strong *ahimsa* campaign against the British. He toured the country with the poor in filthy, third-class railroad cars, held mass meetings and fasted for extended periods to protest the violence on both sides and bolster the flagging resolve of his people. Gandhi insisted that the British system be attacked, not with force, but with "the energy of God."

As World War II approached, Gandhi was horrified at the brutality of Hitler, Mussolini and Stalin. Though he gave moral support to the Allies, Gandhi would not participate in this war in any way. In one of his respectful but truth-telling letters, he wrote to U. S. President Roosevelt, pointing out how hollow it sounded to be fighting to make the world safe for democracy, when the British were exploiting so many people in India and Africa and when there was so much oppression of the Negroes in America! Gandhi continued to speak out against the evil of killing. He maintained that inequality was at the root of violence, and that only equality would bring with it peace and happiness.

Gandhi taught his followers that their training for nonviolence must begin with a living faith in God. He wrote:

> He who has a living faith in God will not do evil deeds with the name of God on his lips. He will not rely on the sword but will rely solely on God.... He alone is a man of God who sees to God in every soul.[43]

Genuine truth identifies God with all humans and does not allow that anyone be harmed. Gandhi always maintained that punishment should be left up to God.

He encouraged his people to strenuously continue noncooperation. Students left their studies, professionals quit good jobs in the cities and went to the villages to teach literacy and noncooperation. People refused to pay their taxes. Gandhi encouraged his people to spin their own cloth and not buy foreign goods and to defy the rigid salt laws that brought so much revenue to the government at the expense of the people. He urged every Indian soldier to resign from the military and the police, so that they would no longer be part of the government's oppression of the Indians. He asked his people to stop all cooperation with the government. Tens of thousands were flogged and jailed.

Gandhi insisted that nonviolence was not passivity, but a strong force within. He said this soul force could be equated with knowing God. Once one knows God, one is incapable of feeling or harboring anger or fear, no matter how daunting the enemy. Gandhi abhorred killing, and would chide his own people about how they worry about not killing cows, when at the same time they are killing each other with their greed. He maintained that we have no right to destroy life that we did not and cannot create. And he pointed out that we cannot hope to seek and realize God if we kill others who are seekers after truth. Gandhi insisted that killing was such a horrible evil that he would rather be killed than to have to kill another.

But *ahimsa* went beyond "not killing." It also ruled out evil thoughts, lies and hatred. It required an active love and an equal consideration for all living things. Soul force does not seek revenge, but prays for the change of heart for the opponent. It also is prepared to bear any injury from the opponent, but bravely and with a smile, not in a spirit of cowardice or helplessness. Gandhi believed that *ahimsa* could melt the stoniest of hearts, and demonstrated this himself so many times, as he "converted" judges, generals, viceroys and even hardened reporters.

Gandhi was a realist and knew that in spite of his *ahimsa*, violence would remain in the world. Yet, he insisted that violence comes from humans and not from God. That is not to say that he never had his daily quarrel with God about the violence constantly around him. He would wonder if God were cruel, and even if God had failed; but he would always return to the truth that we humans are the ones who fail. It was his conviction that no person can stop the violence—only God could do this. Only God's grace can put an end to violence, and yet God uses people as instruments to end the violence and bring about the peace.

Use of Symbol

Gandhi had a deep understanding of the "sacramental principle," and believed that God comes to us in symbols. He also had a keen sense of timing for integrating such symbols into his soul force. In 1921 he set aside Western clothes and would for the rest of his life wear only a loincloth, the dress of the poor, of the untouchables. Now he was one with the millions, dressing, eating and living simply in total solidarity with the poor. In this image, Gandhi could teach his people as well as their oppressors, the truth—that quiet dignity and godliness which exists in the poor. With this simple garment, he also could reveal the centuries-old beauty of the ancient Indian traditions, which had been mocked and suppressed by the British occupation. The truth of God could be loudly professed in a simple homespun loincloth.

Spinning Wheel. Centuries before British control, the people of the Indian villages had proudly spun their own yarn and made their own clothes. The East India Company, and then the British Empire, had destroyed the village culture, and required that the Indians buy only garments imported from England. This was one of the means the British used to take away the skills and independence of the Indians.

Gandhi restored the spinning wheel to Indian life as a symbol of their great culture and independence. He asked his people to spin their own yarn, make their own clothes and refuse to buy foreign material or garments. From time to time, he would build huge bonfires, where Indians could publicly burn their foreign-made clothes.

Not only was this a brilliant symbol of the power in his people, it was also quite effective in seriously damaging the British fabric and clothing business.

The spinning wheel became one of Gandhi's "sacraments," symbolizing the truth among his people: their dignity, their independence and their power to gain their God-given freedom. Gandhi himself would spin each day, and would wear only homespun garments. He found that the rhythm of spinning was in harmony with the mantra "*rama, rama*" (God forgive), and could easily turn one's mind Godward. Spinning also became a powerful symbol of soul force and Gandhi would wear his homespun garments into the high courts, the offices of the viceroys, and even into the royal court in London. The symbol certainly was not lost on Winston Churchill. He hated Gandhi, was infuriated by what he stood for and wanted to see him destroyed. Churchill once ranted about the "nauseating and humiliating spectacle of this one-time Inner Temple lawyer, now seditious fakir [an Indian monk], striding half-naked up the steps of the Viceroy's palace, there to negotiate and to parley on equal terms with the representative of the King-Emperor."[44]

Salt. Salt would become another one of Gandhi's "sacraments." In 1930 Gandhi, along with the Indian Congress, had prepared a Declaration of Independence from Britain and had sent it to British Viceroy Irwin. When there was no response, Gandhi decided it was time for a symbolic action. After much prayer and discernment, he came upon a powerful symbol of independence: salt. Indians were not allowed to extract their own salt, and had to depend on the heavily taxed salt sold to them by the British.

Gandhi decided it was time for some truth telling along with some action. He reminded the viceroy of the many taxes that were being inflicted on the people, especially the tax on salt. He respectfully reminded Irwin that the viceroy's income was five thousand times what the average Indian makes per year and that the system that supports such an injustice "deserves to be summarily scrapped."[45] Gandhi warned that he was about to begin a massive movement of civil disobedience to combat such evils. Irwin chose not to reply.

On March 12 Gandhi finished singing prayers with his followers, took up a bamboo hiking pole and set off for a two-hundred-mile walk "in the name of God." The British at first ridiculed the march, but as Gandhi was greeted along the way to the sea by crowds of commoners strewing flowers at his feet, it became clear that something "dangerous" was going on. Gandhi arrived at the Indian Ocean after twenty days of walking, defiantly took salt in his hands and encouraged his followers to ignore the salt laws. Gandhi was arrested and imprisoned. While he was in jail, twenty-five hundred of his followers made a nonviolent march on the Dharasana Salt Works. This became one of the most dramatic examples of passive resistance, and demonstrated how well Gandhi had taught and disciplined his people in the art of *ahimsa*. Webb Miller, a well-known reporter, reported the gory details to the world. Wave after wave approached the barbed-wire fence and were savagely beaten on their heads and shoulders with steel-tipped clubs. The area was strewn with broken bodies and the air was filled with loud cries of pain. Not a blow was returned.

After that event, the viceroy asked to meet with Gandhi and offered concessions. That fall, Gandhi would go to London to visit King George V, Queen Mary, and Prime Minister David Lloyd George, and to take part in the Round Table Conference with British officials. There would still be sixteen more years of struggle, but it was becoming evident that this "half-naked fakir" would not stop his efforts until India was free from British rule.

Prayer and Fasting. Prayer and fasting were also integral to Gandhi's spiritual program. He taught that prayer was "the key of the morning and the bolt of the evening," the necessary food for the soul. He encouraged his followers to pray in silence with "words of the heart," rather than word of the mouth.[46] Daily he would gather his followers for communal prayer, and would ask them to pray for the well-being of all God's creatures. It was his conviction that the only way to attain the strength to carry on in their difficult mission was to meditate upon God morning and evening.

It was while Gandhi was on his way to one of his evening prayer services that the end of his life came suddenly and tragically. He was stopped by a young Hindu who was angered at Gandhi's tolerance toward Muslims. The young man feigned a tribute, and then pulled out a small pistol and fired three bullets into the seventy-eight-year-old Gandhi's chest. Gandhi raised his hand in a gesture of forgiveness and with the mantra that was often on his lips, he murmured, *"Rama, rama, rama"* ("I forgive you, I love you, I bless you"). He then fell into unconsciousness and died. Some time before, he had written these prophetic words:

Have I the nonviolence of the brave in me? My death alone will show that. If someone killed me and I died with prayer for the assassin on my lips, and God's remembrance and consciousness of His living presence in the sanctuary of my heart, then alone would I be said to have the nonviolence of the brave.[47]

Gandhi had been so gifted. Now, this extraordinary man, who had spent his entire life seeking and telling the truth, was one with truth itself.

CHAPTER TWO

The God of the Homeless

DOROTHY DAY

W hen Dorothy Day died in 1980 at age eighty-
three, she left behind an extensive collection of
retreat notes entitled "All is Grace." Day's life is a story
of God's amazing grace calling a girl from the tenements
of Chicago to be a woman who would change the course
of American Catholicism. The story begins with ordinary events and tiny impulses during childhood.
Dorothy was led one small step at a time to an adolescent faith, a faith which seemingly collapsed for a
decade of wandering and a tempestuous love affair, an
abortion and a failed marriage. Yet through it all, this

young woman was haunted and hounded by God, until she ultimately had to give up the man she loved so that she and her daughter could be followers of Jesus Christ in the Catholic Church.

Day's search continued as she found God in the streets among the destitute and homeless, and then invited them into her own "houses of hospitality" for food, shelter and care. This woman so strongly believed that all people are God's children that she was willing to stand valiantly against all the horrific wars that occurred during her lifetime. She was a lonely person who found God in Jesus Christ; a woman who took her God at his word when he asked his followers to serve "the least of the brethren" and to love their enemy. What were her steps toward conversion, and what role did her experience of God play in her spirituality?

Childhood Glimpses of God

In Day's childhood home, religion was seldom mentioned, but a general faith in God was evident. Her father carried a Bible with him and often quoted from it, yet he had had no use for organized religion. Her mother also read the Scriptures, but had little to say about religious matters. Somehow, Day knew of God from the very beginning. She wrote: "How much did I hear of religion as a child? Very little, and yet my heart leaped when I heard the name of God. I do believe every soul has a tendency toward God."[1] In retrospect, Day believed that a succession of events gave her "glimpses of Him" and gradually led her to a faith, which she says "was always in my heart."[2]

As a child, Day was not engaged in a search for God;

she simply took God for granted as she recited traditional prayers at bedtime or promised she would be good when she was frightened by a violent storm. She recalled her first days in school, when she bowed her head to a desk smelling of varnish and recited the Our Father. She mentioned a time when she found a musty old Bible in the attic, and read it with "the sense of holiness in holding the book in my hands."[3] Day said little about such matters at the time because she noticed early on that the two topics by which people were embarrassed were sex and God.

During her childhood years in Oakland, California, Day was influenced by a Methodist family next door. She says that during this time she began to sing hymns, say prayers and go to church, becoming "disgustingly, proudly pious."[4] During this time, Day also began to be afraid of God, and anxious about such things as death and eternity. She felt terror thinking about the immensity of God, and at night would "wake up crying out, frightened by the immensity of the universe, of the heavens, overcome by a sense of the loneliness of God, the impersonality of God...."[5]

After a severe earthquake in Oakland, the family moved to Chicago, where Day for the first time experienced the poverty of the tenements. There she became acquainted with some neighboring Catholic families. Mary, a friend, told her stories about the saints, stories that deeply stirred Day's mind and heart. Day later wrote that these stories made her heart "almost burst with desire to take part in such high endeavor...."[6] She says that she became thrilled at the possibility of having such spiritual adventures.

On one occasion, Day was running through a

neighboring flat to find a friend when she accidentally came across her friend's mother, praying at her bedside. Day wrote that she had a burst of love for this woman, and a feeling of gratitude and happiness so warmed her heart that she never forgot it. For a while, Day prayed to God at her own bedside.

Another "impulse of grace" came when the local Episcopalian pastor came to the Day home and persuaded the children to come to church. Dorothy's two brothers joined the choir, and she often went to hear them sing. She wrote that she was thrilled to hear the Psalms and canticles sung, and that when she heard the magnificent *Te Deum* she would thank God for creating her.

Teenage Impulses

As Dorothy entered her teenage years and felt the first stirrings of sexuality, she began to see a conflict between the sensual and the spiritual and became increasingly pious and otherworldly. In a letter she wrote as an adolescent, she says: "I have learned that it is rather hypocritical to be so strict on the Sabbath and not on every other day. Every day belongs to God and every day we are to serve Him, doing His pleasure."[7] At the same time, Day wandered through the slums of Chicago and began to feel a call to be linked to the poor. She wrote: "I felt even at fifteen, that God meant man to be happy, that He meant to provide him with what he needed to maintain life in order to be happy, and that we did not need to have quite so much destitution and misery as I saw all around and read of in the daily press."[8]

During her adolescence, Dorothy also discovered several books that would make a deep impact on her.

She read *Imitation of Christ,* by Thomas á Kempis, a book which she would later read in preparation for both her daughter's and her own baptism, as well as throughout her life. The book gave her comfort, created in her a new hunger for God and gave her a strong confidence in God's grace.[9] These passages seem to be glimpses into Day's own spirituality.

> Humble knowledge of self is the surer path to God.

> Consider things carefully and patiently in the light of God's will.

> Do not be ashamed to serve others for the love of Jesus Christ and to seem poor in this world.

> Do not be self-sufficient but place your trust in God.

> Seek a suitable time for leisure and meditate often on the favors of God.

> You have here no lasting home. You are a stranger and a pilgrim wherever you may be, and you shall have no rest until you are wholly united with Christ.

> When Jesus is near, all is well and nothing seems difficult.

During this same period, Day read the *Confessions* of Saint Augustine. She identified with Augustine's struggle between human love and the love of God. Later, she would see parallels in their two conversions from a "life of sin." Her appreciation for Scripture continued to deepen also. In school she had become quite proficient in classical languages, so she bought a ten-cent copy of the Greek New Testament, and wrote out her own translations.

Religion Is for the Weak

At sixteen, Dorothy graduated from high school. In her last year she had become increasingly unhappy at home, especially with her father, who did not approve of her radical political views or of what he perceived to be her "manly" ambition to be a writer. Day was able to leave home at this time because she had won a scholarship to the University of Illinois at Urbana.

For those used to images of Dorothy Day as a matronly woman tending the homeless, it is hard to imagine her as she was in college: leaning on a classroom wall with an air of defiance, a cigarette held high in her fingers, and spouting foul language in order to shock any pious students who might pass by.

An incidental remark in class influenced Day's move away from religion for the next ten years. In one of her classes the professor noted that religion should not be scoffed at because it has given great comfort to many people. Day inferred from the comment that only the weak need such props, and decided that religion was not required of her. She wrote: "In my youthful arrogance, in my feeling that I was one of the strong, I felt then for the first time that religion was something that I must ruthlessly cut out of my life."[10]

College life was not for Day. By this time she had become most sympathetic to "workers" outside of college life, particularly girls who spent their youth working in factories only to marry men who were slaves to the same factories. Since Day herself had to work to pay for expenses at college, she had little time to mingle with the other students or become part of the campus scene. After two years she dropped out and headed to New

York City for a taste of the "real world." Dorothy wandered through the canyons of the city, lonely and without a job or friends. Still, she was determined to harden her heart against God and religion, convinced that such concerns would only impede her from the work she wanted to do. Dorothy would have little to do with religion for some time to come.

Then she took another small step. While working as a journalist in New York, Day was asked to go to Washington, D.C., to demonstrate with the suffragettes—women who fought to secure the vote for women in the United States. She was arrested and hauled off to jail with two of her ribs cracked by a policeman's club. The jail experience, though moderate, was frightening for her, and the hunger strike in which she subsequently became involved was extremely difficult. Dorothy asked for a Bible, and when it was brought to her she says: "My heart swelled with joy and thankfulness for the Psalms."[11] She read about how God brings his people out of captivity and she prayed, "The Lord hath done great things for us."[12] At the same time, she resisted depending on God because that would be a sign of weakness. She later remarked touchingly: "I was like the child that wants to walk by itself, I kept brushing away the hand that held me up."[13]

Labyrinthine Ways

Once out of prison, Dorothy continued to live a Bohemian lifestyle, working as a writer by day and hanging out with friends at night in smoke-filled bars, discussing the latest in books and in politics. She had, for the time, chosen human love, the life of the flesh, over the discipline of religion. Day believed that the strong could make their own laws and live their own lives. Day "belonged to that school of youth which lived in the present, lived the life of the senses."[14]

Even in the midst of all this rebellion, God continued to pursue and haunt Day. One of her favorite bar mates was the famous playwright, Eugene O'Neill. Gene, as she called him, was not a religious man, but did in his own way carry on a serious spiritual search. Day recalls how he would sit drunken on cold winter nights and recite Thompson's *Hound of Heaven*, a poem quite popular among Catholics at the time. Some of the verses are as follows:

> I fled Him, down the nights and down the days;
> I fled Him, down the arches of the years;
> I fled Him, down the labyrinthine ways
> Of my own mind; and in the mist of tears
> I hid from Him...
> ...this tremendous Lover...
> I am He whom thou seekest!...

The poem fascinated her. She resonated with its sentiments and was fascinated with the notion of being pursued by God. She later wrote that it made her feel that inevitably she would have to pause in her mad rush and "remember my first beginning and my last end."[15]

At the outbreak of World War I, Day found herself in transition. She had lost interest in writing, was disillusioned with the labor movement and strongly opposed the war. She decided to train as a nurse and work in a hospital. During the training she befriended a woman she called Miss Adams, and credited the woman's Catholic faith with her goodness, ability as a nurse and healthy attitude toward life. Day thus became much more positively disposed toward Catholicism, and began going to Mass with her friend. In her nursing, Day learned how to serve the poor with dignity and compassion, lessons that would serve her well in the future.

In the Mist of Tears

While at the hospital, Day met Lionel Moise, a brawny, fast-talking womanizer, who swept her off her feet. She fell deeply in love with him, and when he left the hospital, she took leave from work and moved in with him. Moise took control of the young woman's life, made her keep house for him and was ferociously jealous. On one occasion when he left her, she apparently attempted suicide. Day eventually became pregnant with Moise's child, and on his advice, decided to have an abortion. She regretted her decision for the rest of her life, and would keep it from the public until near the end of her life. She described her experience in a thinly veiled way in her novel, *The Eleventh Virgin*. Moise had agreed to meet Dorothy after the abortion, but he never showed up. He left some money and a "Dear Jane" letter (with the advice that she marry a rich man). Her search for love had reached a dead end.

On the rebound, Dorothy did in fact marry a rich older man and traveled with him to Europe. The marriage was brief, and Day tried to resume her relationship with Moise, but to no avail. Meanwhile she had taken a job with a radical Communist newspaper, and one night was caught in a "Red Raid" in 1922 ordered by an assistant U. S. attorney general named J. Edgar Hoover. She was forced to change from her sleeping clothes into street clothes in front of armed men before being thrown into a patrol wagon, and was then booked as a prostitute. In prison she was stripped, given a uniform and put in a cell block where a drug addict perpetually beat her own head on the wall. The horrors of prison made an impression on Dorothy; she gained an appreciation for the many workers who had suffered imprisonment for their strikes. The experience further radicalized her, and when she was released, another "impulse" toward God came to her. She rented rooms in a Catholic household, and came to admire their thanksgiving and worship of God, their deep moral commitment and dedication to prayer. A brief stint in New Orleans in an apartment near St. Louis Cathedral gave her further opportunity to pray to her God and to worship at evening Benediction.

The Hound was at her doorstep. Day's novel *The Eleventh Virgin* had been published, but was poorly reviewed and attracted few readers. Fortunately for her, Hollywood bought the film rights. The film was never made, but Dorothy was paid twenty-five hundred dollars and was able to buy her own place on Staten Island where she could enjoy nature and write. Around the same time, she fell in love with Forster Batterham, an anarchist and atheist with a deep love for nature. Forster returned Dorothy's love and moved in with her. They shared several delightful years together in the cozy beach house.

Though deeply in love, Dorothy and Forster were going in different directions: she toward God, and he away from anything resembling religious belief. Her belief in God was becoming stronger and she was growing more intensely aware of God's presence in creation. At first, they could argue about this in a friendly way because Day had no religious affiliation or commitment to doctrines. When Forster would grumble about the existence of God, she would only say to him: "How can there be no God, when there are all these beautiful things?"[16]

As Day grew more devout, she would say the rosary on the way to the post office, recite the *Te Deum* as she gathered driftwood at low tide and even pray to the Blessed Mother while she cleaned. She found herself praising God throughout the day, and prayer filled her with an intense joy and sense of beauty. She felt a new freedom, much more exhilarating than when she "thought she was free" in the city.

Dorothy began going to Mass on Sundays, and this made Forster even more bewildered and angry. What was happening to his lover? Then came the occasion for a major "grace" in Day's life: She became pregnant. The new life in her put her deeply in touch with God and creation and she threw herself into books on spirituality— some familiar, like *Imitation of Christ,* and some new, like William James's *The Varieties of Religious Experience,* and a life of Teresa of Avila, the Spanish mystic.

The birth of Dorothy's daughter, Tamar, was a turning point in her search for God. She wrote: "No human creature could receive or contain so vast a flood of love and joy as I often felt after the birth of my child. With this came the need to worship, to adore."[17] And not only was she drawn to worship her Creator, but to worship within a church, a community of faithful people. Her experience of socialism had brought her to an appreciation of the power of the masses, and she no longer wanted to worship her God alone. She decided that first she would have Tamar baptized so she would not "flounder as I had often floundered."[18] She wanted Tamar to benefit from the faith, fellowship, teachings and help the church could offer. When Day met an elderly nun named Aloysia and asked if she could have her baby baptized, the die was cast. Day would prepare for the baptism with her own catechism lessons. It was the beginning of the end of her life with Forster.

For a while, Dorothy hoped that Forster would come around. He had grown to love his daughter, Tamar, in spite of his reservations about bringing children into an imperfect world. Day had hoped that they could get married and that she, too, could then enter the church. But Forster would have none of it. He did not believe in marriage, and could not accept her entering the church. They would have loud arguments, and Forster would leave in a huff, only to return later, repentant. The stress disturbed Day to the point where it began to threaten her health. So one afternoon when Forster returned, she refused to let him in the house, even though she said that her heart was breaking. That very day, she made an appointment to be baptized into the Catholic Church. She said she had to choose between God and man.

Actually, Day's baptism turned out to be a disappointment. She says that she had no peace or joy, no conviction that she was doing right. She was losing her lover, betraying all her radical friends and leaving the poor behind for a church that she feared might be lined up with the rich and powerful. A year later, however, Day's uncertainties were resolved when she was confirmed. She wrote: "My confirmation was indeed joyful and Pentecost never passes without a renewed sense of happiness and thanksgiving. It was only then that the feeling of uncertainty finally left me, never again to return, praise God!"[19] God had led her to a church that she would challenge and help revolutionize in the coming years.

Though she had become a Catholic, Day still did not understand the scope of her calling. For the next five years, her challenge was to make a living as a single mother. Somewhat naively, she took a job in 1928 with a Communist-affiliated group that was protesting U.S. military intervention in Central America. She took other jobs, such as cooking for Catholic seminarians, writing movie scripts in Hollywood and a series of articles in Mexico for *Commonweal*. Eventually she returned to New York City.

Once back there, Dorothy found herself amid the Depression, with widespread poverty and unemployment, and with scant Catholic leadership in the labor movement. Pope Pius XI had sadly pointed out that the workers of the world are lost to the church, and Day desperately wanted to serve poor workers as part of her new membership in the church. She was hired to cover the Hunger March on Washington, and during the assignment was appalled at the brutality of the police, the sensationalism of the press and the absence of the church. Day began to fear that her Catholicism would isolate her in quiet self-absorption, while her radical comrades would go on to do the work for justice.

When the march finally came triumphantly to the nation's capital, Day wrote down her thoughts for an article and then went to find a church to pray in. It was the Feast of the Immaculate Conception, and Day knelt in the magnificent crypt that was built long before the national shrine was completed. She was in anguish and in tears as she begged her God for some way to open up for her to use her talents for the poor. It did not take God long to answer her request. The next day she returned to New York to find a stranger waiting for her. His name was Peter Maurin, and he had been sent to her by her editors at *Commonweal* magazine. Her life would never be the same.

Beginning a New Life

Day said that her life really began when she met Peter Maurin in 1932. Peter was a cross between Saint Francis of Assisi and silent movie star Charlie Chaplin. Maurin was a simple but bright man who lived to change society and serve the poor, a troubadour in rumpled suits, his pockets stuffed with books and pamphlets. Day said he was "one of those people who talked you deaf, dumb and blind."[20] Peter tirelessly taught the social teachings of the church and was dedicated to change the very structures of society so that people could live in peace and happiness. He was widely read in European religious and political thought and could in his own quirky way synthesize these notions with the gospel teaching. Peter was able to give Day a more intellectual basis for her faith, and shared a vision with her on how the poor could be served and educated for a better future.

Peter had been looking and praying for someone who could implement his vision, someone who could help him reform society and the church. Once he met Day, he knew that he had found his partner. He began to share with her a vision of a society where workers would be cocreators with God through their work, rather than the alienated and impoverished cogs in the wheel they had become. He taught her that the gospel, with its teaching on love and the works of mercy, had the power to bring this about and showed her how the church was keeping all this power under lock and key. Peter served as Dorothy's most important mentor and worked by her side until his death in 1949.

Together Dorothy and Peter founded the Catholic Worker Movement, started the newspaper *The Catholic Worker* and opened houses of hospitality for the poor across the country. They also established commune farms, and worked tirelessly in both the labor and peace movements. Peter and Dorothy shared a vision to change the very structures of society so there would be more room for gospel equality, justice and peace. Both were deeply committed to the gospel way of life and both placed a great value on community. They wanted to capture the early Christian sense of community in their houses of hospitality, which grew in number to thirty in the first ten years.

Dorothy once lamented: "It is strange, to live in a world of so many strangers."[21] She wanted to have a community life that was based on the Sermon on the Mount, where the hungry would be fed and the homeless given shelter. She felt that through such communities people could be in touch with the earliest Christians and also with generations to come. Day often displayed a mystical approach to time, so that it seemed to her that it was only yesterday that Jesus walked the earth. The "nearness of God" linked her to past and present. She once said:

We are communities in time and in a place, I know, but we are communities in faith as well—and sometimes time can stop shadowing us. Our lives are touched by those who lived centuries ago, and we hope that our lives will mean something to people who won't be alive until centuries from now.[22]

Love for the Poor

Day had a great love for the poor. "These are Christ's poor. He was one of them,"[23] she wrote. She could be strident on this point, believing that if people were really leading Christian lives, the sight of ragged hungry people would not be possible. She once remarked that the impoverished were far dearer in the sight of God than the "smug, well-fed Christians who sit in their homes."[24] Day was disappointed with the many Catholic young people coming from Catholic schools and colleges concerned mainly with security and wages. It was her conviction that no one has a right to security when "God's poor are suffering." She would say: "What right have I to sleep in a comfortable bed when so many are sleeping in the shadows of buildings?"[25]

The line in the gospel that was seared into Day's soul was "...just as you did it to one of the least of these who are members of my family, you did it to me" (Matthew 25:40). She believed that all humans are made in the image and likeness of God and are temples of the Holy Spirit. She took Jesus on his word that how we treat others is how we treat him. Day was one of those rare figures in Christianity who can shine a new light on gospel teachings and actually live according to Jesus' word and example.

Even as a child, Day had been amazed that people were not taking off their coats and giving them to the poor, or inviting the lame, halt and blind into their banquets. Day once commented that not just the Salvation Army, but everyone should be kind to the poor and open to helping the lame. Jesus would become her role model for serving the poor, since he, too, was a poor man without a place to lay his head. He had directed his message to the poorest of the poor and died between two thieves.

To serve the poor with shelter, food, clothes and care, Day first opened her own apartment and then rented larger spaces for her houses of hospitality. She wanted to reach out to the unemployed and the destitute during the time of the Great Depression, and help them realize that God was present within them and was on their side in a special way. She wrote: "God is on the side even of the unworthy poor, as we know from the story Jesus told of His Father and the prodigal son."[26]

Dorothy was realistic about poverty. She practiced "voluntary poverty" which meant she lived simply, wore hand-me-down clothes, traveled by bus and had few possessions she could call her own. For her, poverty meant being dependent on God, detaching herself from systems that exploit and being ever available to those in need. She was careful to distinguish between the dignity and freedom of such a choice and the bondage of destitution in which so many of the poor she served lived. This latter poverty was not freely chosen, but was the result of injustice and oppression, a sign of institutional sin.

The Catholic Worker, which is still sold today for a penny a copy, was directed primarily toward the poor, the dispossessed and the exploited. Day wrote: "We felt a respect for the poor and destitute as those nearest to God."[27] The paper was directed to worker's issues, unemployment, unjust wages, strikebreaking and oppression in the workplace and peace issues. She cried out when employers treated their workers as animals rather than as children of God. She urged the workers to realize that they were brothers and sisters in the Lord, and encouraged them to have courage and hope in their struggles for better wages and working conditions.

Day's voluntary poverty was also a protest against injustice toward workers. She wrote: "Poverty means not riding on rubber while horrible working conditions prevail in the rubber industry. Poverty means not riding on rails while bad conditions exist in the coal mines and steel mills.... Railroads have been built on robbery and exploitation."[28]

She urged her followers to rejoice in poverty and live with the poor workers because they are specially loved by Christ. "Even the lowest, most depraved, we must see Christ in them, and love them to folly. When we suffer from dirt, lack of privacy, heat and cold, coarse food, let us rejoice."[29] She often wryly said: "The less you have of Caesar's, the less you have to render to Caesar."[30]

Day believed that Jesus' words were addressed to the common folk, the workers and the poorest of the poor. She saw the outcasts of Jesus' time as those people who were unemployed, those standing in bread lines, those who needed a place to live, health care and clothing. Indeed, what attracted her to Catholicism was the notion that God dwelled in the world, actually had become one of us as a poor person. She also saw the Catholic Church as primarily a church of the poor who came or were brought to the United States, only to end up serving the prosperous, moneymaking developers and exploiters of this country.

Long before Vatican II urged Catholics to do so, Dorothy and Peter decided that they would be church advocates for peace and justice in the modern world. They hit the streets as laypeople and preached the gospel of mercy. They declared their solidarity with those who were suffering, and announced to the world that Jesus did indeed call us to be our sisters' and brothers' keepers. They redefined the Catholic conscience in terms of justice, freedom and the nonviolent struggle for peace. Day believed that if God had found the world good enough to die for, she, too, would sacrifice herself for this same world. She could see in others that "which is of God," and therefore never tired of serving them through the works of mercy.

Providence

Dorothy's faith in the providence of God developed gradually through her life. In her walks through the poor neighborhoods of Chicago she felt that God wanted more for those people and that somehow she was called to tend to their needs. In her voluntary poverty, Day tried to be totally dependent on God. Early on, Peter had taught her, "In the Catholic Church one never needs any money to start a good work. People are what are important. If you have people and they are willing to give their work—that is the thing. God is not to be outdone in generosity. The funds will come in somehow or other."[31] For the workers, true security would mean having trust that God would provide.

Of course, such trust in God was not new to Day. Had she not put her life in the hands of God at her baptism, confused and distraught over losing her lover and her friends, and yet trusting that God would guide her? Once she met Peter, she felt that God had sent him to take her by the hand on her mission, and she never turned back. No matter what failure or resistance came her way, Day always believed that God could take failure and turn it into victory. In the midst of the Depression in the 1920s she wrote a letter to her friends who supported her: "God is with us, the saints protect us. Each time we have asked for aid, the money was immediately forthcoming to pay each and every bill.... God seems to intend us to depend solely on Him."[32]

Often Day would receive criticism, even from within her own ranks, about inefficiency, lack of organization or even poor hygiene (her houses often had no hot water or place to bathe). There was grumbling from the homeless, complaints from her own workers, and at times harsh criticism from the clergy. Day often felt a deep loneliness and depression, yet she carried on against tremendous odds, at times without money to pay the bills or to even buy meager supplies. She would say: "However the thing is to bear it patiently, to take it lightly, not to let it interfere with your work. The very fact that it is hard shows how weak I am. I should be happy, however, to think that God believes me strong enough to bear these trials, otherwise I would not be having them."[33] When things got desperate in her work, she would invoke the statement: "It is a terrible thing to fall into the hands of the living God."[34] She truly believed that everything we think and do can be used by God to bring us closer to him. And she used to warn her followers to be careful what they promise to God, because God takes us at our word.

This is not to say that Dorothy advocated a naive passivity to the will of God. She was critical of the poor who had little ambition for bettering their condition. She did not approve of those who did not work hard to succeed or to get an education. Day opposed patient acceptance of suffering with humility and hope for a better life with God ("pie in the sky"). She would say that such people mistakenly thought that God meant suffering to be. Hers was a God of love and mercy who wanted people to be whole and happy, and action needed to be taken to gain such conditions. Thus she believed in strikes, protests and aggressive action against greed and oppression. She taught that the choice for God meant a choice for life, justice and peace. Day spent her life in extending charity, but she also actively fought for justice. Hers was the notion of Augustine: "Pray as though everything depended on God and work as though everything depended on you."

God in Creation

Robert Ellsberg, a long-time associate of Dorothy's, points out that creation spoke to her of God. Whether it is the sunlight on water, children playing in the street, a long line of hungry people waiting for their soup, or the world going by through a bus window, Day felt God's presence. She knew better than most the dark side of life and all its suffering, yet she maintained a deep faith that the loving-kindness of God would prevail. She was fond of saying that the world must be good if God found it good enough to die for.

Even as a teen, Day had been attuned to beauty, even in the destitution around her in the city streets. She loved tiny flower gardens and vegetable patches in the yards, and the odors coming from the drab neighborhoods. She wrote of: "The odor of geranium leaves, tomato plants, marigolds; the smell of lumber, of tar, of roasting coffee; the smell of good bread and rolls and coffee cake coming from the small German bakeries. Here was enough beauty to satisfy me."[35]

Day's special love for nature often served her as a bridge to the divine. She loved her little cottage on Staten Island and would go to the shore whenever she was able. She often quoted Russian novelist Dostoevsky's words: "The world will be saved by beauty." We have seen how Forster loved the sea, and opened a new world of beauty for her during long weekend walks along the beach. In the winter months, he charted the stars for her and showed her the magnificence of the night sky. She wrote that this was a very happy time for her and that she began to consciously pray more.

Day sustained this love of flowers and birds, the sky and the water, and came to see the final object of this love and gratitude to be God, a God worthy of praise. She wrote:

> I was "born again by the word of the Spirit," contemplating the beauty of the sea and the shore, wind and waves, the tides. The mighty and the minute, the storms and peace, wave and the wavelets of receding tides, sea gulls, and seaweed and shells, all gave testimony of a Creator....[36]

Day's love of nature led her to see a correlation between the transcendent and the immanent in a God that was both living and personal. She was later to reflect in retrospect what was happening to her during those happy days on Staten Island:

> I did not know then [while at the beach], as I know now, that in a way, it does not enter into the heart to understand the love of God, that over and over again it comes, this quality of in-loveness when we see an individual as God sees him, in all his beauty, and all the earth seems transformed.... Suddenly all around me the world has lightened, the fog has lifted, and the air has cleared and one understands what man is capable of becoming and in how many ways he is indeed an image of God.[37]

Through most of her life, Day lived among the impoverished and broken people of the world, and yet she was elated that there is so much beauty in the world, and was convinced that "beauty will save the world."[38] At the same time, she realized that creation cannot be an end in itself. "When we search for love in creatures, when we turn from God to creatures, instead of seeking God *in* creatures, then all is perversity."[39] Day maintained a certain detachment from material things, wanting to ultimately be stripped and emptied of all things so that she could give herself to the poor. Moreover, she believed that material things were for all, even the poorest of the poor. Once she was criticized for giving a beautiful donated diamond ring to a bag lady and she answered: "Do you suppose God created diamonds only for the rich?"[40]

Later on, at retreats by the sea, this awareness of God's presence would mature. The immensity of the sea would lead her to stand in awe of and want to worship and adore the greatness of God. She came to understand that there was a spiritual dimension to life, a Kingdom of the Spirit, which was beyond everyday suffering, and yet which was accessible to every one, even the simple folk. She often referred to Augustine's notion that there was a light, a melody, a fragrance and embrace in life which can never disappear, and that is what we love when we love God. And she often quoted Saint Paul's wonderful line in Acts 17:28 about the God in whom "we live and move and have our being."

This Tremendous Lover

Day, as a Catholic Christian, saw her God incarnate in the person of Jesus Christ. Christ for her was God made human, and therefore was the way for living human life. She found him in Scripture, in the sacraments and profoundly in the outcasts of society. Christ was a real presence to her: "It is no use to say that we are born two thousand years too late to give room to Christ.... Christ is always with us, asking for room in our hearts."[41] For her, Jesus was the worker, the poor man without a place to lay his head, and Day was able to see the Lord in the homeless person, the worker trying to get a just wage or without a job. Jesus' commitment to the outcast was the model for Day's dedication to alcoholics, prostitutes, drug addicts and convicts. Many know how to recite the works of mercy; Day took them literally and lived them. This was the way to making life better for people here on earth. "We are not expecting utopia here on this earth. But God meant things to be much easier than we have made them.... Eternal life begins now. 'All the way to heaven is heaven.'"[42]

For Day, the Incarnation was ongoing. She believed that God had assumed humanity once and for all, and that as a result divinity could now be found in our neighbor. Sharing bread with the hungry, clothing with the naked and shelter with the homeless were indeed intimate contacts with God for Day and her followers. As Ellsberg puts it: "In the gospels she learned that God Himself had walked among the poor, had known hard work, exile, and the life of a wanderer. He had revealed Himself to those who were abused and unwanted, and had become one of them Himself, laying down His life, an enemy of Church and State alike."[43]

At the houses of hospitality, the poor and destitute were respected as those nearest to God, as those specially chosen by Christ for his compassion. She stood in wonder at the great mystery of the Incarnation. The fact that Jesus actually walked the earth made Dorothy want to kiss the earth in worship. Day's charism was that all this was vividly real for her. She once remarked about the Hunger March on Washington: "I watched that ragged horde and thought to myself... 'These are Christ's poor. He was one of them. He was a man like other men, and He chose His friends amongst the ordinary workers.'"[44] Christ was a worker and what attracted her to Marxism early on was their dedication to workers. She believed that people who work with their hands are cocreators who take the raw materials God provides and make those into all manner of things to make life better.

Dorothy knew well that loving God is the first commandment, but she often wrestled with the problem of *how* a person can actually love God. She wanted to have the feeling that she loved God, and yet was aware that as humans we battle hardness of heart. She took comfort in Pascal's saying: "Thou wouldst not seek Him if

thou hadst not already found Him." She concluded that
the mere desire to love God indicates that we love God,
and yet she was aware that there had to be more. She
said one of the most disconcerting facts about the spiritual life, is that when we say we love God, God takes us
at our word and gives us a chance to prove that love.
For her, the love of nature, the poor masses, and
beauty all lead to the love of God. For her, dedication to
serve the poor, to demonstrate with workers, to struggle against violence, were all ways of proving the
love of God. She describes this love in mystical terms as
"delicate and kind, full of gentle perception and understanding, full of beauty and grace, full of joy unutter-
able."[45] She believed that we can only experience the
flavor of such love in our love for other people. Such
love brings us to see all things new and helps us to see
people as they truly are, or "as God sees them."

Christian love was not romantic or sentimental for
Day. It meant laying down her life for her neighbor; it
meant sacrificing "our bread, our daily living, our rent,
our clothes."[46] In her last major speaking engagement,
Day spoke of this love of God and said that love must
be taken into all of creation. She recalled how the love
of the material world had led her to the love of God, and
that now the love of God had led her full circle to see
the world itself in a new light.[47] For Day, to live unin-
terrupted in such love is heaven, whereas hell is "not to
love anymore."[48]

Day's personal life and her life among the unloved
and forsaken had taught her that being in love with God
can often include the painful experience of "the absence
of God." She wrote about such absence, the horrible
darkness that can come over one's soul, where the soul

appears to cease loving. It is her conviction that the person must go on loving the emptiness, and at least continue to *want* to love. "Then one day God will come to show himself to this soul and to reveal the beauty of the world to it...."[49] And Day's mission seemed to be to bring love and joy into the lives of so many who lived in the hellish lack of love, in the darkness of need and addictions. Having known the darkness herself, she was never afraid to plunge into the lives of the abandoned and to bring hope and love to them.

Day held that a true mystic is one who not only *loves* God, but is *in love* with God. This did not come easily for her, and she recalls how when young she many times "turned away almost in disgust, from the idea of God, and giving myself up to Him."[50] After her conversion, when many Catholics were given to a legalistic approach to Catholicism, Day saw love rather than the law at the heart of the gospel. She believed that God's love should be infused into every thought, word and deed. She often quoted John of the Cross's saying: "Love is the measure by which we shall be judged."

She was convinced that the only way we can know that we love God is to show love for other people. She believed that love makes us want to give, and if we look at the measure by which Day gave, we have some notion of the largeness of this woman's heart. Day identified with the mission of Saint Thérèse of Lisieux, who said, "My mission is to make God love, and make Love loved." She could see the identification between the divine and love. She wrote, "What else do we all want, each one of us, except to love and be loved, in our families, in our work, in all our relationships? God is love."[51]

Day believed that when people seek love, as all do,

they are indeed seeking God. Sin is a turning from love, a turning from God. True love is so strong it casts out all fear, even of enemies, and it can be a force so strong that it can overcome war.[52] However, she insisted that we should not love our enemies because we fear war, but rather because God loves our enemy. A skeptical Mike Wallace once interviewed her about this and asked if God loves murderers like Hitler and Stalin. She answered: "God loves all men, and all men are brothers."

Of course, she realized the enormous challenge in such a love and could only query: "Have we begun to be Christians?" But no matter how difficult, she believed that we have to keep striving. Both Dorothy and Peter wanted to see a new social order where all people love God and each other because they are all children of God. They sought to help establish peace, tranquility and joy in work. Yet they knew that these were ideals that required a lifetime of commitment, and both were realistic enough to know that "We are never going to be finished."[53]

Resistance to the Church

Day's Marxist friends had influenced her in her youth to think of the Catholic Church as a controlling institution that dispensed religion to the weak as an "opiate." We saw earlier that the image of her neighbor Mrs. Barrett on her knees, of the Catholic nurse in the hospital where she worked, and of Sister Aloysia who instructed her, gave her more positive images of the Catholic Church. She wanted her daughter to be baptized into the church so that she could take part in its stability and tradition, its discipline and morals.

Day herself was ultimately attracted to the church because of its notions of an immanent God, an incarnated God and its time-honored traditions. She loved the church's devotions, its traditions of spirituality, its great saints and its sense of community. Yet she entered the church knowing that she would lose her lover, Forster, and would again be alone. She had been fearful that she was betraying the class to which she belonged, as well as the workers, the poor of the world, the people Christ most loved and spent his life for. Even after her conversion, Day felt that often Communists served the poor better than most Christians did. She was indeed relieved when Peter Maurin introduced her to the social teachings of the church, and showed her that the church's gospel mission was to bring the works of mercy to the poor and to labor to overcome poverty, injustice and violence.

Because Day was so devoted to Christ's church, many of her followers were often disturbed at her wholehearted acceptance of the church's hierarchical structure and its rigorous teachings. She loved the church's sacramental life and its doctrinal and spiritual heritage, but balked at its political and social views. She was always respectful toward the hierarchy, but never afraid to take them on. The powerful Cardinal Spellman was not able to have the word "Catholic" removed from her paper, and was stung when her followers sided with the Catholic cemetery workers against him in a wage dispute.

Although Day was committed to her church, she could be critical of its failure to live up to Christ's teachings. She was often disillusioned at the church's identification with the wealthy, and criticized the luxurious rectories of the clergy in America as the scandal of her day. Day could be sardonic when she saw hundreds of people begging in the street and then noticed well-dressed people proudly coming out of church in their fine clothes "as complacent as could be in their conviction that God was *theirs*—that an hour at Mass on Sunday had put Him in their corner."[54]

Dorothy believed that the church was of Christ, but she was also well aware of the human dimension of the church. This is revealed in one of her strongest statements: "I loved the Church for Christ made visible. Not for itself, because it was so often a scandal to me. Romano Guardini said the Church is the Cross on which Christ was crucified; one could not separate Christ from his Cross and one must live in a state of perpetual dissatisfaction with the Church."[55]

Dorothy never grew bitter about the human failures of the church, and she resisted being judgmental about individuals. Her mission was to call the leaders and members of her beloved church to be faithful to the heart of the gospel—the promotion of peace, justice and mercy. At the same time, Day always kept her sense of humor about Catholicism. She once said the old horse who helped deliver the bundles of her paper in downtown Manhattan was a Catholic horse because her assistant, Dan, told her that when they went up past St. Patrick's Cathedral on Fifth Avenue "the horse genuflects."[56]

Nonviolence

Day's pacifist views did not cause much of a stir between the world wars. Many of her *Catholic Worker* readers were convinced that America had been duped into entering that war by munitions workers, bankers and British propaganda. But when the Spanish Civil War broke out in 1935, that was a different matter. Most of the Catholic press supported Franco, as though he were fighting a holy war against the atheistic Communists who persecuted the church. *The Catholic Worker* declared itself neutral, pointing out the Fascist commitment of Franco and its alignment with Fascists in Germany and the atrocities of the Loyalists. At this time, Day's pacifism ignited an outrage among most Catholics.

In 1938 Day wrote an editorial answering those who said it was madness for *The Catholic Worker* to oppose the use of force in national or international disputes. She said that the views of her movement were the "folly of the Cross," the same "folly" which characterized Jesus' refusal to use violence. She said that she took Jesus at his word that we are to love our enemies, and refused to pray for victory for either side. She wrote: "We are praying for the Spanish people—all of them our brothers in Christ—all of them Temples of the Holy Ghost, all of them members or potential members of the Mystical Body of Christ."[57] Her workers would accept the leadership of Christ, and carry on a "Christian revolution" of their own, without the use of force.

The Catholic Worker movement would pay a price for its pacifism. Many orders for the *Worker* were canceled and the circulation dropped by more than a hundred thousand. To those who told Day to stick to her work with the impoverished and stay out of politics, Day replied that the works of mercy and peace cannot be separated. She believed that whatever you do to the least, whether to deprive them of food or drink or to do an act of violence toward them, is an offense against God. She applied these same pacifist principles to the labor movement. She felt that the beating of scabs and strikebreakers, as well as the use of force against employers were offenses against God. "The use of force has lost more strikes than it has won them," she wrote.[58]

World War II put Day's commitment to pacifism to its ultimate test. A year before the war broke out, Day opposed those who wanted to enter the war. She wrote: "There are so many who hate war and who are opposed to peacetime conscription who do not know what they can do, who have no sense of united effort, and who will sit back and accept with resignation the evils which are imposed upon us. This is not working for God's will...."[59]

After Pearl Harbor, when the nation was caught up in extreme patriotism and propaganda, Day often seemed to be a lone voice against the war. Day knew better than most the evils of Hitler and Nazism: She had protested against them and against anti-Semitism earlier than most. Still, she firmly believed that there were powers stronger than brute force, and was convinced that the powerful weapons mounted to defeat Hitler would only lead the world to more devastation.

Many of Day's own followers turned on her because of her opposition to World War II, and saddened her when they joined the war effort. A good number of her houses of hospitality had to be closed and the circulation of her paper fell precipitously. On the other hand, many of Day's followers remained pacifist, and spent the war years in prison, in work camps or serving as medics.

Day remained adamant in her conviction that people are children of God and that God wants us to love our enemies. She was not afraid to be a lonely outsider, for she had been there many times before. On this, she would quote philosopher Simone Weil: "The idea of the despised and humiliated hero which was so common among the Greeks and is the actual theme of the gospels is almost outside our Western tradition which has remained on the Roman road of militarism, centralization, bureaucracy and totalitarianism."[60]

She had hard words for those who accused her and her fellow pacifists of being soft, sentimental or afraid of suffering in the war. She challenged her critics should "come to live with the criminal, the unbalanced, the drunken, the degraded...with rats, vermin, bedbugs, roaches and lice."[61] Then they would understand that it takes toughness and courage to serve poor outcasts in the name of God. Her followers would rely on the power of love, not hatred and violence, to conquer. She wrote passionately about this: "We will be pacifists—I hope and pray—nonviolent resisters of aggression from whomever it comes, resisters to repression, coercion, from whatever side it comes, and our activity will be the Works of Mercy. Our arms will be love of God...."[62]

And when some would challenge her pacifism, asking what she would do if a maniac threatened her daughter she would answer: "Restrain him, of course, but not kill him. Confine him, if necessary. But perfect love casts out fear and love overcomes hatred."[63] Day never faltered in her opposition to the violence and destruction during the War. And when the ultimate weapon, the atomic bomb, was developed, she considered it a blasphemy not to stand against weapons that threatened to destroy all the life the Creator has given us. She winced at there being a "chapel" at Oak Ridge, Tennessee, where the material for the bomb was processed, and rejected using the name "Trinity" for the site where scientists prayed as they first tested the atomic bomb. She wrote with passion: "God is not mocked. We are held in God's hands, all of us, and President Truman, too."[64]

When atomic bombs were dropped on Hiroshima and Nagasaki in 1945, Day was horrified to hear that innocent men, women and babies, God's own children, had been vaporized and "scattered to the four winds over the seven seas. Perhaps we will breathe their dust into our nostrils, feel them on our faces in the fog of New York, feel them in the rain on the hills of Easton."[65] She sharply played on President Truman's name, saying that the true man came to save and not to destroy. "We refer to Jesus Christ as true God and true Man. Truman is a true man of his time in that he was jubilant about destruction. He was not a son of God, brother of Christ, brother of the Japanese, jubilating as he did."[66]

Day's pacifism was another experience of loneliness, where she had to stand against the crowd and ask herself "What does God want me to do?... Can I stand against state and church? Is it pride, presumption, to think I have the spiritual capacity to use spiritual weapons in the face of the most gigantic tyranny the world has ever seen?"[67] She wondered if she was capable of standing alone and facing suffering or even martyrdom for her beliefs.

In the 1950s members of Day's community occupied missile bases, refused to pay taxes or cooperate with the draft. Day was jailed several times for refusing to participate in the civil defense drills. She saw all war as sin, as estrangement from God, and recognized that in some way we all participate. Thus she viewed her fasts during wartime and her time spent in jail as gestures of repentance to God for any participation she might have had in the sins at Dachau or Hiroshima. She identified with the early Christian martyrs in that she would only "conquer" with love and was willing to lay down her life in martyrdom rather than shed the blood of other children of God. During the 1960s, Day protested the Vietnam War. She was appalled at the slaughter of innocent Vietnamese citizens, especially children, who were being scorched with napalm. Day was also severely critical of those who grew wealthy through manufacturing armaments and described articles supporting such profit as "satanic." She supported her workers who had burned their draft cards and encouraged conscientious objectors. She was sympathetic to those who were willing to lose their freedom to do acts of resistance, but she was at the same time troubled by the destruction of property they caused in their protests. Day wrote passionately against war at this time: "I accuse the government itself, and all of us, of these mass murders in Vietnam, this destruction of villages, this wiping out of peoples."[68] She called for penance for what we have done to these children of God and prayed for the knowledge and love necessary to contribute to the peace. She challenged the American bishops to acknowledge their role in the Vietnam War, and cited the prophet Hosea's writing on God's steadfast love for *all* people.

During the 1960s and 1970s, Day also continued to demonstrate against the arms race, proclaiming that: "God's grace is more powerful than all the nuclear weapons that could possibly be accumulated."[69] At times there were so many with her in the struggle against war and the arms race that she grew concerned—she was used to the lonely position of pacifism.

Day's last campaign was with the nonviolent protests of Cesar Chavez with the migrant workers in 1973. She said: "Remember the boycott and help the strikers.... Their struggle has gone on for years now. It is the first breakthrough to achieve some measure of justice for these poorest and most beloved of God's children."[70] There is a touching picture of Day is sitting, quite thin and elderly, wearing a straw hat, a hand-me-down dress that is pinned at the top with the eagle symbol of the United Farm Workers. She is framed with the flag of the Union in the background and on either side by two policemen, armed with pistols and clubs. Day sits there nobly, sternly staring at the two officers of the law as though they are two misbehaving children. Day was seventy-six years old and it was the last time she was arrested.

Day deeply appreciated Pope John XXIII's work for peace and went to Rome on a pilgrimage for peace with the "Mothers of Peace." She was thrilled when the pope acknowledged her group in St. Peter's Basilica. She mourned John XXIII when he died soon after that and would have agreed with what one of the cardinals said: "He left us closer to God." Vatican II's emphasis on solidarity with the poor and suffering greatly encouraged her.

Loneliness

Loneliness was characteristic of Day's life. She experienced it in the tawdry streets of Chicago, on the bustling campus during her college years, amid the rotting tenements of New York and in long nights in saloons. The loneliness was almost tangible when she lost Forster and her friends, when she faced the world as a single parent, surrounded herself with the poorest of the poor, marched in unpopular peace and labor demonstrations, and languished in jail cells. She points out that conversion is a lonely experience, because other people, and often we ourselves, do not know what is really going on in the depths of our hearts. Yet she says that this loneliness was not so much an isolation that drove her to God as a "hunger for God," which was filled when she experienced the love of nature, of people, of her world. Indeed, Day fell in love with God in the midst of what she describes in her autobiography as a "long loneliness." It was as though her God had come to her in her darkness and restlessness and filled her heart with love and compassion for others. She wrote: "We have all known the long loneliness and we have learned that the only solution is love and love comes from community."[71]

Day wrote of the "psychology of the soul," wherein we are alone when we ask ultimate questions. She said that all her life she asked "why," and that when you ask "why?" you are alone. Day felt alone because she was asking unanswerable questions; she was always restless for something more. Day saw the same struggle going on in her soul mate Peter. She describes him as a person always on the go and surrounded by people who loved him, yet as lonely because "he missed being near God all the time." Day says that many of us are lonely because of what we see ahead, the joining of the human and the divine. One author describes Day's loneliness as "transcendental loneliness," the experience of being unable to be fully united to God in this life. Day knew well that she would have to be satisfied with "glimpses" of her God. She wrote the glimpses of God always came most when she was alone, and describes moments in a strange church or city, when she felt "God nearer than ever."[72]

In many ways Day was a contemplative who craved being alone, and yet her busy urban life often seemed to belie that calling. Robert Coles comments on these apparent contradictions, saying that Day was always trying to be alone with God, and yet lived in a community where it was hard to find even the conventional privacy of the comfortable bourgeois life. Day seemed to be always trying to get time alone with God, with Jesus, and yet she loved the crowds in Catholic churches. She craved secluded study, and time for thought and prayer near the ocean, and yet she lived in the noisy city and was constantly taken up with challenging projects. At times Day seems to be overwhelmed with the chaos around her: "[I am worn down] because I have been harried...all day yesterday by a consciousness that we were inundated by an ocean of unemployed and unemployable, black and white human beings, searching for food, warmth, comfort, and a momentary surcease from suffering."[73] Still, so often this amazing woman was able to find God vividly present in these very situations.

Prayer

We have already seen how Day began to pray as a child in traditional ways. We saw the little impulses of prayer in her youth and how these gradually led toward her conversion. Her prayer life deepened during her years on Staten Island, and as she carried Tamar she began to pray daily. Her diary at the time reveals still a great deal of doubt on prayer, concern that she was giving in to "the opiate of the people." Then she would reassure herself: "But I am praying because I am happy, not because I am unhappy. I did not turn to God in unhappiness, in grief, in despair—to get consolation, to get something from Him."[74]

In later years, Day learned to integrate her work and her prayer. Deeply influenced by Benedictine spirituality, she was able to pray not only formally but also to see her work with the poor as a prayer. She came to see her sewing, cooking, sheltering and caring for others as cocreation with God. The Mass was the supreme prayer for Day. She believed that the Mass is where one comes into the closest contact with God in Jesus Christ, and it was here that she was most conscious of the gospel teaching "without me you can do nothing."

During the 1940s Day turned to Teresa of Avila's mystical writings on prayer. Day's writings reflect a great deal of Teresian influence on how to integrate prayer and action, the contemplative with the active. She also resonated with the feisty attitude and humor of Teresa and saw parallels in how they both had at one time turned from God. Day wrote:

> The shadow of death that she spoke of was the life she was leading, purposeless, disordered, a constant

> succumbing to second-best, to the less-than-perfect....
> As a convert I can say these things, knowing how many
> times I turned away, almost in disgust, from the idea of
> God and giving myself to Him.[75]

Along with her friend Thomas Merton, Day saw mysticism as accessible to all. For her, a mystic was simply someone who is in love with God. Jim Forest, who knew Day well, points out that anyone who was in sight of Day for more than a few hours would recognize that she was a woman of prayer. He says: "When I think of her, I recall her first of all on her knees.... She prayed as if lives depended on it."[76] Prayer was an integral part of her movement to feed the hungry and give clothes and shelter to the poor. She once observed that if outsiders came to visit her place and did not pay attention to the prayer, they would miss the whole point of her work.

Day had a very broad notion of prayer. She wrote: "Does God have a set way of prayer, a way that He expects each of us to follow? I doubt it."[77] She maintained that people can pray through the witness of their lives, the work they do, the friendships they have, the love they offer and receive from others. Day did not think words were the only acceptable form of prayer. Day's prayer was often a simple thank-you. She did not believe that prayer had to be connected only with sadness and misery, but should also be an expression of gratitude, joy and fulfillment. She would often say: "I just can't believe there isn't someone to thank." As age and sickness began to wear on her, Day could no longer work for the poor; she was confined to her room. At that difficult time she would say: "My job is prayer."

Day had a unique notion that since God is eternal—beyond time—prayer could also somehow transcend time. When she heard about the suicide of a friend, she immediately prayed for the person, believing that these prayers could still help the person turn to God. She used to say that a thousand years are as one day in the sight of God, and that only in death will we see clearly. She believed that for now we must be satisfied with small glimpses of what is to come, glimpses gained in "play, in suffering, in serving."[78]

Day's biographer, William Miller, points out that in the final accounting of Day's life, her great power was in her faith. Day lived and died as a tough-minded, indefatigable woman of faith. She believed that the just person lives by faith in God and that faith works through love. Day believed in God, in the creed of her church and in eternal life. She believed in the amazing grace of a God who chased her, caught her up in divine love and mercy, called her to serve the poor and homeless and, in the end, embraced her forever.

Dorothy Day died on November 29, 1980. All sorts of people—beggars, workers, bag ladies, executives, addicts, priests and nuns—gathered in the church and in the streets to pay their respects. Miller describes the scene:

> At the church door, Cardinal Terence Cooke met the body to bless it. As the procession stopped for this rite, a demented person pushed his way through the crowd and bending low over the coffin peered at it intently. No one interfered, because, as even the funeral directors understood, it was in such as this man that Dorothy had seen the face of God.[79]

She left behind no instructions for carrying on her work; it was now in the hands of God. And she was not keen on talk of her being a saint, commenting, "Don't call me a saint. I don't want to be dismissed so easily."[80]

Dorothy was buried in a plain pine coffin, near her beloved sea on Staten Island. The inscription on the simple stone reads *"Deo Gratias"* (Thanks be to God).

CHAPTER THREE

The God of the Mountain

MARTIN LUTHER KING, JR.

In 1954 a dapper twenty-five-year-old preacher, finishing his Ph.D. in systematic theology at Boston University, came to offer a trial sermon to the tiny congregation at Dexter Baptist Church in Montgomery, Alabama. Before assuming a career as a university professor, the bright minister was planning a return to the South for a few years of pastoral experience. He preached on the need for world peace, proclaiming in his deep baritone voice: "We must somehow...lead men and women of a decadent generation to the high mountain of peace and salvation."[1] The congregation voted to hire him. Newly married to a lovely vocalist named Coretta, he assumed his pastoral duties and joined the local chapter of the NAACP (National Association for the Advancement of Colored People).

He had served just one year, when a black seamstress named Rosa Parks refused to obey the segregation laws in Montgomery and give up her seat to a white man on a city bus. The minister was immediately swept up in the bus boycott, and then into a maelstrom of racial protest. Martin Luther King, Jr., would soon become the central figure in one of the most significant movements in the history of the United States. He would lead the black people of his country in their struggle for freedom and justice. Like Moses and Abraham, he would answer the call of El Shaddai, the God of the mountain, and lead his people toward a new promised land of dignity and equality.

Early Formation

In his autobiography, King says that it was always easy for him to associate God with love because of his family background. He wrote: "It is quite easy for me to think of a God of love mainly because I grew up in a family where love was central and where lovely relationships were ever present."[2] His mother Alberta was soft-spoken, easygoing and warm, a devout Christian. King liked to think that his gentle, sweet side came from her. She taught him to have a sense of being "somebody," even in a world that treated him as inferior. She explained to her four children the history of slavery and segregation, stressing that this was not the natural order but an unjust social system. She told them that they were children of a loving God.

Martin's father, "Daddy" King, was a big, strong, dynamic man, a dedicated preacher and pastor. Martin, Jr., felt that he got his strong personality and determination for justice from his father, who was the son of a sharecropper. From his youth, Martin, Sr., had been unafraid of oppressive whites, and would set them straight in no uncertain terms. He served as president of the NAACP in Atlanta, where he grew up, and was a formidable foe to segregation in that city. Daddy King provided his son with a strong role model for integrity and good moral principles, as well as conscientious and courageous service of God.

Young Martin became a Christian at age five, and remembered the day all his life. Mother played the organ, while Daddy presided, and little Martin "joined God's house." King says that he was too young to experience any dynamic conviction or deep religious experience at that time. He wanted to be part of his family's religious environment, true, but he was even more concerned that he not be surpassed by his three-year-old sister, who joined the church on the same Sunday.

The church became the place for meeting friends, attending succulent Sunday dinners, studying Scripture and (always with a bit of discomfort) swaying and shouting at the Sunday service led by his dad. The church was only three blocks from the King home, a sedate Victorian house, where Martin enjoyed a normal life of sports, games and bike riding. Early on, King concluded that God was looking out for him, since he survived a long fall over the upstairs banister, was twice knocked down by cars, and was clubbed over the head with a baseball bat by his brother!

Two incidents deeply affected King's early formation. One was the death of his grandmother. He blamed
her sudden heart attack on himself, thinking that it was
a punishment for his "sin" of running off without permission to watch a parade. Fortunately, his father
explained that Martin was not to blame and that "God
has His own plan and His own way."[3] King came face
to face with providence and mortality for the first time.
The second was King's first encounter with racial prejudice: The father of a white friend forbade his son to
play with King. When Martin told his parents, they
shocked him by telling him about racism and how they
themselves had suffered insults because of their color.
For the first time, he was faced with a question with
which he would struggle all his life: "How can I love
those who hate me?"

As King grew up, he would encounter more racial
prejudice firsthand. He experienced segregation in
restaurants, hotels, theaters and buses, even at water
fountains. Blacks were sometimes restricted from voting
(rules requiring literacy made many blacks ineligible)
and had to attend separate and inferior schools. King received abuse from some white people, saw Ku Klux
Klansmen beat up a black man and walked by places
where blacks had been lynched.

Once King entered adolescence, he became skeptical
about religion. He began to question the literal way his
church interpreted the Bible, doubting that all those leg-
endary stories about God could really have happened.
At the same time, he became disillusioned with all the
stomping and shouting at church. He also began to feel
that such religion was neither intellectually respectable
nor emotionally authentic. He began to rebel against the

controlling ways of his father. King looked upon his father's overemotional ministry as irrelevant, and announced that he would not follow his father's wish that he become a minister of God and succeed him at the Ebenezer Baptist Church.

At fifteen, King entered Morehouse College, hoping to become a lawyer who would fight for the legal rights of his people. Majoring in sociology at Morehouse, King was able to break out of biblical fundamentalism, and was trained to think critically about social issues. His professors helped him realize that he could be a well-educated, socially conscious, thinking man and at the same time be a minister of God. At seventeen, King changed his mind, and decided he would be a minister. He wrote: "I came to see that God had placed a responsibility upon my shoulders, and the more I tried to escape it the more frustrated I would become."[4] At the same time, King points out that he did not experience his calling from God as miraculous or supernatural; he says he simply had an inner urge to serve humanity.

His father was delighted at Martin's decision, and invited him to preach his first sermon at Ebenezer Church. That same year, 1947, eighteen-year-old Martin was ordained and made assistant pastor of his father's church. But the struggle with his father's stern ways was not over. King enjoyed going out to dances. His father believed that God did not approve of dancing, and thus made his assistant pastor get up and humbly apologize for his behavior before the entire congregation. King began to plan his escape from his father's control.

In 1948 King began studying at Crozer Seminary in Chester, Pennsylvania. He studied the work of Walter Rauschenbusch, a turn-of-the-century theologian, who linked the gospel with social concerns. This provided King with a way of linking his belief in God with his concerns for social justice. King also studied the work of Karl Marx—the political philosopher who developed the theory behind Communism—and Vladimir Lenin, a Russian revolutionary. Though Marx echoed King's criticisms of capitalism, he was repelled by his ideology's materialism, ethical relativism and abuse of freedom; it seemed to reduce human beings to mere cogs in the wheel of production. Most of all, King rejected Marxism for its exclusion of God. He wrote:

> This I could never accept, for as a Christian I believe that there is a creative personal power in this universe who is the ground and essence of all reality—a power that cannot be explained in materialistic terms. History is ultimately guided by spirit, not matter.[5]

After hearing a lecture on pacifism at Crozer, King felt that war could never be a positive good, though he maintained that it could be a negative good, in that it could stop an evil force, like Nazism or Communism. As for social conflicts, such as the fight against segregation, King still believed that only armed revolt could solve such a problem.

A key breakthrough in King's views on pacifism came when he attended a lecture on Mohandas Gandhi by Dr. Mordecai Johnson, president of Howard University. Johnson had just returned from India, and his talk on Gandhi electrified King and moved him to study Gandhi in more depth. Gandhi took gospel teachings familiar to King, like "turn the other cheek" and "love your enemies," beyond their usual application to individual conduct and turned them into a powerful force for social change. King studied Gandhi's "soul force"—the application of love and nonviolence to social transformation.

King also was fascinated with the work of Reinhold Niebuhr, an American Protestant theologian. Niebuhr's critique of pacifism tempered the young preacher's idealism. From Niebuhr, he gained more depth of understanding of the complexity of human nature and the reality of sin in all of human life. Ultimately, King came to disagree with Niebuhr's rejection of the universal use of pacifism, and concluded that Niebuhr was wrong in characterizing pacifism as simply nonresistance to evil. King was convinced that nonviolence was extremely active and universally applicable. Later on, King would discover a need for these convictions in situations he could never have anticipated.

The years at Crozer turned out to be most formative for King. He wrote that during this time he had come to appreciate that religion can give meaning to life. He now saw God, not as a doctrine, but as a treasured experience. In a paper at Crozer, he wrote:

> As I reflect on the matter, however, I do remember moments that I have been awe awakened; there have been times that I have been carried out of myself by something greater than myself and to that something I gave myself. Has this great something been God? Maybe after all I have been religious for a number of years, and am now only becoming aware of it.[6]

In 1951 King was prepared to move on to more intensive theological study in graduate school at Boston University. He began his classes for a Ph.D. in theology. King's studies in personalistic philosophy strengthened his convictions that the meaning of ultimate reality is to be found in personhood. This gave King further grounding in his belief in a personal God and in the dignity of all humans created in the image of that God. This conviction would be a foundation notion in his later struggle to remind blacks of their inherent dignity—their "somebodiness."

During his years at Boston University, King explored the writings of the most prominent theologians on the God question. His study of Karl Barth, an important European Protestant theologian, sharpened his understanding of God's transcendence and incomprehensibility. King confronted the paradox that God seems so near, and yet in reality lies ahead in vision. King put much more stock in God's immanence than did Barth, and yet he was willing to grant that so much of God's nature and plan remains hidden to us. At this time, King wrote: "What is the ultimate way out of this paradox? It is found in God. The contradictions will be solved not in time, nor on this plane of earth, but 'from God who is our Home' prior to, subsequent to, Creation—'not now, but in a Better land'."[7] Such thinking would be the basis of his later "I Have a Dream" theology.

At Boston University, King continued his intense study of biblical criticism. By now he had moved far beyond the nineteenth-century literalism of his Baptist tradition, and now viewed the Bible as the living Word of God, always open to new interpretations and applications. In one of his comparative studies of Protestant reformers Martin Luther and John Calvin on Scripture, King gives his preference to Luther's openness to a living God carrying on his revelation. He thought that Calvin tended to mummify and embalm God in the pages of the Bible.[8] King was critical of both Luther and

Calvin for their stress on the sovereignty of God at the neglect of God's love. He points out that Luther at least gives the love of God a nod, while Calvin so stresses the justice and power of God that God becomes a "monster of iniquity." King rejected this image of an angry, vengeful God. He wrote: "God is first and foremost an all loving Father, and any theology which fails to recognize this, in an effort to maintain the sovereignty of God, is betraying everything that is best in the Christian tradition."[9] The God of love, of course, would be central in King's work for racial justice.

King continued to focus on the God problem in his dissertation. He chose to do a comparative study between the work of Paul Tillich and Henry Nelson Wieman, two twentieth-century theologians who, in the 1930s, engaged in a heated controversy over their views on God. After a thorough study of these two theologians, King would ultimately find both their notions of God wanting. King points out that Wieman seemed to view God as a process or unifying activity, while Tillich described God as "being itself" and the "ground of being." All of this was too impersonal for King, who firmly believed in a personal God. He wrote: "The religious man has always recognized two fundamental religious values. One is fellowship with God; the other is trust in his goodness. Both of these imply a personality of God."[10]

King could not warm up to either a process or a ground of being. He was committed to a living God, a God with feeling and will, a God who is "responsive to the deepest yearnings of the human heart; this God both evokes and answers prayer."[11] Moreover, King firmly believed in a God of love, and he did not think that either Tillich or Wieman dealt with love in God in a personal enough way.[12]

The Mission Begins

King was awarded his Ph.D. from Boston University in June 1955. He was already established as pastor for eight months in the Dexter Baptist Church and was a preacher and speaker who was very much in demand. His congregation adored their short minister with the deep voice and fawned over him as their "boy pastor." Some called him "Little Lord Jesus!" King says that he had to constantly remind himself to be humble. He would say to himself: "Keep Martin Luther King in the background and God in the foreground and everything will be all right. Remember you're a channel of the gospel, not the source."[13] As he gained celebrity throughout his career, he would have to repeat this to himself often. He had learned from Gandhi to be critical of self, to admit mistakes and to confess them publicly. He admired and imitated Gandhi, who said to his people: "I'm not perfect, I'm not infallible, I don't want you to start a religion around me. I'm not a god."[14]

At the end of the first year at Dexter Baptist, King was well-established as a pastor, and served as the vice-president of Montgomery's NAACP, working alongside the organization's secretary, a middle-aged seamstress by the name of Rosa Parks. Martin and Coretta had their first child, daughter Yolanda.

In December 1955 an event occurred which would change King's life forever. Rosa Parks was arrested in Montgomery for not giving up her seat on the bus to a white man. Though she was a prominent member of the local NAACP, her action was not planned; she merely felt that she could not take segregation any longer and decided on her own to resist. Upon Rosa's arrest, local leaders decided to finally launch a long-discussed boycott of the bus system, which over the years had been extremely oppressive to its black customers. The Montgomery Improvement Association was formed to manage the boycott, and King was elected president. (Young and newly arrived, King had no enemies to contest his leadership, and his public speaking skills were sorely needed.) He now had to stand up and give what he described as "the most decisive speech of my life."[15]

King's speech was magnificent. He reviewed the sad history of oppression of his people and showed how contradictory all this was to the Constitution of the United States and the teachings of Jesus. Using sweeping metaphors from nature and the Bible, King advocated unity, courage and legal protest. In closing, he summed up what would be the basic vision of his leadership:

> We, the disinherited of this land, we who have been oppressed so long, are tired of going through the long night of captivity. And now we are reaching out for the daybreak of freedom and justice and equality. May I say to you, my friends...that we must keep...God in the forefront. Let us be Christian in all of our actions. But I want to tell you this evening that it is not enough for us to talk about love. Love is one of the pivotal points of the Christian faith. There is another side called justice.[16]

King's vision, and the entire Civil Rights Movement, was beginning to take shape: A God of love and justice would restore the dignity of his children and lead them through nonviolent resistance out of the slavery of segregation to the promised land of freedom and justice. Whether or not King realized it, he would be called to be a new Moses, and for the next twelve years would lead his people through the deserts of Montgomery, Atlanta, Albany, Birmingham, Washington, Selma, and then finally Memphis, toward freedom.

Divine Providence

King points out that even as a child he had an inner urge to serve humanity, no doubt influenced in part by his dedicated parents. From the beginning of his work with the bus boycott in Montgomery, King seemed to have a sense of destiny and mission. He told his people in beginning the struggle: "If we are wrong, God Almighty is wrong. If we are wrong, Jesus of Nazareth was merely a Utopian dreamer who never came down to earth."[17] King came to see that he was in the midst of a unique *kairos*, a special moment in history, an opportunity to write a new chapter in the history books about the dignity of the black people in the United States and how they courageously stood up for their God-given rights. He felt that his people were caught up in this historical moment—a "great hour for the Negro." His people were to be privileged instruments of a great idea. He quoted English historian Arnold Toynbee, saying, "It may be the Negro who will give the new spiritual dynamic to Western civilization that it so desperately needs to survive."[18]

King proceeded ever more conscious that blacks were part of the *Zeitgeist*, the spirit of the times, a special and unique time when his people were being called to challenge the consciences of those who thought that segregation and racial discrimination were God's will. For King, the very purpose of life was to stand up for the truth of God and to do the will of God. In one of his sermons, he proclaimed: "The end of life is not to be happy. The end of life is not to achieve pleasure and avoid pain. The end of life is to do the will of God, come what may."[19]

For King, God was clearly on the side of this movement. King often spoke in cosmic tones about the God who sustains the vast scope of the physical universe, and is likewise able to subdue the power of evil and conquer the evils of history. This same God was able to give the civil rights movement the interior resources it needed to face the trials and difficulties that would come its way. He said: "The God that we worship is not some Aristotelian unmoved mover who contemplates merely upon himself. He is not merely a self-knowing God, but an other-loving God. He is working through history for the establishment of his kingdom."[20]

King's faith was in the God of the universe who lasted throughout all the ages. This was a God whom he believed had given black people a mandate for becoming better people and making a better world. This God commanded an ultimate allegiance to this mandate. King preached: "Let us remember that there is a great benign Power in the universe whose name is God, and he is able to make a way out of no way, and transform dark yesterdays into bright tomorrows."[21]

King often used the image of a march. His people were on a relentless and inexorable march of destiny with their God. Nothing could stop this march. Beatings, killings and bombings could not stop the people as they marched for freedom, integrated housing and schools, poverty relief, food and fair voting. In his famous speech "How long?" King cried out, quoting from old spirituals: "He has sounded forth the trumpets that shall never call retreat. He is lifting up the hearts of men before His judgment seat. Oh, be swift, my soul, to answer Him. Be jubilant, my feet. Our God is marching on."[22]

A Personal Calling

King gradually saw that he was being singled out by God to lead this march. From the beginning of the struggle in Montgomery, he seemed to have a sense of his vocation. At one point, when there was the real possibility that King would be murdered in Montgomery, his father wanted him to return to the safety of Atlanta. King told his father that he would have to pray through this himself. He told him, "This I've got to do."[23]

Such a call had its difficulties for King. There is a touching story of one night when King had received a threat that his house would be blown up. He was overcome with fear for his life and for that of his beloved wife and child. That night he told God that he was at the end of his power and could not face this alone. At that moment, he said that he felt something, a presence, and heard an inner voice telling him to stand up for righteousness and that Jesus would be with him through it all. His trembling and tears stopped, his fear left him and God was no longer a theological notion, but someone very close to him, "a living God who could transform 'the fatigue of despair into the buoyancy of hope' and who would never, ever leave him alone."[24] Three days later his home was bombed, but he was able to accept it calmly and go on to lead the movement with courage and dedication.

The responsibility of such leadership and the burden of being a celebrity often weighed heavy on King. He was warned of the possibility of succumbing to seductions and greed. From the very beginning in Montgomery, the FBI and other groups made a concerted effort to discredit him. Some of his own followers were concerned about what the hero worship might do to King. But he was quite conscious of this himself and made serious efforts to remain humble and to stay close to his people. He said that his regular prayer was: "Oh God, help me to see myself in my true perspective. Help me, oh God, to see that I'm just a symbol of a movement. Help me to see that I'm the victim of what the Germans call a *Zeitgeist* and that something was getting ready to happen in history."[25]

As for the celebrity status going to King's head, one local minister said that people did not have to worry about their leader being deified, because everyone, especially King, knew that Jesus was the captain of the ship. "He has a sense of humility and awe at what has happened to him, but he also has a sense of destiny. He sees himself as an instrument of history—of God—and is very earnest about finding and doing his duty."[26] Toward the end, King certainly seemed to have things in perspective when he said, "Yes, if you want to say that I was a drum major, *say* that I was a *drum major* for justice. Say that I was a drum major for peace."[27]

A National Movement

King believed that the destiny of the blacks in this country was somehow bound up with the future of the nation itself—the destiny of freedom. America had been founded on the principles of freedom, and King believed that blacks as well as whites were losing freedom from the sinful system of segregation. He wrote: "We will continue to insist that right be done because both God's will and the heritage of our nation speak through our echoing demands."[28]

Later, after King had received the Nobel Peace Prize in 1964, he pointed out that he had an abiding faith in the future of this country. He said it was the destiny of his people to overcome, and not to be swept along, or tragically bound to their fate. History in the future would show that so many of these nameless people had followed their calling to make a more noble civilization. All of America would benefit if his people enjoyed freedom.

An International Movement

King's vision eventually went beyond the civil rights of black people in this country. He said that God was not interested in the freedom of black, yellow or white men. Rather, "God is interested in the freedom of the whole human race and in the creation of a society where all men can live together as brothers, where every man will respect the dignity and the worth of human personality."[29]

International travel had enabled King to realize that the racial movement was worldwide. He saw that people all over the world were being swept along in the spirit of the time and were calling for freedom. Not only American blacks, but the black people of Africa, and the brown and yellow people of Asia, South America and the Caribbean, were "moving with a sense of cosmic urgency toward the promised land of racial justice."[30] King believed that God demands that we respect the dignity and worth of all humans. He preached about this God: "Be still and know that I am God. And if you don't, I will rise up and break your power."[31]

God Is with Us

For King, God was not some old man in the sky or Tillich's ground of being. Rather, God was the personal God of history, deeply involved in everyday life and walking alongside his people. King's deep faith in such a God is what enabled him to face the daily threats on his life: the humiliations, the constant surveillance by the FBI, the beatings and killings of his followers. Even in the many times he was in jail he did not feel alone. "God had been my cellmate,"[32] he would say. He believed that God was with him every step of the way, and that he could "walk through the dark night with the radiant conviction that all things work together for good for those that love God." He could stand up to whatever came his way, and even lose all fear of death because he believed that God was with him and his people in their daily struggle.[33]

King often reminded his followers of God's presence in their midst. He preached that when it seems that we are down and under attack, we should remember that God is with us. We are never alone. He told his people that God is always a majority and has a way of transforming a minority into a majority. He proclaimed: "We need to know that in this universe is a God whose matchless strength is a fit contrast to the sordid weakness of man...." When we are weak and afraid and mired down and frustrated, "we need to know that there is someone who loves us, cares for us, understands us, and will give us another chance."[34]

Toward the end, this awareness of God's presence seemed to intensify for King. Reflecting on his amazing mission, he reflected that after giving his whole life to the will of God, he had come to feel that both he and his followers experienced a "cosmic companionship" as they struggled together.[35]

We saw earlier how King was influenced in his college days by the social gospel of Rauschenbusch. This perspective gave King a vision of the future, a "glad tomorrow," where love and justice would prevail. While King did not agree with Rauschenbusch's identification of this future with the kingdom of God, he did go along with the commitment to activism needed to achieve such social goals. He was always critical of pastors who preached a remote God and saw their job as getting people to heaven, while they did nothing to change things on earth. He believed that a religion is dry as dust and spiritually moribund if it professes concern for the souls of people and is not concerned about the slums to which they have been condemned, the poverty that strangles them and the social conditions that cripple them. Love was central in King's vision. He often spoke about the different kinds of love, distinguishing among *eros* (romantic love), *philia* (friendship) and *agape,* which he understood as goodwill to all people, an overflowing, creative and redemptive love which asks nothing in return. It is "the love of God operating in the human heart." With this love in our own hearts, King believed we could love everyone, even those who persecute us. We love them for the simple reason that God loves them.[36]

We have seen that from his childhood, King identified God with love, and eventually came to see that this was the key to gaining freedom for his people. They had to be taught that they were lovable, and that they had the force of love within them, which could transform their hate-filled enemies. King called his people to an all-embracing, unconditional love for all people. It was his belief that such love is the supreme unifying principle of life and the force in all the great religions. It is the way to God and a godly life. He wrote: "Love is the key that unlocks the door which leads to ultimate reality."[37]

King knew from his own experience that only God could empower people to carry such love in their hearts. Therefore, he constantly reminded his followers that they did not struggle alone, but had God and God's power of love with them every step of the way. "You do not struggle alone, but God struggles with you." [38] It was the power of this love that would bring in a new age and a new creation.

King linked love integrally with justice. He believed that the universe was on the side of justice and that there was a creative force at work in the universe which works to overcome evil and injustice. His oft-quoted line was: "The arm of the moral universe is long, but it bends toward justice."[39]

Like every great prophet, King had a sharp eye for injustice and hypocrisy. He knew that his country was founded on commitment to the God-given rights of all people. Though called a democracy with a commitment to equality, it supported the horrendously unjust systems of slavery and segregation. King insisted that his people lovingly but ever so vehemently stand against such injustice. And he constantly reminded them that the God of love and justice would guide, strengthen and accompany them in their struggle.

King had a great sense of drama and knew when to make his points about injustice. On one occasion he was arrested in Montgomery, physically abused and thrown into jail. At the trial, he refused to pay the fine, made a statement and handed out a press release. He said that his actions were because of his deep concern for the injustices inflicted on his people. He added that he did this out of love for America and its principles of liberty and equality, and that he had come to awaken the dozing conscience of America before it is too late. The next day a newspaper pointed out that King and his people had unlocked the revolutionary resources of the gospel.

In 1965 when the historic march from Selma to Montgomery concluded, King gave a powerful speech on justice. He pointed out that segregation had been a travesty of justice, and that he and his people would continue to be on the move in spite of the burning of churches, bombing of homes, arrests, beatings and killings. He spoke of the courage of his people, the little folk who will never be famous, but who selflessly suffer for justice in a finer and nobler future. King proclaimed:

> Let us march on ballot boxes until we send to our city councils, state legislatures, and the United States Congress men who will not fear to do justice, love

> mercy, and walk humbly with their God. Let us march
> on ballot boxes until all over Alabama God's children
> will be able to walk the earth in decency and honor.[40]

King's prophetic view of injustice expanded as he became more experienced. As he traveled to Mexico, India and Africa he began to realize that the injustices inflicted on the poor children of God were worldwide. He observed that all the peoples of the world were children of God and thus interrelated. He realized that all over the globe people were revolting against old systems of exploitation and oppression. The "shirtless and barefoot people of the earth" were rising up.[41] King called for a worldwide fellowship that would go beyond tribe, race, class and nation, and struggle for peace and justice for all. By 1967 King's dream had expanded to the whole world: "With this faith we will be able to speed up the day when there will be peace on earth and good will toward men. It will be a glorious day, the morning stars will sing together, and the sons of God will shout for joy."[42]

You Are Somebody

Integral to King's strong faith in a loving God was his belief that all human beings were children of God. Part of his mission was to reclaim that realization for the people of his own race. He would point out that before the arrival of the pilgrims, slaves were brought to America from Africa, a continent that had been raped, plundered and demoralized. Often he would review for his people the horrible history of slavery, where the slave was reduced to property subject to the dictates of the owner, a mere cog in the plantation machinery. After the Civil

War, the blacks were told that they were free, but were left penniless, illiterate and homeless. They were told to lift themselves up by their own bootstraps, but as King sardonically pointed out, they had no boots! He would review how, after emancipation, blacks were then subjected to the oppression of segregation, a system under which they were separate, but never equal as promised. Many blacks had lost faith in themselves, often feeling that they were less than human.

Migration north brought many African Americans to take a look at themselves and see themselves as somebody. Religion was a contributing factor to this recovery of dignity. King wrote: "His religion revealed to him that God loves all his children."[43] King reminded his people of the Declaration of Independence, which declared that all are created equal and have certain God-given and inalienable rights. He would quote Frederick Douglass's point on the Constitution: "We the people" means *all* the people. And King would repeatedly stress that segregation is diametrically opposed to the principle of the sacredness of personality. It reduces the person to a thing, instead of the "Thou," that Martin Buber had stressed. King declared: "So long as the Negro is treated as a means to an end, so long as he is seen as anything less than a person of sacred worth, the image of God is abused in him...."[44]

King had both the education and historical perspective to do serious damage to traditional notions of racial superiority. He adamantly opposed those who used the Bible and religion to show that people of color were inferior. He ridiculed the notion that blacks were inferior because of Noah's curse upon the children of Ham. And he mocked the logic that said that all are created in the image of God, but God is not black, so blacks are not in the image of God. He also attacked the notion that blacks were not culturally ready for integration, and destroyed the arguments that they are criminal by nature. He pointed out how poverty, disease and ignorance are the main factors in crime, not race. He said that the theological position that racial prejudice is part of original sin and cannot be changed was simplistic. Progress toward equality was possible and was already in the making.

King constantly urged his people to reevaluate themselves and realize that everybody is somebody. He reminded them that their religion revealed that God loves all his children and the important thing about a person is not the texture of hair or color of skin but his or her eternal worth to God. They are all God's children, and they must come to see that every person "from the bass black to the treble white, is significant on God's keyboard."[45] King spoke of the "New Negro," and he announced his "Dream" that all God's children would be free.

King revised the American Dream to include all people. He called for equality of opportunity, a fair distribution of privilege and property, an environment where color would not be more important than character, a country where love and justice prevailed. King's words could be majestic on this point: "Whenever it is fulfilled we will emerge from the bleak and desolate midnight of man's inhumanity to man into the bright and glowing daybreak of freedom and justice for all God's children."[46] At the same time, King could be "down home" and quote an old slave: "We ain't what we ought to be and we ain't what we want to be and we ain't what we're going to be. But thank God we ain't what we was."[47]

Critique of Churches of God

King was often critical of the Christian churches for not being advocates for justice for their people. In his famous letter from the Birmingham jail in 1963 he addressed his fellow clergymen. He challenged their criticism that his protests were "untimely" by pointing out that blacks had been waiting for 340 years for their God-given rights. He reminded them that the laws of segregation are unjust, and that he and his people are indeed standing with Jesus, who also was crucified for his devotion to God's will. King expressed his deep disappointment with the many churches, especially white churches, for their lack of support. He had seen the laxity, the pious irrelevance and had said to himself: "What kind of people worship here?" He loved the church but expressed his deep disappointment with it and lamented that its leaders had been guilty of social neglect. He warned, "If today's church does not recapture the sacrificial spirit of the early church, it will lose its authenticity, forfeit the loyalty of millions, and be dismissed as an irrelevant social club with no meaning for the twentieth century."[48]

King pointed out that the church was the most segregated institution in America, and that Sunday morning was the most segregated time of the week. He reminded the churches that it was their responsibility to challenge the status quo. King saw the task of conquering segregation as an inescapable goal for the church of his day. It was important that churches get to the roots of prejudice, move away from their fears, and come to realize that people of color simply want to live as first-class citizens. The churches needed to keep their people's minds and visions "centered on God," and then they will realize the fellowship that exists among all people.

King could be critical of the churches serving his own community. He said that often they were too emotional, and used their worship for entertainment. They commonly confused muscularity with spirituality. Moreover, King did not think that many of these churches had enough vitality or relevance to feed hungry souls with the life of God. Others had their own exclusive class system, and were not interested in the poor or in social issues.

King urged all churches to supplement the gospel of individual salvation with the social gospel. He called upon the ministers to provide spiritual leadership and not simply to extol the glories of heaven, while ignoring social conditions that are an earthly hell for so many. At the same time, King called the churches to a faith that God is good, loving and just.

In an address given in Geneva in 1966, King brought this criticism of the churches to an international level. He said that many have come to the churches for bread and for the bread of economic justice and have left frustrated and deprived. He challenged the churches to "proclaim God's son, Jesus Christ, to be the hope of men in all their complex personal and social problems," and to listen to the cries of their people.[49] King maintained that justice was indivisible, and insisted that it must be honored all over the world—injustice anywhere is a threat to justice everywhere.

The God of Nonviolence

We saw earlier how in his seminary days King had reservations about the power of Christian love and non-violence. He thought that this approach had not been effective in overcoming slavery. Neither had pacifism been able to stop Hitler, or segregation in this country. So in his earlier days, King thought that segregation could only be solved by armed conflict.

It was only after intense study of Gandhi that King realized that pacifism could bring about social transformation. He figured that if Gandhi could use pacifism to free India from the domination of the British Empire, it ought to be useful in bringing about better racial conditions in the South. King was impressed with how Gandhi set out not to defeat the British but to redeem them through love. King interpreted this love to be *agape,* a disinterested love for all humankind, a forgiving love, without bitterness and hatred. This love perceives that all life is interrelated, part of a single family and process. The "broken" community could be cemented together again and become the community of love. Gandhi showed King how to subdue his temper, harness his anger, overcome his hatred and channel all of that emotion into a positive force of love. King was also struck with how Gandhi used Henry David Thoreau's teachings on civil disobedience and put them into action with strikes, boycotts and protest marches. Of course, this was all fine in theory in the rarefied atmosphere of the seminary. Once King was thrown into the trenches of a highly controversial bus boycott in Montgomery, that was a different story, and King would have to think long and hard about strategy.

Actually, in the heat of the bus boycott in Montgomery, King did not think explicitly about pacifism. It was only when a white librarian, Juliette Morgan, wrote a letter to the local newspaper noting the apparent influence of Gandhi and Thoreau in the boycott that the light went on for King. It was time to connect his seminary theories on nonviolence to real life. King called in some expert pacifists, began in-depth study and then devised thorough training programs in nonviolence for those involved in the boycott. King now knew that Gandhi lifted the love ethic of Jesus to a powerful social force on a large scale, and made love a potent instrument of social and collective transformation. This method of loving nonviolent resistance would become King's main instrument for overcoming segregation.

King knew that he would have to sell nonviolence to his people. Some still thought that if they killed some whites they would get results. Others wanted to kill whites, to let everyone know that blacks were not afraid. And many were adamant that if they were attacked, they would fight back in justified self-defense. Most were not familiar with nonviolent resistance, and thought of it as being passive to evil or even as cowardice. Only their respect for King and other leaders held back those inclined toward violence.

King began to formulate his position. He began by sharing his belief in God: "This belief that God is on the side of truth and justice comes down to us from the long tradition of our Christian faith."[50] Moreover, he proclaimed that the God of love ruled the earth, and holds all people to be his children. That was the love that his followers were to carry in their hearts.

King believed that hatred and violence only beget more hatred and violence, so there must be no violence of any kind—physical, verbal or even mental. He warned his people in apocalyptic tones: If they succumbed to the temptation of using violence in his struggle, unborn generations would "be the recipients of a long and desolate night of bitterness and our chief legacy to the future will be an endless reign of meaningless chaos."[51] He pointed out how history was filled with accounts of those who failed because they did not follow Jesus' command to put up the sword. Their movement now must be done in with love in their hearts and determination to protest courageously but nonviolently.

King made it abundantly clear that he was not advocating passivity, or a "do nothing" approach. On the contrary, he was proposing active resistance to evil. He was aware that freedom would not be handed over to them; they would have to actively struggle for it. He also noted that nonviolence was not for cowards. While not physically aggressive, nonviolence is vigorously active mentally, emotionally and spiritually. Such action does not set out to defeat the enemy, however, but to win the enemy's friendship. Evil forces are to be attacked, not people. King's views would be challenged day after day as blacks and their sympathizers were beaten, killed, sprayed with power hoses and bitten by trained dogs.

The nonviolent resister, naturally, must be willing to undergo suffering of all kinds: abuse, imprisonment, even death, without returning hatred or violence. The objective was to win over the enemy with love, with agapic love, which King describes as spontaneous, nonpragmatic, groundless and creative. He says that such love is the love of God operating in the human heart. It is a love that recognizes that all life is related, and so that if a man harms another, he is harming himself. In the process, he is teaching his enemies that if they harm him, they are also harming themselves. In this specific situation, the lesson is that racial segregation is harming not only black children, it is doing harm to white children also. King's movement was for the freedom of all people.

Nonviolence is not aimed at humiliating or defeating the enemy. Thus King resisted the blacks who spoke of power and violence. He believed that black supremacy was as dangerous as white supremacy. He said: "God is not interested merely in the freedom of black men and brown men and yellow men. God is interested in the freedom of the whole human race...."[52]

King said that he was calling the white man to open himself to the gift that God has given him for loving and relating. Make the enemy realize how hatred, revenge and violence demean the human person and stifle the human heart. In the process the nonviolent win a double victory, freedom for themselves and freedom for the enemy.

Nonviolence also has a kind of "wearing down" aspect, saying to an enemy that no matter how much he beats us, defames us or even kills us, we will still love him. King put it this way: "Be assured that we'll wear you down by our capacity to suffer, and one day we will win our freedom."[53] Clearly, this was not a strategy for the faint of heart!

Redemptive Suffering

King spoke of the redemptive quality of the suffering that the nonviolent endure. He encouraged his people to suffer with the belief that Good Friday may reign for a day, but that ultimately it will give way to Easter.[54] In an unusual article published in 1960 King shared the sufferings he had endured in the previous few years. He reviewed how he had been arrested five times and put in Alabama jails; his house had been bombed twice, and almost daily he and his family had received death threats, and on one occasion, he had been nearly fatally stabbed. He said at times he felt he could no longer bear the burden and was tempted to retreat to a quieter life. He came to realize that he could respond to his sufferings in one of two ways: He could react with bitterness or he could find ways to transform the suffering into a creative force. He decided to see his suffering as a virtue, to see his ordeals as an opportunity to transform himself and to heal the people involved in the tragic situation. King found that unearned suffering was redemptive. He discovered that the cross contains the power of God for both individual and social salvation. He concluded: "The suffering and agonizing moments through which I have passed over the last few years have also drawn me closer to God. More than ever before I am convinced of the reality of a personal God."[55]

As they prepared for Sunday school in Birmingham in 1963, four little black girls were killed instantly by a bomb set off in their church basement. At the eulogy King said that God has a way of wringing good out of evil and that the innocent blood of these little girls may serve as a redemptive force on the city. It may cause the white South to come to terms with its conscience and transform this darkness into a bright future.

King told his followers that they must be willing to suffer and sacrifice. When acts of violence are inflicted on them, the enemy must know that many more potential victims will show up. The oppressor must face a deep religious faith in God and a unity that will ultimately overcome. "Forced to stand before the world and his God splattered with the blood of his brother, he will call an end to his self-defeating massacre."[56] He taught that nonviolence was a way of humility and self-restraint, and he often commended his followers who had been beaten and jailed for being veterans of creative suffering.

The nonviolence was extraordinarily effective. Those who have seen the innocent men, women and children being beaten, attacked by dogs and blasted with fire hoses in Birmingham know the power of such loving resistance. At one point in Birmingham, while the people were marching, the infamous police commissioner of the city, Bull Connor, called for more hoses and dogs. Suddenly the police and firemen fell back as though hypnotized. Some of the firemen were crying. One marcher remarked: "You would have to say that the hand of God moved on that demonstration." Another said, "For the people who went through the line without being caned or kicked or beaten, well, it did something to them. They had experienced nonviolence in its truest form."[57]

At one point, King, realizing the effectiveness of nonviolence in Birmingham, wrote the heroic civil rights leader in that city, Reverend Fred Shuttlesworth:

> Keep living by the principle of nonviolence. If necessary,
> fill up the jails of Birmingham. Remember, God lives!
> They that stand against him stand in a tragic and an al-
> ready declared minority. They that stand with him stand
> in the glow of the world's bright tomorrows.[58]

Much had now been achieved. King had accepted God's call to be a prophet for his people. He had stood up for his people and demanded their rights as children of God and citizens of the United States. He persuaded President Kennedy to consider civil rights legislation. After Kennedy's assassination, King found an ally in President Johnson, who was able to push through Congress the Civil Rights Act in 1964 and the Voting Rights Act in 1965.

Opposition to the War

When King began to oppose the Vietnam War, even some of his own followers were confused. He had established himself as a civil rights leader. Why did he want to get involved in the peace movement? King's critics simply did not understand that his position against Vietnam was consistent with his principles and vision.

First, King worshipped a God of history who loved all people as his children. King's vision for freedom and justice was now global. Second, King opposed violence as a solution to any problem, whether personal, national or international. Moreover, he saw that no one could win a nuclear war. So now that African Americans had become proficient in nonviolence, this was their great hour to teach nonviolence to their countrymen and to the world.[59]

King's opposition to the Vietnam War was absolute. It was an unjust war and he vehemently opposed it. He decided to speak as a child of God and brother to the suffering poor in Vietnam, whose land was laid waste, homes destroyed and culture subverted. He spoke for the poor in America who had to fight in a war they did not understand and pay the price of poverty at home.

The Vietnam War, according to King, had derailed America's "war on poverty" by drawing people, money, skills and resources into a "demonic destruction tube." Most of the people sent to die were from the ranks of the poor. Blacks and whites were dying for freedom next to each other eight thousand miles away, when they could not sit together in school or live in the same block in a city.

King also decried the fact that we were teaching our young how to be violent and how to kill. He says that these concerns were well within his mission as a civil rights leader. King was passionate about America, and believed that this war was poisoning its soul. Moreover, King pointed out that his call to minister peace and justice for the children of God was a call that goes beyond race, nation or creed. It was the vocation to serve all children of God and to be concerned especially for the suffering, outcast and helpless. For King, this included the voiceless, the victims of the nation, and its enemies.

King complained that only twenty billion dollars would provide a guaranteed annual income for the poor, and yet America wasted thirty-five billion dollars a year on the war in Vietnam. He noted that we spent twenty billion to put a man on the moon, but we refuse to spend the money needed "to put God's children on their own two feet right here on earth."[60]

King called for the rebirth of America, saying we must have

> ...divine dissatisfaction with creeds and no deeds, with poverty and despair in our cities, slums, segregation, racial injustice, and war. We have to move beyond talk of white power, black power, American power and talk until our leaders walk humbly with their God, move beyond white power and black power and will talk about "God's power and human power."[61]

This was his dream: "I still believe that one day mankind will bow down before the altars of God and be crowned triumphant over war and bloodshed, and non-violent redemptive goodwill will proclaim the rule of the land."[62]

The Final Speech

In King's last speech in Memphis he spoke almost mystically of unfulfilled dreams and gave instances where leaders did not live to see their dreams fulfilled. Gandhi died while his country was divided and caught up in violence; Woodrow Wilson did not live to see the League of Nations established; and the Apostle Paul was not able to take the gospel to Spain. King spoke of the perennial tensions between illusion and reality, body and soul, the god of light and the god of darkness, between God and Satan, and God and humans. He marked the internal struggle we all endure as we try to be faithful.

King had lost all fear of death. It was as though he momentarily stood beyond space and time, ready for a panoramic view of history. He hoped to witness Moses and the exodus from Egypt; wanted to see the ancient

Greek philosophers Plato, Aristotle and Socrates gathered around the Parthenon. He would like to have seen the great Roman emperors, the famous artists of the Renaissance, and watch his namesake Martin Luther tack up his ninety-five theses on the church door at Wittenberg. King desired to watch Abraham Lincoln sign the Emancipation Proclamation; and then listen to Franklin D. Roosevelt rally the American people against fear during the Great Depression. King would have liked to live in the second half of the twentieth century to witness the global struggle for freedom. Then, he returned to the scene in Memphis, and said that he was happy that his people were gaining their rightful place in God's world.

In this speech, King admitted that he was a sinner, but said that he wanted to lead a moral life and desired to hear God say: "I take you and I bless you, because you tried." Since his first efforts in Montgomery, the FBI and many others had made constant efforts to discredit King. At one point a series of tapes, purportedly proving that he had adulterous affairs was sent to his home. He immediately gave the tapes to his wife, Coretta, who said that the tapes were inconclusive. However, King did admit that these tapes "were a warning sign from God" that he had not lived up to his responsibilities toward his wife and his people.[63] In this last speech in Memphis, the night before he was assassinated he reflected on how there is a tension in all of our lives between God and Satan. He admitted that he was not a saint, but offended God like all God's children. He said:

> In the final analysis, God does not judge us by the separate incidents or the separate mistakes that we make, but by the total bent of our lives. In the final analysis,

> God knows that his children are weak and they are frail. In the final analysis, what God requires is that your heart is right.... I want to be a good man.[64]

He continued his recollection of memories past, and then began his closing remarks with the classic words that he said he did not know what the future would bring, but it does not matter because "I've been to the mountaintop." King said that it would be nice to live a long life, but he was not concerned about it. "I just want to do God's will. And He's allowed me to go to the mountain. And I've looked over, and I've seen the promised land. I may not get there with you." King was happy, and had no fear. "Mine eyes have seen the glory of the Lord."

Then King began to reflect on his own death, and on what he would want said about him at his funeral: "I'd like somebody to say that day, that Martin Luther King, Jr., tried to give his life serving others...tried to love somebody...tried to be right on the war question...did try to feed the hungry...clothe those who were naked... visit those who were in prison. I want you to say that I tried to love and to serve humanity."[65]

The next day, April 4, 1968, King was shot to death on the balcony of a motel in Memphis. King had followed a call from the God of the mountain to preach a message of justice and peace, and lead his people out of segregation toward a land of freedom. He had fought injustice with only the soul-force weapons of Jesus and Gandhi, and like them, he gave his life to save his people.

CHAPTER FOUR

The God of the Cosmos

PIERRE TEILHARD DE CHARDIN

It was a simple funeral in New York City for a French priest who had spent nearly half of his life in exile. Only a few people were present, and when the service was over, the coffin was taken upstate to a Jesuit seminary and left in a vault until it could be buried in the spring. Many officials in the Vatican and in the Jesuits' community hoped that this would be the end of this man and his dangerous ideas.

Such hopes were dashed when that same year, 1955, the priest-scientist's works began to be published and he gained recognition as one of the most profound religious thinkers and visionaries of the twentieth century. Pierre Teilhard de Chardin had uniquely linked the scientific study of evolution with the Christian tradition. As a visionary far ahead of his time, Chardin had proposed a God of the Cosmos.

Childhood Formation

Pierre Teilhard de Chardin was born in 1881 in central France, an area surrounded by volcanic rocks and wooded mountains. Pierre came from the same area as the seventeenth-century philosopher Pascal, and was related to eighteenth-century satirist Voltaire. Auberge, the province where Teilhard was born, was formed by volcanic activity. The now inactive volcanoes gave the area a mysterious moonscape atmosphere, and provided an ideal place for collecting ancient rocks and unusual plants. Pierre inherited his passion for such activities from his father, Emmanuel, a wealthy landowner, country gentleman and armchair scholar. The father passed on to Teilhard his love for insects, birds, rocks, plants and stars. He also taught his son how to use maps and charts, and to keep careful records of his discoveries. From his mother, Berthe-Adele, the boy learned to appreciate religious devotion and Christian mysticism. It was she who taught him his catechism and gave him an appreciation for the church.

One of eleven children, Teilhard early on showed signs of being extraordinary. Even as a child he had what he describes as a "passion for the Absolute."[1] He was saddened, sometimes even moved to tears, that the rocks and pieces of metal which he collected were all ultimately perishable. He longed to discover that which was both tangible and eternal. He began his lifelong search for the absolute.

A fire was enkindled within him as he wandered amid the volcanic rocks. All the nature around him seemed to glow with activity, with a wonderful "withinness." Early on, he began to experience God within the depths of the matter around him. He wrote:

> Since my childhood, and in later days ever more fully and with a greater sense of conviction, I have always loved and sought to read the face of Nature.... It seems to me that every effort I have made, even when directed to a purely natural object, has always been a religious effort....I am conscious that my aim has been to attain the Absolute. Science and Religion have always been for me one and the same thing.[2]

Teilhard developed a cosmic sense, a unique and mystical awareness that the Divine was somehow glowing in the world around him and was indeed "the heart of matter." Ultimately, he would come to discover this presence in the entire universe.

At eleven Teilhard was enrolled in a Jesuit boarding school near Lyons, which was well known for its program in natural sciences. There, he did well in science and won a prize in religion. At the same time, he encountered the intense spirituality of the Jesuits and their quest "to find God in all things." Already, he was learning how the study of science and religion can "sanctify" each other. In his summers, Pierre would continue to pursue his fascination with rocks during vacations at home.[3]

While at school, Teilhard began to feel the stirrings of a religious calling. He wrote of this to his parents: "It does seem to me as though God is offering me a vocation to leave the world."[4] At that time, religious life was still quite otherworldly, and the boy somehow perceived that by entering the Jesuits he would be stepping into another zone of reality.

Two years later, he became a Jesuit novice, "Brother Pierre." The studies were rigorous, the spirituality intense. He wrote to his parents and asked them to keep praying that he would be equal to whatever God asked of him. Little did he know how extraordinary these challenges would be.

In 1901 Teilhard began his studies in philosophy and theology on the English Channel island of Jersey. (The French government at the time was repressing religious orders, so the seminary had to be established away from France.) Pierre spent four years on the island preparing for the priesthood and enjoying further training in geology and zoology. As he walked the wind-blown shores of the island, he once again was in touch with the magic within the rocks and the sea. He was becoming more intensely aware that somehow God and the natural world were intimately linked. He recalls this profound insight when he wrote: "The reconciliation and fusion of the two fundamental loves (love of God and love of the World) was realized in me."[5] The young seminarian was actually perceiving God "as the extension of the attributes (magnitude, intimacy, unity) in the universe."[6] For him, the two centers, God and world, seemed to need and complete each other. According to Teilhard, God actually uses the world so that the divine might attain us, and that we might attain God.

Traditional spirituality taught that one had to "leave the world" to find God; that one must reject material things and live the life of the mind Teilhard had been taught to flee the tangible and the corporeal. Some even told him that matter was cursed and evil, that it would poison him and kill him. As a result, he considered giving up his scientific studies at one point, and joining a contemplative order. Fortunately, a wise novice master advised him to combine his science with the religious life. Pierre decided that it was all right to surrender himself to science and to the world in order to find God. He would not have to leave the world to find God. Indeed it was possible for him to immerse himself in nature, and thereby be immersed in God. However, later he would have to suffer rejection from many in his church, including some of his fellow Jesuits, for this decision.

Teilhard continued to see more deeply the unity of all reality. He wrote: "Nothing is precious save what is yourself in others and others in yourself."[7] He now wanted to steep himself in matter and "bathe in its fiery waters," because he believed that matter was the source of life. He could freely plunge himself into matter, "for it cradled you long ago in your preconscious existence; and it is that ocean that will raise you up to God."[8] Pierre wanted to see himself as part of the cosmos, and to be able to meet his God in that very same cosmos. He was embracing a unique spirituality which was quite out of step with the church of his day.

After his studies in Jersey, Teilhard was sent to teach science in a Jesuit high school in Cairo. This was a splendid opportunity to be able to dig in some of the oldest archaeological sites in the world. He could explore the ancient areas of the Nile valley and help uncover lost civilizations in the land of the pharaohs. Besides his high school duties, he took every opportunity to join caravans for digs, to gather the fossils, flora and fauna of Egypt. His stay also served to familiarize him with some of the early places of Christianity, other Christian rites and the Islamic religion.

Teilhard's time in Egypt developed his fascination with creation's vast expanses of time and place. He continued to find God and Jesus within matter. He later described "how the universe, in all its power and multiplicity, came to assume for me the lineaments of the face of Christ."[9] He saw how the divine dimensions of reality were intimately intermingled with the reality of the world.

From Egypt, Teilhard was sent to Hastings, England, to study theology. Fortunately, this area was also rich in geological and paleontological opportunities, so in his free time, he was able to study the ancient rocks and the dinosaur fossils in the area. At this time, he intensely studied the great cosmic passages in the writings of Saint Paul and Saint John, and began to build bridges between biblical perspectives and his scientific discoveries. Both the Bible and the laboratory revealed to him that in the complex and ever-changing cosmos there existed a divine life and energy. Scripture and science taught him that there was a "Universal Being" in nature, a "blood stream or nervous system running through the totality of life."[10]

During his years at Hastings, Teilhard deepened his understanding of the evolutionary perspective, and continued to integrate his scientific and theological views. Until now, his education and religion had indicated to him that there was a dualist separation between matter and spirit, body and soul, the unconscious and the conscious. Matter, body and the unconscious were often seen by the religious-minded to be suspect, inferior and even dangerous. Spirit had been presented to him as a shadow, which he was told to venerate, even though he notes that it often held little interest for him.

Teilhard was beginning to be convinced that his own experience of spirit existing within matter was authentic. He wrote:

> I took my first still hesitant steps into an 'evolutive' Universe, and saw that the dualism in which I had hitherto been enclosed was disappearing like the mist before the rising sun. Matter and Spirit: these were no longer two things, but two states or two aspects of one and the same cosmic Stuff...[11]

Teilhard's reading of French philosopher Henri Bergson helped him reject traditional notions of a static cosmos and accept a dynamic evolutionary understanding of the universe. His contacts with Father Joseph Marechal, a scientist, philosopher and expert on mysticism, also helped him understand his own mystical experiences of the oneness of the finite and the union of matter and spirit as authentically mystical. Teilhard was moving toward seeing the cosmos always in the process of becoming—a "genesis" produced by the divine energy within all things. He would later reflect on this process:

> It was during the years when I was studying theology at Hastings...that there gradually grew in me, as a presence much more than as an abstract notion, the consciousness of a deep running, ontological, total Current that embraced the whole Universe in which I moved; and this consciousness continued to grow until it filled the whole horizon of my inner being.[12]

More and more, he realized the centrality of spirit in matter, and how the future would be determined by how that spirit evolved. The cosmos was vibrant for this young visionary, and all matter seemed to glitter with what he describes as an illuminating brightness, a rich plenitude. This moved him to proclaim: "God, who is eternal Being-in-itself, is, one might say, everywhere in the process of formation in us. For God is also the heart of everything."[13] For Teilhard, the God above and the God ahead were the same; he saw his mission as helping modern believers to integrate the two.

In 1912 Pierre finished his theological studies and was sent to Paris to continue his studies in geology and paleontology. His graduate work, as well as opportunities to study fossil data at the Museum of Natural History and work in excavations in France and Spain deepened his understanding of and commitment to evolution. At the same time, he continued to have profound experiences of God as the heart of matter.

Called to the Front

When World War I broke out in Europe in 1914, Teilhard joined the service as a medical orderly and asked to be a stretcher-bearer at the front. He had spent the first thirty-three years of his life in the security of his idyllic home life and in the otherworldly, protected life of the seminary. Now he would be thrown into an entirely new world of diverse people, bloodshed, suffering, death and courageous action. This period would test his mettle and bring him to new depths of human experience and insight.

Teilhard served his country for three challenging years at the front, carrying the wounded and dying from the battlefield. During this time, he encountered the devastation from bombardment, as well as the savagery of hand-to-hand combat in trench warfare. He would serve at the brutal battles of Ypres, Verdun and Marne.

At Verdun, he experienced one of the worst battles in history. Over seven hundred thousand casualties were incurred on both sides in less than a year. Teilhard gained a reputation for being fearless and courageous. Amazingly, he came through the horrors of war without disease or even a scratch. The men in his division, mostly Muslims, gave him an Arabic name which meant "a person closely bound to God who is blessed with God's favor." At the end of the war he was given several war decorations, including the Legion of Honor.

Teilhard's tour of duty left a profound impression on him. It put him it touch with the depths of human feelings—patriotism, fear, courage, determination, endurance, hatred, loss. He felt himself to be part of an enormous movement of human effort, as though he were at the "'front of the wave' carrying the world of man towards its new destiny."[14] In the war, it seemed to Pierre that millions were marching forward in a massive cosmic surge. He even experienced at times a sense of a spiritual grandeur about battle. Enormous moral energies were released as soldiers were driven by instinct to live, and by noble pride to win victory for their countries.

In spite of the suffering and death, there was something about the experience of war which gave Teilhard a clarity, energy and freedom that he had never before experienced. Day-to-day civilian life seemed almost slavery compared to the nobility and rightness he felt being part of a cause. As a soldier, he became part of something much larger and more sublime than himself.

He was free of the worries about health, family, success and the future. He often felt as though he was living in a new zone of serenity, liberated from all the conventions of life. At night, as the poisonous vapors from gas attacks still lingered in the hollows, and the mortars were silenced, he would put himself back in touch with the nature around him and feel safe and free. He had survived another day and felt that his life was more precious than ever. After the battle of Ypres, he wrote his sister: "I hope I shall have emerged more of a man and more of a priest. And more than ever I believe that life is beautiful, in the grimmest of circumstances—when you can see God, ever-present in them."[15]

The war also helped Teilhard delve even more deeply into the energies and secrets of the world, and strengthened his resolve to reconcile his love of the earth with his love of God. The war also moved him to extend the dimensions of God to a now much larger world.

Pierre often found in war the absolute for which he had searched so earnestly. War not only put him in touch with the massive energies within humanity and matter, it also made him appreciate the value of peace. Those who survived could devote themselves to peace "religiously, with the consciousness of forwarding, in God and for God, the great task of creating and sanctifying a humankind that is born above all in hours of crisis but can reach its fulfillment only in peace."[16] Those who have given their lives in war have taken responsibility for a freedom greater than their own, and they have been "elevated to the very frontier of the World—close to God."[17] Teilhard had seen this firsthand, and had glimpsed in the faces of dying soldiers the "divine eyes revealed."[18] He had accepted that he himself might come to such an end and prayed: "And if I am destined not to return from those heights I would like my body to remain there, molded into the clay of the fortifications, like a living cement thrown by God into the stonework of the New City."[19]

Amazingly, Teilhard was able during lulls in the fighting to reflect on his vision of the earth, integrate his experience and write a number of reflective essays. Those writings contain the seeds of his later thoughts: seeing the cosmos as the Body of Christ, communing with God through the earth, seeing evolution as a process holy in that it contains God's spirit. Already he sees that "God, the personal and loving Infinite, is the Source, the motive Force and the End of the universe,"[20] and that all the world has emerged from the heart of God's creative power. He sternly warns that people will turn away from a religion which offers them a God who is cut off from themselves and the world in which they live; a God who makes them condemn the world.[21] He has entrusted himself to a God who is deep within matter, life and the ocean of energies which surround him. He is fully engaged in the conquest of the world for the cosmic Christ.

The war had put God on a bigger screen for Teilhard. His world was now larger, his experience of life broader and deeper. More than ever before he could see that one could find the divine where it was least expected. God was everywhere—in the trenches, in the night sky after a battle, in the eyes of an agonized soldier on a stretcher. The war had offered him many new insights into his growing belief that "God is also the Heart of it all."[22]

Return to Civilian Life

After the war, Teilhard returned to Paris to pursue a degree in natural science at the Sorbonne and seek work as a professor. He gained his doctorate with the highest honors in 1922, and began teaching geology at the Institute Catholique in Paris. During this period he continued to write about his experience of God in matter, and pointed out that as a priest, he now understood the expression "this is my body" in a whole new way. For him, the material world was now like an ocean in which he wished to struggle, bathe and drink, an ocean that would raise him up to God. The fullness and unity in the universe thus contrasted sharply with the trite human pretentiousness around him. He felt that his God was bringing about a deep process of renewal in the world, and that he was being called to play a part in this new creation.

Teilhard's writings became more mystical as he described how

> ...a Being was taking form in the totality of space; a Being with the attractive power of a soul, palpable like a body, vast as the sky; a Being mingled with things yet distinct from them; a Being of a higher order than the substance of things with which it was adorned, yet taking shape within them. The rising Sun was being born in the heart of the world. God was shining forth from the summit of that world of matter...[23]

He described the material world as blessed, in spite of the fact that it can also be harsh, stubborn and perilous. He perceived the march of evolution to be ever irresistible and new, ever forcing him to further pursue the truth of it. At the same time, what he called "universal matter" was boundless and immeasurable, capable of revealing the dimensions of God. Teilhard could be lyrical as he wrote of matter: "You who batter us and then dress our wounds, you who resist us and yield to us, you who wreck and build, you who shackle and liberate, the sap of our souls, the hand of God, the flesh of Christ: it is you, matter, that I bless."[24] The universe had become the divine milieu for Teilhard, an ambience charged with creative power and the Spirit of God.

We Are Moving

Teilhard gave his wholehearted approval to the movement of evolution and the modern progress emerging after the war. He used the image of earth as a raft in space with two opposing camps on board. One group is filled with excitement and faith and they cry out: "We are moving! We are going forward!" The other group, whom he calls the "immobilists," don't share this enthusiasm, and with their characteristic inertia and pessimism insist that "Nothing changes. We are not moving at all." They believe that progress contributes to evil and that change undermines tradition. In defense of the sacred established order, the immobilists deny change and forbid the earth to move.[25]

Obviously, Teilhard identified with those who accepted change, progress and evolution. He said that he joined them in their excitement over new ripples in the water, fresh scents in the air, and guiding lights in the sky. He embraced the notion that Nature is a "becoming," and that all the universe, even the human spirit is changing. All along there has been an ascent in living creatures to consciousness, and now both the universe and the human spirit continue to evolve.

Teilhard pointed out that the human spirit has moved from self-knowledge to an ever-growing capacity to understand its place in space and time. We are becoming more and more conscious of "our place and responsibility in relation to the Universe."[26] We are discovering our relationship to the whole universe, and at the same time, we are awakening to our responsibilities to the universe. The human race is maturing, becoming adult, with new freedoms and responsibilities.

A new choice emerges in this maturity: Do we become arrogant in our autonomy or loving in our service? Do we revolt against our world, or stand in adoration of it?[27] To choose the latter would mean that we strive to know more and be more, to envision all that can be. True progress, for Teilhard, then, is not simply ease and well-being. It is a force which moves beyond the individual and acts in unity and collectivity. He pointed out that it was evolution which produced the human brain and opened the possibility of human holiness; now is the evolution of collective thought which can bring us to the fullness of human consciousness, and to our ultimate goal in Christ.

To accomplish this ultimate goal, Teilhard believed that there would have to be a new church. A quarter of a century before Vatican II, he spoke of religious people gathering from the four corners of the world. Their task would not be to build a new temple on the ruins of the old, but "the laying of new foundation to which the old church is gradually being moved."[28]

Evolution

It was, of course, quite controversial for a Jesuit priest to be accepting evolution, a theory many derided as "godless." Early on, Teilhard had to spend time explaining how evolution could be compatible with the Christian tradition. This would come to be his most enduring contribution. As early as 1921, Teilhard pointed out that the early evolutionists—Jean Baptiste de Monet de Lamarck and Charles Darwin and many others—were on to an authentic truth, but that their efforts to explain this truth often went astray, especially when they used strictly biological explanations.

He thought that early explanations of evolution were oversimplified, showing quick and continuous development along zoological lines through natural adaptation and selection. Already, he showed, we could see that evolutionary development is much more complicated. He compared it to a flowing river, continually reshaping itself to the various banks along which it flows, and at times slipping into mysterious crevices. He saw the process of evolution as complex, much older than first thought, and holding states of stability which were difficult to comprehend. There are many "leaps" and "gaps" to study, much movement and dispersion to chart. Yet, one thing was quite clear to Teilhard: There is a physical connection between all living beings. He wrote: "Living beings hold together biologically."[29]

In 1921 Teilhard maintained that the theory of evolution would only be dangerous to Christian faith if it claimed that the whole process worked automatically and ruled out the action of a creator. He pointed out that many materialists made that mistake and therefore abolished any reference to God or spirit.

Evolution in itself "proves nothing for or against God,"[30] he held. Evolution deals in fact, not faith, and simply points to a chain of connection. It presents an anatomy of life, and says nothing of ultimate sources or goals of this reality. At the same time, he said, rather than ruling out Christian beliefs, the theory of evolution actually is quite suited to this religious tradition. After all, Christianity teaches that there is a divine power pursuing its purpose in creation and that humans come to fulfillment in Christ. Therefore, the Christian tradition better fits the unity, interconnectedness and direction of reality, than theories that teach reality is here merely to be useful or ornamental. The Christian tradition is quite compatible with design, and ultimate purpose.

For Teilhard, evolution was a simple law of creativity within the universe and did not rule out a creator. For him, accepting a creator means "that when the primal cause operates, it does not insert itself among the elements of this world but acts directly on their natures, so that God, as one might say, does not so much 'make' things as 'make them make themselves.'"[31]

The Universal Christ

Teilhard believed that Christ was the center of the creative process, indeed, "the organic center of the entire universe."[32] This notion of Christ, which goes beyond the historical Jesus and even beyond the risen Christ, is the center on which all development, whether physical or spiritual ultimately depends. He maintained that this was the cosmic Christ of whom both John and Paul wrote. This is the great Christ of tradition and mysticism, whose redemption touches all of the universe. All progress ultimately depends on this Christ, even though humans can cooperate in this movement forward. This Universal Christ is within evolution, and within all those who take part in advancing the process. Christ is the "vast all-embracing Reality—that remodels and recasts every belief, every observance and every system, adapting them to its own service."[33] This is the Christ that is seen in the depths of human hearts. The power of this Universal Christ is operative in all, not only through the natural impulses of life, but also in experiences of defeat and death.[34]

Teilhard's objective was to help people understand science in a Christian way. While he granted that analytical science by its nature can lead away from divine realities, he held that science can "turn us back to the unique center of things, which is God our Lord."[35] The human mind is driven to gain more knowledge, but at the same time humans have a deep need to understand the profound significance and the secrets of the world. Underlying our research there is a mystical hope to penetrate to the heart of reality. So, as scholars go deeper into reality, it is possible for them to see the upward thrust of the process.

Teilhard addresses scientists whose research concludes in endless series of states of matter, large numbers of statistical laws, and many elements of chance. He regrets that their analysis often moves them to eliminate any notion of God, morality or spiritual purpose. He feels that such materialism comes from a fundamental error in not perceiving the unity, the rich synthesis in reality, failing to recognize the eternal depth of things, the absolute and immortal center. He urged scientists to penetrate to the heart of things, to the spirit within matter. At the same time, scientists must be aware that they cannot save us, unify us, or give the world direction. These goals can only be brought about by collaboration between humans and God. He wrote:

> Life has made us conscious collaborators in a Creation which is still going on in us, in order to lead us, it would appear, to a goal (even on earth) much more lofty and distant than we imagined. We must, therefore, help God with all our strength....[36]

Teilhard had established himself in Paris as a serious researcher, popular professor and much sought-after lecturer. His vision of how evolution can be integrated with Christian belief now had all its components, and he would now, through a constant stream of essays, explore new facets of this vision throughout his life.

At one point in 1922, Pierre was invited to come to Belgium to speak to Jesuit seminarians on evolution. After his lecture, he was asked how these views could be compatible with the traditional teachings on Adam and Eve, the fall and original sin. Pierre was quite open in his answers and pointed out that these matters could not be taken literally as they had been in the past. Several of the faculty questioned Pierre intensely, and then asked him to put his views into an essay which they could study. Pierre honored their requests, and the essays soon found their way to the Vatican in Rome. The writings shocked the Vatican censors, and the machinery was put in place to stop the dangerous ideas of this upstart French Jesuit.

Without realizing what was going on behind the scenes to stifle him, Teilhard accepted an invitation to travel to China to examine some exciting discoveries in the Yellow River Basin. As was the case in Egypt, China offered him an extraordinary opportunity to go to an ancient and exotic land and explore areas where sage emperors ruled over an endless number of dynasties. It was a chance to do some firsthand excavations in one of the cradles of humanity.

It was during this brief expedition in China that he wrote his famous *Mass on the World,* a creative and now classic expression of his union of the world and his religious faith. The setting is early morning, and since he has neither an altar nor bread and wine, he chooses to make the earth itself his altar and hold up the labors and sufferings of the people of the world as his offering. He wrote:

> I will place on my paten, O God, the harvest to be won by this renewal of labor. Into my chalice I shall pour all the sap which is to be pressed out this day from the earth's fruits.
>
> One by one, Lord, I see and I love all those whom you have given me to sustain and charm my life... I call before me the whole vast anonymous army of living humanity.
>
> Receive, O Lord, this all-embracing host which the whole creation, moved by your magnetism, offers you at this dawn a new day.
>
> Because I know myself to be irremediably less a child of heaven than a son of earth, therefore I will this morning climb up in spirit to the high place, bearing with me the hopes and the miseries of my mother...
>
> Over every living thing which is to spring up, to grow, to flower, to ripen during this day, say again the words: This is my Body.
>
> Through your own incarnation, my God, all matter is henceforth incarnate.
>
> So, my God, I prostrate myself before your presence in the universe which has now become a living flame.[37]

Soon after he returned to Paris, a letter arrived from his Jesuit superior informing him that Rome vehemently opposed his views on original sin. He was to go to Jesuit headquarters and sign a document promising that he would never again challenge the church's teaching on original sin. He made appeals and continued his teaching, drawing huge crowds of students and seminarians to his public lectures.

But the pressure against him began to build. Articles attacking his views appeared in journals, and a bloc of conservative French bishops complained about him to Rome. The Jesuit General offered him little support, and soon ordered him to sign an agreement on the literal truth of Adam, Eve and the fall, leave his post at the university, and get out of France as soon as possible. Teilhard was devastated. He believed that God was in all things—how was God in all of this? He wrote to a friend: "Help me! If I show defiance I will betray my fundamental faith in the fact that everything that happens to me is animated by God...I'll compromise the religious value of my ideas....I'll be accused of pride, estrangement from the Church, who knows what else!"[38]

He signed the agreement out of sheer obedience and prepared to leave his friends, his university and his native land for exile in China.

Teilhard was forty-five when he took up exile in China. His lifetime ambition to be a professor of science in a university had been snatched from him. Moreover, he was not allowed to publish any thoughts on his extraordinary vision of how science and religion might be integrated. Pierre would remain in China for twenty years, amid constant political turmoil, another world war and a Japanese invasion—events that would seriously curtail his work. The stress would often cause him to be depressed. Still, he persisted as best he could in his work and writing and in the development of his vision. He participated in important archaeological expeditions in China, including the discovery of Peking Man. He researched in Africa and India, studied the Java Man in Burma, and visited Paris and the United States several times. He continued to write a steady stream of essays on his vision, and circulated them to his friends and colleagues.

The diversity in Beijing gave him a new sense of being a citizen of the earth, but his roots were still in Paris and he hoped to eventually return for more than just brief visits. He began to write a short work called *The Divine Milieu*, which he hoped would enjoy a wide readership and restore his superiors' confidence in his orthodoxy. The title of the book says it all. The French word *milieu* can mean "middle" or "environment." The book says that God is in the middle of things—that the world is the divine environment. Teilhard offered a new piety that was not otherworldly or world-denying. His was an earthy spirituality, which recognized that the world is shot through with the Divine presence. He wrote: "God truly awaits for us in things...the whole of our world is full of God."[39] He felt that God was revealed "everywhere, beneath our groping efforts, as a universal milieu, only because he is the ultimate point upon which all realities converge."[40]

In Teilhard's view, we are all intimately connected with our universe; we live in the center of cosmic influences. It is *through* this universe, not in spite of it, that we meet the creator. All are able to discover God as the center of creation, if they will but open their eyes.

Teilhard wrote that he was quite certain God does not hide himself so that we should have to look for him—nor that God allows us to suffer in order to increase our merit. He believed that God reaches out of creation and works to beautify and illuminate it, as creation gradually makes its way back to the creator.

As a Christian, Teilhard believed that through the Incarnation the Word has penetrated all of matter. It was possible, therefore to love God through the world. He made a statement which has touched many hearts: "Nothing is here below profane for those who know how to see."[41]

Teilhard felt that we could accept the theory of evolution if we could see that God is somehow building a new creation within the evolutionary process through the power of love. God is not only out to "save souls," but to save the whole world.

He also observed that we are privileged to join our God as cocreators: "It is the collaboration, trembling with love, which we give to the hands of God."[42] We actually help build the earth, complete the world. The Incarnation continues and we participate in it through uniting our work with that of Christ to bring the world to its fulfillment. He wrote: "Then the presence of Christ, which has been silently accruing in things will be suddenly revealed—like a flash of light from pole to pole."[43] Pierre urged his readers to cleave to the creative power of God and merge their hearts with the very heart of God. God awaits us "at the tip of my pen, my spade, my brush, my needle—of my heart and my thought."[44] He urged us not to live on the surface, indifferent to our world, but to plunge into God.

Imagine how some curial eyebrows were raised

when Vatican officials read Teilhard's prayer to matter:

> Matter, you in whom I find seduction and strength, you
> in whom I find blandishment and virility, you who can
> enrich me and destroy, I surrender myself to your
> mighty layers.... Let your whole being lead me towards
> Godhead.[45]

Teilhard pleaded with his superiors to allow him to come to France so that he could have *The Divine Milieu* published. For a time, it seemed that he would prevail, for he was allowed to bring the manuscript with him to Paris in 1927. In the end, though, he was not given permission to publish the book. Moreover, his superior told him that either he confine his work to science, or he would be sent to some remote mission.

Critique of the Church

Teilhard returned to China bloodied, but unbowed. On the way back, he wrote an essay denouncing the church's failure to address the modern world, and said: "The time has come for us to save Christ from the clerics, in order to save the world."[46] He sent the essay to his friends who discreetly passed it around to others.

He would continue his criticism of the church for not recognizing that God was at the center of the world. He pointed out that the church presented a narrow Christianity, which had lost its attraction for many. The church called for indifference to and renunciation of human progress, instead of sharing in the enthusiasm for the accomplishments of humanity. The church presented a static view of fallen nature, while many saw a radiance in the universe and were excited about the future. Teilhard criticized the church for its negative and sterile approach to the world. He says the church was not spreading, as a true religious movement should. As a result, the church was making no headway in advancing God's truth.[47]

He further pointed out that the church cannot expect to keep its believers in a cocoon of orthodoxy. Catholics remain loyal, for the lack of anything better, but they cannot be prevented from eventually "drawing from the common reservoir of human vigor the natural religious energy which feeds their 'supernatural' faith in God."[48] Catholics, he said, were mentally alert and were already sincerely looking for a new gospel that coincided with their human experience and the world in which they live.

Teilhard felt that the church had never properly respected science because it contained new elements which disturb the church's dominance over people. When church leaders saw signs of progress, they sought to suppress, condemn and ridicule. In its constant condemnation of errors, the church had shown that it had never understood the fine pride of humans, nor the sacred passion for enquiry. Instead of sharing the life of the world, the church rejected the world and clung to antiquated apologetics. As a result, he said, a great part of the world had lost confidence in the church.

He proposed a renewal in the church. He challenged the church he loved to restore a zeal for creation, and to participate in the human effort to develop and build the earth. He urged its leaders to stop advocating passivity to human suffering, and to actively fight pain and suffering in the world. The church needed to move beyond individual salvation and be concerned with the collective work of the people of the world. Such recognition of future progress and scientific discovery would not eclipse God's revelation, but would instead show the gospel to be at the core of human endeavors. The church needed, therefore, to turn to "a God conceived as the supreme center...."[49] The church needed to accept evolution and the belief that God creates by immersing himself in creation.

Exile had some advantages for Teilhard. At least he was able to focus on his scientific work and continue writing about his vision without interference. True, he was not permitted to publish any of his religious views, but this did not stop him from writing a regular series of articles and circulating them among his friends and colleagues, and giving addresses during his travels. More than ever, he saw himself as a citizen of the earth, a person called to share his unique vision of a God whom he perceived to be the center of the world.

The Human Phenomenon

In 1928, during a visit to Paris, Teilhard drafted an essay called *The Phenomenon of Man,* which he hoped would develop into his major work. After ten years of painstaking effort in the midst of difficult circumstances, Teilhard asked the Vatican for permission to publish it. His request was denied.

The human phenomenon was an area which had particularly fascinated him. It was his position that the human race should not be separated off as a world on its own, but should be seen as a part of the universe, an amazing phenomenon of evolution. He believed that the gradual appearance of humans could be seen in continuity with the general development with the rest of life.[50]

He maintained that there was a unity of cosmic evolution, and that the earth gradually became hominized, or conscious. The current of spirit emerged uniquely in the human and humans were the "thinking zone" in the world, though still part of the organic whole. With the explosion of thought, the universe could now begin to understand itself and be developed in new directions. This thinking envelope, which has so uniquely appeared in humans, had now progressed to a network of communication of thought around the globe, which he calls the "noosphere."[51]

Teilhard did not accept the traditional dichotomy between matter and spirit. For him, the whole of existence was matter becoming spirit. The very stuff of the universe was spirit-matter. God, of course, is spirit itself, and is the focus of this drive toward personhood. For Teilhard, God was the center of centers, the supreme center of personalization.[52] The human person was the result of God's own self becoming cosmic, and the evolution of that cosmos toward the personal.[53]

Teilhard's God was supremely personal, and therefore not only created but animated and gathered to itself all the forces of evolution. Within the evolutionary process, God is the gatherer, the consolidator, the one who stands ahead of the process drawing all things to the divine self through love. God is the someone toward which creation advances.[54] In Teilhard's vision, the earth and God were conjoined in an upward process wherein the earth opens and flowers, with God as both the root and the goal. In the Incarnation God enters the process uniquely, and Christ stands ahead of all creation, drawing it to omega, ultimate fulfillment.

For Teilhard, the human person is the ultimate expression of God's drawing reality toward the personal. He described God as the first nucleus of consciousness and maintained that the advent of human consciousness was the peak of God's process.[55] The human is the phenomenon which now reflects on itself and seeks meaning. Humans not only know, they know that they know! The human consciousness is the culmination of spiritual transformation. It represents a stage where a creature can discover God in the heart of matter and actually participate in the converging process whereby all creation becomes one with God.

It is clear that Teilhard believed that the human phenomenon was not a chance accident, but was "inspired by the creator."[56] He wrote about the time before humans appeared on earth: "If by some miracle a traveler had been transported to our planet at that period (that even so is not so very distant—a couple of million years or so in the past), he could have covered the whole earth and met *nobody*: I mean *literally nobody*."[57] He points out the strangeness and contrast to the time when humans cluttered the whole earth. What happened in between? The answer is obvious, he states: There was over time an explosion of consciousness. There was the gradual appearance of the human phenomenon.

The human phenomenon quickly spread over the earth in the first stage of what he called planetization. He saw the next stage as the inward development of a cosmic spiritual center "upon which all the separate consciousness of the world may converge and within which they may love one another; the rise of a God."[58] It is this God who gave the impulse for humans not only to live, but to have an essential joy in living.

For Teilhard the driving energy within the process of evolution is love, and God is the center of that love, the presence of love, and indeed can be called love itself. He saw a special role for Christianity in bringing the message of love to the world, and in helping to bring about the ultimate goal of creation—"God finally becoming all in all within an atmosphere of pure charity."[59]

As we have seen, in Teilhard's vision the world is filled with God. Therefore, for those who can see, God becomes intelligible and lovable in everything around us. Conversely, we can come to see that "everything becomes lovable in God." He believes that God drives the world with a "love-energy" and watches over creation like a mother.[60]

Teilhard must have startled his critics when he wrote: "If, as a result of some interior revolution, I were to lose in succession my faith in Christ, my faith in a personal God, and my faith in spirit, I feel that I should continue to believe invincibly in the world."[61] He could surrender himself to the world and confidently go where the world might lead him. His work as geologist and paleontologist would reveal to him his God. He wrote: "The God whom I seek must reveal himself to me as a savior of human work."[62]

He discussed the human urge for life and living, encouraged people to have faith in the world, and held high the hope that such faith in the world would indeed bring about a more profound recognition and adoration of God. Religion, for Teilhard, is not something alien to humans, but rather is an integral part of the evolutionary process. Religion "represents the long unfolding, the collective experience of all humankind, of the existence of God—God reflecting himself personally on the organized sum of thinking beings...."[63]

As we have seen, Teilhard spoke of God guiding the universe with loving and attentive care and revealing the divine self to the unique intelligence possessed by humans. The growing awareness of the human race, through science, about its origins in no way threatens religion. On the contrary, evolution strengthens the world's need for religion and God, rather than diminishes it. The acceptance of evolution, according to Teilhard, makes the existence of God even greater and more necessary than ever. He wrote: "evolution has preserved our God for us."[64]

Teilhard maintained that Christianity has presented a personal God who thinks, loves, speaks, punishes and rewards. But we have reduced creator and creature to a juridical level, and see the soul as a transient guest in the cosmos and a prisoner of matter. Salvation becomes personal success without reference to cosmic evolution and without interest in human progress.[65] Christianity in not an opiate, but rather is an animator of action. The gospel should awaken believers, give them a zest for life, and move them to build the earth. It is not simply a religion of individuals and of heaven, but a religion of all people and of the earth.

He saw that Christianity is unique in that it professes the Incarnation of God. He maintained that the Incarnation is the culmination of personal evolution. As a medic in World War I, he wrote of the link between the natural process of evolution with Christ. Through the Incarnation the divine penetrated our nature, renewed and restored all the forces and powers of the universe. Jesus Christ is the best to which evolution can possibly ascend. Moreover incarnation continues and is God's means for unifying the world. Through ongoing incarnation, nature is led back to God. Therefore, he could worship Christ as "the God of progress and evolution."[66]

Creation, incarnation and redemption are all of a piece and are true dimensions of the world. Teilhard could project the face of Christ onto the universe in its evolutionary process and see Christ as both the peak and axis of universal maturing. Christ is the animator. Christ is the evolver.[67]

He used the term "Universal Christ" to denote the synthesis of Christ and the universe. Here Christ envelops the world in divine life. Salvation here is establishing unity with the universe. He wrote: "I can be saved only by becoming one with the universe."[68]

In this classic summary, Teilhard makes his act of faith:

> I believe that the universe is an evolution.
> I believe that evolution proceeds towards spirit.
> I believe that spirit is fully realized in a form of
>   personality.
> I believe that the supremely personal is the
>   Universal Christ.[69]

When World War II ended, Teilhard was finally permitted to return to his beloved Paris. To his pleasure, he found that many scholars were aware of his work, and once again he was a popular lecturer. Still, no permission was given for him to publish religious thoughts, and the Jesuit General threatened to put his scientific writings on the Index of Forbidden Books. His scientific colleagues were more accepting, and in 1947 he was given the Legion of Honor citation from the French

Government for his scientific work. In the citation, he was recognized as "one of the glories of French science." He was also enrolled as a member of the prestigious French Academy of Sciences. Unfortunately, around the same time, he had had a heart attack, was in poor health, and had begun a period of convalescence.

In 1948 he visited the United States, and received offers to lecture at Harvard and Columbia. That same year, he went to Rome seeking permission to publish *The Phenomenon of Man*, to lecture in the United States and to accept a professorship in France. The answer, ultimately, was no on all counts.

Teilhard relentlessly continued writing his essays, but soon became restless for fieldwork. In 1951, he traveled to South Africa to study some significant sites there. Before he left, he made his secretary Mademoiselle Mortier executor of his writings. He wanted to ensure that his work would not be destroyed after his death. (Soon after his death, she released his works for publication.) He had said that he was willing to accept the world's judgment on his work. He said: "If my writings are from God, they will go on. If they are not from God, they can be forgotten."[70]

After several months in South Africa, now seventy and in poor health, he began his final exile—in the United States. He vigorously continued his writing, did some traveling and shared his visions of a new face of God in the cosmos.

He continued to speak of humanity's need to make the "Grand Option," which for him meant a choice to accept "being" in the cosmos, and through that to be led to oneness in the Supreme Being. He encouraged people to choose spirit, and the future, and to actively participate in building the earth. He urged people to hunger to live in God, to allow themselves to be embraced by God in the world, and to do their part in helping to make themselves more spiritual in the embrace of God. He continued to write of his hunger to live in God and to help the God of evolution to divinize the world.[71]

Toward the end, he focused more and more on what he called Christogenesis, the process wherein the cosmic nature of Christ gathers the whole of creation, bringing it gradually to immortality and unification. He speaks of the Christic, the saving and unifying energy within the universe, which will bring the entire cosmos to its fulfillment.[72]

Shortly before he died Teilhard remarked to a friend that he felt he was always living in the presence of God. He believed that he was surrendering himself to a God who would bear him away to become one with the divine. Consistent with his vision, he pointed out that his own personal happiness was not important. He simply wanted to be part of God. He wrote: "It is enough for me in that respect that what is best in me should pass, there to remain forever, into one who is greater and finer than I."[73]

As he had hoped, he died on Easter, the feast for celebrating spiritual transformation. The date was April 19, 1955. Earlier he had written what might be his epitaph:

> I throw myself, my God, on your word. The man who is filled with an impassioned love of Jesus hidden in the forces which bring increase to the earth, him the earth will lift up, like a mother, in the immensity of her arms, and will enable him to contemplate the face of God.[74]

In 1981 the Vatican issued a letter to the rector of the Catholic University of Paris, written on behalf of Pope John Paul II on Teilhard's one-hundredth birthday. In the past, Teilhard's acceptance of the theory of evolution as it applies to human beings challenged the historicity of Adam and Eve and traditional views on original sin. His views on the immanence of God were interpreted by some church officials as pantheistic. Now that evolution, as well as modern biblical studies, had come to be accepted by the church, the Vatican could better understand his views. The letter from the Vatican pointed out that Chardin's research, personality and richness of thought has left a lasting mark on our age. He was praised for "his insight into the deep value of nature, a keen perception of the dynamism of creation, and the wide view of the becoming of the world." The letter pointed out that his synthesis offers hope to so many who are in doubt as to how to relate science to the faith.[75]

Teilhard left a great legacy to his church. He showed Christians that they can comfortably accept science, especially its discoveries of evolution and astrophysics. He demonstrated that these discoveries can be compatible with the church's teachings on God as the creator of all things, because God is the power of love, goodness and creativity within all of reality. He presented a dynamic God who is within the universe—a God who is its source, its sustaining power and its ultimate goal.

CHAPTER FIVE

The God of the Prophets

OSCAR ROMERO

The Archbishop of San Salvador stood over the stiff-ened, blood-drenched bodies of a priest—his closest friend—an old man and a teenaged boy. The three had been killed with high-powered military weapons as they drove along a country road. Suddenly he saw his circumstances more clearly. He had been telling himself that the violence in his country was due to renegades and leftist rebels. He had opposed those priests who had taken a radical stand against the government and the rich landowners. He had taken a very cautious, con-servative position and tried to keep his mission to the people spiritual, avoiding political matters. Now, at last he saw that his own government was murdering its own people and that he must stand in solidarity with the poor and oppressed of his country. At that moment, Archbishop Oscar Romero felt the same call so many of the ancient prophets had heard: to speak for God against injustice to the poor, even if it meant the sacrifice of his own life.

A Prophetic Voice

Prophets do not come along very often, and when they do, they usually burst on the scene and catch us all by surprise. After all, they have the awesome and dangerous job of speaking for God. More often than not, prophets are uncommonly outspoken individuals, and they bear news that most of us are simply not prepared to hear.

We often associate the prophets with the Hebrew Scriptures. The Jewish prophets did not separate religious and secular matters as we do today. They spoke for a God of history, a God of freedom and liberation from injustice and oppression. Prophets were to lead their people to conversion and freedom.

Those Old Testament prophets were feisty, and often confronted those in power. They spoke for a creator outraged over injustice and oppression. Prophets are not usually called from the high and mighty, or from the rich and famous. Rather, they are called from unsuspected places and from the most unlikely of candidates. They are called from the masses to stand in solidarity with the oppressed. We call these figures "seers" because they could see into the hypocrisy and evil around them and could call sinners to conversion to the peaceful and loving ways of God.

We revere such great prophets in the New Testament as well. The austere precursor of Jesus, John the Baptist, denounced Herod for his immorality, and invited the sinners to the river Jordan for a baptism of repentance. Jesus of Nazareth, the humble carpenter, stood up to the Herods and Pilates of his day, condemned the oppression of outcasts, and blessed those who struggled for justice. He announced a reign of God that was within, invited his followers to repentance and reconciliation with their creator, and offered to share with them a new life of joy and freedom here and hereafter. Both John and Jesus were executed.

In our own times, Oscar Romero was such a prophetic figure. As theologian Virgilio Elizondo expresses it:

> In moments of great suffering and crisis, God has always raised great prophets among us to straighten the ways of humanity.... In our own day and time, out of a small and relatively unknown country of the world, El Salvador, God has raised a great prophet in the person of Archbishop Oscar Romero.[1]

Humble Beginnings

Oscar Romero, like many of the great prophets, had his roots among the common folk. He was born in 1917 in a thatched adobe house in an isolated village accessible only on foot or on horseback in the tiny country of El Salvador. Romero's family lived in cramped conditions, so much so that the children had to sleep in a common bed. His mother, Guadalupe, was a simple, square-jawed woman who seemed resigned to a life of hard work and patient suffering. She gave birth to seven children. His father, Santos, was the local postman, who seemed to have had an eye for the ladies. (Some of the other children who lived in the barrio were rumored to be products of Santos's trysts.)[2]

At the outset, Romero was exposed to a God who seemed rather parochial and private. Santos was not a religious man, but he taught his son the standard prayers and the traditional notions about God. God lived in heaven; God transcended everyday life. His image of God had been imported, and had been enforced, by the Spanish conquistadors. This conquering God was often on the side of the rich and powerful, and yet a God from "a world beyond," whose church was not to get involved in matters of this world. The poor and oppressed were encouraged to be patient and long-suffering with the evils of this life so that they would be rewarded with life hereafter. The many trials of the people were often seen to be tests by their God, and the poor were encouraged to "carry their crosses." The people were often taught that if they could not find happiness here, they could hope that they would at least find happiness after death. Life was a "vale of tears," a time to endure until they went to their true home in heaven.

God was often portrayed as an old man with a long flowing beard, sitting on a throne in heaven with a large book on his lap, where he kept track of everyone's good and bad deeds. He was often thought of as an "old man in the sky," who was all-knowing, all-powerful and present everywhere. Such a God was often presented as harsh and judgmental, sending people to hell for mortal sins. Most Catholics, even though they firmly believed in the mercy and forgiveness of Jesus, hoped at best to make it to purgatory for a long stay before getting into heaven.

Romero was taught that religious life was centered in the parish church where he worshipped on Sunday. Catholics had a strong commitment to the Mass, Jesus' presence in the Eucharist and private devotions, but did not commonly relate their God or religion to social or political problems. Even though Romero had a deep regard for God's presence in nature, even though the church had a growing tradition on social justice, the Dorothy Days of the world were rare. Few prophets rise out of that kind of otherworldly spirituality.

Early on, Romero's father told him that he was to be apprenticed as a carpenter, and Romero quickly became accomplished in that trade. From the outset, however, the young craftsman felt that he had a priestly calling. The mayor of his town had told him that he would make a good priest, and soon after that, a young priest came to town to say his first Mass. Romero was deeply impressed with the whole experience and expressed his desire to become a priest. In spite of his father's strong resistance, Romero left for the seminary at the tender age of thirteen.

Oscar Romero was an ideal candidate for church work. He was bright, pious, prayerful, idealistic and obedient. At twenty he was sent to Rome, where he was caught up in the mystique of the Vatican. He became deeply devoted to Pope Pius XI, especially for what he considered the pontiff's brave stands against Fascism and Nazism.[3] There were many lessons for the young seminarian as he studied in the midst of the ominous beginnings of a second world war and watched the pope's anguished struggle against brutal dictators Perhaps here he began to have an inkling that God was not so removed from this world, but rather was one whose kingdom was truly of this world. Romero could see that, at times, church leaders had to speak for a God whose message has relevance for the worldly matters of politics.

Perhaps without fully realizing it, he saw Pius XI as a role model. Throughout the pontiff's ecclesiastical career he faced the tyranny of oppressive governments. Early on, as a Vatican representative to Poland, Pius had experienced the horrors of the Russian Communist regime as they invaded Poland, slaughtering and exiling thousands of people in efforts to destroy religion. He saw the ruthless repression of religious people in Spain and Mexico. In his own country, Pius watched the rise of Il Duce, Benito Mussolini, and eventually learned the hard lesson that one cannot accommodate and compromise with dictatorial regimes. In spite of his concordat with Mussolini, ultimately the pope was forced to condemn the oppression of this Fascist regime.

Pius had learned the same painful lesson of betrayal in his dealings with Adolf Hitler. Days after the Vatican had signed a concordat with National Socialism, fierce repression and killings of Catholics began. Ultimately, Pius would bravely distribute his famous *Mit brennender Sorge* to all the Catholic pulpits so that the evils of Nazism could be condemned in all the churches. Later, when Hitler asked for a papal audience in Rome, Pius was "unavailable" and publicly compared Hitler to the Emperor Nero. There were many lessons to be learned here for Romero, for in his own life he would face some of the same challenges and betrayals from ruthless politicians.

Romero was deeply moved when Pius died in 1939. He wrote that this was the death of his hero, and he recalled the deep sadness and sense of loss he felt as he stood in the long line to view the body. When it was his turn, Romero put his hand tenderly on Pius's arm and bid farewell to the man who had inspired him so deeply. He later said that of all the popes who reigned throughout his life, he most admired Pius XI. Perhaps it was because Pius had given him a glimpse of a God larger and more actively involved in the world than he had ever seen before.

Young Romero's secure "hothouse" seminary existence would soon be disrupted by the onslaught of World War II. Romero later wrote of those years that Europe and almost the whole world were a conflagration during World War II. Fear, uncertainty, news of bloodshed and dread enveloped the seminarians. Romero's pious and sheltered seminary world was shattered, and Romero had his first taste of the violence and oppression that could be brought on by repressive governments! He was called home in 1943, and on the way had another experience of oppression when he was briefly thrown into a horrible Cuban prison as a suspected enemy agent. His reflections on the priesthood at the time indeed augured his future destiny. He wrote that the priesthood means "to be, with Christ, a crucified one who redeems and to be, with Christ, a risen one who apportions resurrection and life."[4] Jesus would always be central to Romero's experience of God, and his understanding of the saving power of God would, in time, become more radical and political as he was drawn into the turmoil of his own country. Much to the dismay of many of those around him, he would eventually come to see Jesus as a liberator of the poor, as the incarnation of a God of justice and freedom.

When Romero was able to return to his country, he was appointed secretary of his diocese and remained in this position for twenty-three years. He also acted as pastor of the cathedral parish—hardly the resume for a prophet! Yet, Romero became known as a strong pastoral figure: a powerful preacher, a distributor of food to the poor and a frequent visitor to the local prison. His devotional and sometimes testy bearing offended some, especially many Protestants who did not think he was open to ecumenism. Throughout this time, Romero seems to have sustained his conventional notion of God, a rather exclusive God of the church who worked through ecclesiastical hierarchies. As a representative of this God and his church, Romero was not comfortable with other churches or religions. For him, the Catholic Church was the one true church and the only way to salvation. Nor was Romero comfortable, as a representative of the church, getting involved in political or other worldly matters.

Romero eventually rose to be the most powerful priest in the city of San Miguel. His parish was the center of activity; he had considerable influence as the bishop's secretary, edited the diocesan newspaper and was rector of the minor seminary. Some priests resented Romero's uncompromising and severe ways. Although Romero accepted Vatican II's call to church renewal, he was resistant to change from the traditional ways, and did not approve of young priests appearing without cassocks, their familiarity with women, or their involvement in worldly matters, especially politics.

Romero did not agree with the spreading liberal views on the church's role in the modern world. Nor was he willing to accept the Vatican Council's statement on the "signs of the times," if that meant that God was calling the church to get directly involved with such modern issues as politics and class struggle. For Romero, God's kingdom still was not of this world.

By 1967 Romero celebrated his silver anniversary as a priest, and his role as a traditional ecclesiastical leader grew more extensive. That year he was appointed secretary-general of the national bishops' conference. Three years later he was asked to be the auxiliary bishop of San Salvador. Though he accepted these posts dutifully, it seems he had some misgivings. He wrote that he was a perfectionist, and often felt immature, uncertain of his priestly call, scrupulous about his lack of fervor, and at times was filled with self-doubt about his desire for God. Perhaps Romero was beginning to perceive God as a "horizon" far beyond sacristy and sanctuary, a God whose kingdom he gradually recognized as transcending all realities, even the church. This was a God "who does not let anything contain him, but who contains all...."[5] Possibly he was learning more of what it might cost him to speak for such a God. It seems he wondered whether he would be strong enough to respond to what God might ask of him.

Romero's consecration as bishop was held in a high school gym, and it was planned by his close friend, Jesuit Rutilio Grande. Not everyone was thrilled with the new auxiliary bishop. Some felt that he was wedded to the old pre-Vatican II ways, and others pointed to his resistance to many of the liberation views that were embraced by the Conference of Latin American bishops at

Medellin in 1968. Some objected to Romero's close rela-
tions with Opus Dei, which still today is a controversial
and conservative movement in the church.

Others remembered that when Romero took over
the archdiocesan newspaper, the focus became more
traditional and addressed social questions very cau-
tiously. Once Romero had written a thinly veiled attack
on the local Jesuit high school, where the teachers spoke
of a God intent on liberation, who stood with the poor
in their struggle against government oppression. Such
teaching was threatening to Romero, and he sharply
condemned the "demagogy," "false liberating education" and "Marxism" in the school.[6] He could not yet
grasp this "theology from below," which listened to the
voice of God as it arose from the tortured and the "disappeared"—those who had been taken from the streets
or even their own homes, never to be heard from again.
He could not yet hear the voice of a God who called the
people to free themselves from oppression by their government and by their church as well.

In the end, the majority of parents backed the Jesuits
and the school was exonerated. But Romero persisted,
attacking in his editorials those who supported the
school and insisting that the teachings of Medellin were
being misunderstood and mutilated by many. Romero
persisted in his stand for conformity and unquestioning
submission to the traditional hierarchy. He refused to
acknowledge that God could support revolution and
political liberation.

In 1974 Romero was made bishop of his home diocese and began to put the area in order. True, he had
begun to see the hardships and oppression of the rural
peasants as he rode on horseback or mule to the remote

areas of his diocese. But his world was still too neat, and he still trusted institutions, believing that the church and the state would ultimately do the right thing. He still believed that, through the traditional structures, everything would work out. God had a plan, and if we prayed and followed the rules as good Catholics, all would work out for the best—if not here, then at least in the hereafter.

That same year there were ominous signs of the chaos that was to come: Peasant cottages were sacked and robbed, *campesinos* were massacred, and priests were arrested. When the government's police massacred five peasants in his own diocese, Romero consoled the families, said Mass for the victims and even condemned the actions from the pulpit. But his protests to the authorities were quiet and respectful. At this point, Romero assumed that public authorities had God-given authority, were not responsible for the violence and would do something to stop the abuses. Neither did he want to get the church directly involved in these public and political affairs. His writings at this time were still flowery, idealistic. His concerns for justice usually called for prayers or expressed a pious wish that the landowners would be more generous. Romero knew that his God was deeply concerned, but still could not allow himself as a man of God to intervene in secular affairs.

The Vatican recognized that Romero was indeed a trusted "company man." In 1975 he was named a consultor of the Pontifical Commission for Latin America. He would now attend meetings in Rome and rub shoulders with curial members in the higher echelons of the church. At one meeting, he offered his views on the politization of the clergy in his country. He singled out the

Jesuits at Central American University, in the seminary
and the local high school. He was severely critical of the
Jesuits' political theology, liberating education, new
Christology and vigorous challenges to the government. He chastised any of his priests who criticized
landowners, investors and government officials. And he
spoke against groups of priests, religious and laity who
were spreading their liberating ideas in development
centers, using Marxist analysis in their thought. Perhaps
without realizing it, Romero was criticizing the gen-
uinely prophetic voices in his country, the very
voices that he would eventually be called to join. He
strongly called for a spiritualization of the clergy so
that they could give witness to the "transcendence of
Christianity." Romero's God and church still seemed to
be far removed from worldly economic and political
conflicts.[7]

Gradually there were signs that a new and challenging call from God was being born in Romero's
spirit. First, he received the news that forty students
were massacred by government troops for demonstrating at the university. During the same period, Pope Paul
VI wrote on evangelization and said that liberation from
temporal evils was essential to the spreading of the
gospel. As Romero attended conferences, studied,
tended to his people and worked for land reform, he
began to consider the notion of liberation, but still in the
context of harmony, love and trust in the good will of
all—never in terms of conflict. He was yet unaware that
he was destined to stand with a God who challenged
worldly powers, a God who would call him to be locked
in conflict with his government, and even with many
leaders of his own church.

Archbishop

In 1977 the revered old bishop of San Salvador, Luis Chavez, was about to retire. Chavez had vigorously supported the liberal reforms of Vatican II and the Latin American bishops, and encouraged preaching and action for social justice. The retiring bishop had for years believed in a liberating God, linked faith in God with justice, and had vigorously supported the peasants' right to organize and exert political pressure.

The priests of the diocese wanted Arturo Rivera Dumas to be the new Archbishop. Dumas had been the auxiliary bishop for seventeen years and had supported the liberating policies of Chavez. Romero, on the other hand, was not acceptable to many of the clergy because he was perceived to be politically and theologically out of touch, cautious, even rigid.

The Vatican chose Romero. While many of the clergy winced at this selection, the appointment was received with great enthusiasm by the wealthy. The prominent families who controlled most of the land and money in the country believed that Romero would remain pious, studious and, most importantly, would keep his nose out of political matters. They even offered to build him a new episcopal palace, where he could live in splendid and pious isolation. In their excitement, the landowners and politicians seemed to miss indications that Romero was undergoing a change.

In his early interviews he spoke of keeping to the center and holding with tradition. He told his people:

> As Christians formed in the gospel, you have the right to organize, to make concrete decisions inspired by the gospel. But be very careful not to betray those

> evangelical, Christian, supernatural convictions in the
> company of those who seek other liberations that can be
> economic, temporal, political.[8]

He urged his people to work for the kingdom, but stressed that such a struggle did not mean to get involved in politics. He denounced social abuses, but was not yet ready to take on the government as being responsible for such sinfulness. And along with his strong stands for justice, Romero began to defend priests who were struggling for social justice, insisting that they not be viewed as subversive. Romero was beginning to see a new meaning for Jesus' teaching that the kingdom of God is within, and that his disciples would be "persecuted for righteousness' sake" (Matthew 5:10). As for his "palace," Romero chose to live in the sacristy adjacent to the hospital chapel where he served. That should have been a signal to those who had hoped that Romero would be a "domesticated prelate."

The Gathering Storm

Romero assumed the office of archbishop in the midst of great turmoil. A new president had just been elected in an outrageously fraudulent election. Strikes and rallies were organized to protest the election, and in response soldiers fired on the crowds, killing many of the protesters. Some priests who were considered revolutionary were arrested, tortured or exiled. Many people were gathered up and became part of the "disappeared."

The Salvadoran bishops met to offer some reaction to such atrocities, many of them wanting to issue a strong statement regarding human rights and the suffering of the majority of the nation's people. Romero was to read such a statement in public, but a week later he began to have reservations about the bishops' statement, thinking it to be untimely and too partial toward the poor. Eventually, Romero agreed to read the statement in the cathedral Mass, but not in the parish where his offices were located and where some of the wealthy landowners would attend. Romero was still cautious and reluctant to offend the government or the wealthy oligarchy. Attacking the wealthy and powerful as responsible for social and political injustice still seemed imprudent for a representative of God's church.

Up to this point, Romero thought perhaps he was leaning more toward liberation thought, but was still a centrist, a traditionalist, a company man whose dedication was to order, both in church and government. He was still a man who followed the traditional dualisms of church and state, piety and politics, material and spiritual and he was proud to be a man of balance and prudence.

But the center was losing its hold and Romero felt himself drawn to the margins along with the oppressed and his priests who fought for justice in solidarity with their people. His prophetic calling was becoming more apparent. His God would no longer be a God of order and perfection, who observed oppression and chaos from a distance, but a creator who stood in the midst of oppression and violence as an active force for love and justice. This Lord of history unmasked power, privilege and profit gained at the expense of the poor. This was a God whose dominion was one of peace, justice and truth. More than ever, Romero was encountering this saving presence in the faces of refugee children, in the mangled bodies of victims of the death squads, and the pained faced of the Madres—the mothers of the disappeared—who had lost their loved ones. The archbishop was also becoming more aware that to respond to such a God would be a dangerous decision indeed.

Chaos suddenly invaded his neatly organized world. The turning point was the brutal murder of his closest friend, Father Rutilio Grande, s.j. Romero had met him when they both lived in the diocesan seminary. Grande had planned and led Romero's consecration as bishop. Even today, if one visits the simple rooms where Romero lived, there can be found the large picture of Grande which the archbishop had hung over his dresser.

Grande had been working as pastor of a rural parish in Aquilares. He had courageously denounced the government for expelling and murdering priests. He and other Jesuits in the area had organized the peasants and were raising their awareness about their oppression by the wealthy landowners. In his sermons, Grande denounced the wealthy for exploiting the peasants. As a result, both he and his companion priests were censured by the media as subversives and communists.

When Romero heard the tragic news of the three brutal murders, he was devastated. Until now, he had tried to convince himself that the priests who were politically active had gone too far. He may have hoped that the violence and oppression was coming from mavericks and renegades, whom the government would eventually bring under control. Now Romero had to face the fact that his closest friend, whom he trusted completely, had been right in standing with the peasants and denouncing the government. It would become clear that his Grande had been cut down along with two innocent people by the military police. Romero would now have to take sides and stand as the representative of God against many powerful leaders in the state, and in the church itself.

On the evening of the killings, Romero demanded that the president investigate the crimes, and then set out for church in Aquilares to view the bodies. At Grande's church, Romero led a moving liturgy for the dead, a ceremony that lasted until near midnight. Many noted a new determination awakening in the archbishop during that eucharistic celebration.

The following morning Romero proclaimed the bishops' statement on social justice, not only in the cathedral but also in the parish where some of the wealthy landowners lived. He spoke of his close friendship with Father Grande and of his support for the Jesuit's work for the poor. There was a new tone in his voice, as Romero spoke of Christian liberation. There was no bitterness in his sermon and he emphasized that the church still loved the murderers and asked for forgiveness for them. At the same time, it was obvious Romero was now determinedly on a mission to see that justice would prevail. There was now a new tone in his preaching: "When we preach the Lord's word, we denounce not only the injustices of the social order, we denounce every sin that is night, that is darkness...."[9] God's word could no longer be segregated "from the historical reality in which it is proclaimed." Romero was now in solidarity with the "holy suffering of so many homes that suffer unjust orphanhood," and it was now his conviction that such suffering could inject life and the love of God into the very bloodstream of the church.[10]

Romero soon learned from an examining doctor that the wounds of Grande and the other two victims appeared to have been made by police weapons, so he confronted the president himself with this news. The archbishop strongly insisted that there be a thorough investigation, and did not hide his anger when his own lawyer later reported that the government was showing indifference to the matter and was even allowing a known suspect to go unprosecuted. Romero, the company man, was now being drawn by God to take a radical stance within his own land and his own church. This man of order and propriety was now being asked to take a radical stand against his own government, a position that would be opposed by the papal nuncio in El Salvador, by many in the Roman curia, and even by most of his fellow bishops.

Conversion

Romero never accepted the word "conversion" to describe the change that took place in him after Grande's murder. He knew that some in the Vatican smarted at the thought that an archbishop could be "converted," so he avoided that term, and pointed out instead that an "evolution" of something deep within him had taken place. In an interview at the Puebla meeting in 1978, Romero said jokingly: "Would that I were converted!" He admitted that events had "changed" him, but pointed out that conversion was turning to the true God, and he had never followed a false God. Romero said he had always wanted to be faithful to what God wanted of him and he had always loved the poor. But the new desperate plight of the poor and needy had led him to a unique sense of the need for God in our everyday lives. He said that the simplicity of the poor now taught him that without God one can do nothing. Their bloodshed and deaths "touch the very heart of God."[11] He wrote: "The poor person is the one who has been converted to God and puts all his faith in him, and the rich person is one who has not been converted to God and puts his confidence in idols: money, power, material things...."[12] He constantly reminded his people that without the true God they are nothing.

The cruelty of the government had shown him the brutality of godlessness. He preached: "Without God, humans are wild beasts. Without God, they are deserts. Their hearts have no blossoms of love. They are only the perverse persecutors of their brothers and sisters."[13] He was called in a new way to put his trust in God and through God provide a word of consolation and compassion to the oppressed in his country. He now began to tell the rich in his country to stop worshipping idols and to "search for the God of the poor."[14] Romero would call the rich and the powerful of his country, and indeed his own church to conversion from sinfulness. He called wealth one of three principal idolatries, defining it as, "The idolatry of wealth and private property, which inclines persons toward the ideal of 'having more'; and lessens their interest in 'being more.' It is this absolutism that supports the structural violence and oppression of our people."[15] This was not a popular message.

Romero's writings indicate that he was aware that a profound change was taking place within his spirit at the time. A new experience of God and a new calling—which ran counter to his own personality—was developing. In 1978, when John Paul II became pope, Romero wrote to him and described this new calling:

> From the beginning of my ministry in the archdiocese, I genuinely believed that God asked of me and gave me the pastoral strength that contrasted with my "conservative" inclinations and temperament. I believed it a duty to take a positive stand in defense of my church and, on the part of the church, at the side of my oppressed and abused people.[16]

Jon Sobrino, S.J., a liberation theologian who knew Romero, comments on how the archbishop, at age fifty-nine, had a new experience of God. He wrote: "Never again would he be capable of separating God from the poor, or his faith in God from the defense of the poor.... Among the poor he discovered that God is God become small—a suffering God, a crucified God."[17] Romero now embraced a God who was indeed partial toward the poor, who loved them in a special way and vigorously took up their cause. This was not a God of death, but a God of life; one who is deeply touched by the violation of his people.

This "new" Romero became more than simply the pastor of the poor; he became one of the poor himself, and stood in solidarity with them as "God's humble echo of this people."[18] He was suddenly challenging the rich and the powerful, and proclaiming publicly the sinfulness of their misuse of money, political influence, weapons and power. He chastised them for "establishing the reign of hell on earth" through their torture and killing. He pointed out that he was willing to accept the conflict and persecution that arises when the burning prophetic word of the church accuses sinners and calls them to tear sin from their hearts. He encouraged his people to follow his example: "If someday they take away the radio station from us, if they close down the newspaper, if they don't let us speak, if they kill all the priests, and the bishop too, and you are left a people without priests, each one of you must become God's microphone, each one of you must become a messenger, a prophet."[19]

Romero no longer settled for pious considerations that did not bother anyone. Instead he proclaimed a gospel that unsettled people and brought the divisions that Jesus predicted. Romero criticized preachers who avoided the thorny issues so they would not be harassed or have to encounter conflicts and difficulties. He pointed out that it can be easy to be a servant of the word when the preacher neither disturbs anyone nor makes any commitments. But when one accuses and confronts, then the word brings conflict and persecution. Then the word, "burning like the word of the prophets," requires hard work and danger.[20]

Romero saw his role as one of service to the poor, and reminded his fellow bishops and all his people that they too were called to serve as obedient prophets of God. He declared: "I am not a master, I am not a boss, I am not an authority that imposes itself. I want to be God's servant and yours. The prophetic mission is a duty of God's people. So, when I am told in a somewhat mocking tone that I think I am a prophet, I reply: 'God be praised! You ought to be one too.'"[21]

God of the Times

Romero criticized many of the wealthy and powerful of his country for having a "pocket God," a God they carried with them as a kind of talisman who approved of their greed, self-righteousness and persecution of the have-nots.[22] He pointed out that such a God could be manipulated to be satisfied with the way the rich underpaid their workers, and even to approve of the atrocities he saw committed in support of the wealthy and powerful.

In contrast, Romero preached a God who was in the hearts of all, the true God who asked people to give up things when they become sinful. This was a God of the times, who powerfully and vigorously struggled for peace and justice and worked to save all people from enslavement. This was not a deity who could be cut down to size or shaped in our own image, but one who opened the way for people to develop their gifts and write their own histories. This God was "closely present to those suffering, totally involved in their liberation."[23] Romero's creator could use even human error and sins to bring his children out of the darkness into a new heaven and a new earth.

In his later preaching, Romero's most prevalent and powerful image was that of the dominion of God. He saw the dominion of God, not as some ideal world in the sky, but as God's loving and saving rule within human society, a kingdom where all classes of people live together in harmony and peace. In his sermons, he often stressed that defending human rights was integral to this dominion, not a departure from it. He underlined Jesus' teachings that the dominion of God was close at hand, and movingly pointed to this divine presence in those who had vanished, as well as in those who were tortured or imprisoned. As for the church, it is not to be equated with the kingdom, but should work to open the way for this reality. The mission of the church was to prepare the way for the kingdom of God by being "'the voice of the voiceless,' a defender of the rights of the poor, a promoter of every just aspiration for liberation, a guide, an empowerer, a humanizer of every legitimate struggle to achieve a more just society."[24]

There is a story told in El Salvador of a young woman named Maria, who had a deep influence on Romero's thinking. She worked with the poor, trying to secure for them their basic needs, and even tried to organize them politically. On one of the archbishop's visits, it was she who pointed out: "God's kingdom is not in heaven. It is right here with us and He is helping us bring it about!" Romero never forgot those words. Maria was later kidnapped, raped and murdered—an almost predictable fate for those who challenged authority in those dark times. Romero was deeply touched by the example of her life and always kept in mind what she had said to him.

Following in the footsteps of the Master, Romero experienced the dominion of God as being uniquely among the outcasts and persecuted: the campesinos, or farm laborers, slum dwellers, exploited workers, prisoners and those tortured and killed by the military. He preached a God who stood in judgment of those who oppressed the poor, and whose reign was hindered by the idolatrous use of money and power. Romero wrote: "Everyone who struggles for justice, everyone who makes just claims in unjust surroundings is working for God's reign."[25]

Romero's commitment to the immanence of God moved him to submerge himself in the lives of his people: into the world of food, work, health care and housing. He understood that God did not want people to suffer or to be resigned to oppression and injustice. He reminded the rich and powerful that they must constantly ask themselves how they treat the poor "because that is where God is." He once remarked how deeply it pained his heart to see the people tortured, to see the very image of God trampled in them. The poor are often more conscious of the need of God than others, he said, and working with the poor brought him a deep awareness of the presence of God. He called his people to share in his experience. He said: "Everyone concerned for the hungry, the naked, the poor, for those who have vanished in police custody, for the tortured, for prisoners, for all flesh that suffers, has God close at hand."[26]

Romero's God was within creation, within the world, where he liberated his people from exploitation. This was the Lord of freedom and life, who is offended when his people are persecuted. Romero pointed out that such sin becomes visible when one sees a blood-stained corpse. Evil becomes audible when one hears the wailing of mothers of the disappeared. Romero challenged his church to stand against these horrors. Expressing a radically new ecclesiology, Romero proclaimed: "We all have a church within ourselves, our own consciousness. There God is, God's Spirit."[27]

God of Truth

The God of Romero was now the God of truth, and the archbishop set out to arduously discover the truth and then bring it out in the open for all to see. He seriously studied every detail of the injustices which his government inflicted on his people and exposed these injustices in his national broadcasts. He went out of his way to listen carefully to the suffering of his people and then applied the truth of God's word to these horrors. Romero exposed the atrocities that were taking place in dark alleys and in secret prison cells to the light of the gospel, so that all could see their ugliness and evil. Romero discovered God in the "least of the brethren," who were being terrorized and killed by their own government. He spoke out against institutional violence, the day-to-day workings of a system that oppressed innocent men, women and children.

Romero continued to denounce the false gods of wealth and private property, which moved the controlling families in El Salvador to destroy anyone who posed a threat to their greed and selfishness. He opposed the false god of power, which in his country hid behind "national security" so that the authorities could use force to take away human rights and dignity.

Romero exposed the false gods of political organizations that abandoned the interests of the people and used violence and repression to achieve their aims. As a church leader, he felt it his mission to "unmask these destructive absolutisms and guide humankind to the one and only Absolute and to human fellowship."[28]

There could be only one true God for the archbishop, and that is the God who asks us to give up our sinfulness and reach out in love. He wrote: "No one can serve two Lords. There is only one God, and that God will either be the true one, who asks us to give things up when they become sin, or it will be the God of money..." Moreover, this true God is not a distant God, but "a God close at hand here on earth."[29]

The beginning of the year 1979 was a particularly

trying time for Romero. In January, thirty young men were gathered in El Despertar for a retreat with a priest, Father Octavio Ortiz. Security forces came in an armored car, invaded the property and opened fire. They killed the priest, crushed his skull under the wheels of their vehicle, killed four young men and arrested the others. Then the security men put pistols in the hands of those whom they had murdered in order to make the event look like a battle with subversives.

Romero immediately recognized the deception and exposed the blatant lie in his homily the next morning. He said that the security forces were corrupt, did not admit their errors and made it worse by lying and slandering their victims. Romero said that Father Ortiz and his companions were witnesses to the kingdom of God, and he praised the growing numbers of other young men who were courageously coming to the seminary in spite of the dangers. He proclaimed: "This reign of God in the world is a reign of God that makes the noble, the young, truly say, like the one in the gospel: 'Let us also go, that we may die with him'"(John 11:16).[30]

The archbishop became more aggressive as the violence escalated. He pointed out that the killing in El Despertar showed that the president had lied on a visit to Mexico when he said that there was no persecution of the church in El Salvador. Romero also said that the president was not telling the truth when he denied that fourteen wealthy families owned most of the land, and when he refused to admit that political prisoners and "the disappeared" even existed in El Salvador.

As the numbers of murdered and disappeared mounted, Romero cried out more and more vehemently on behalf of his people. As more mutilated corpses appeared in the streets and on the hillsides, Romero called on the government to control "these forces of hell and murder."[31] More and more, Romero sounded like the prophets of old, speaking for a God of history, attacking the rich who acted as though the creator were their servant. Romero had hard words for the wealthy landowners who used the Mass for their "idolatry" of false gods of money and power. He denounced them for using the liturgy to celebrate their greed and economic power, and for hypocritically justifying their sinful abuse of others. Romero spoke often now with great passion: "We have seen torture victims taken to hospitals to die under all sorts of deceitful stratagems. Torturers also are killers, murderers; they do not respect the sacredness of life. No one may raise a hand against another, because humans are images of God."[32] He now spoke for a God who was indignant over such hypocrisy and viciousness, and who gave his people the courage and power to stand toe to toe with the hired guns of the military, as well as with those who paid them.

Romero's religious and political views took on more global dimensions as his homilies reached beyond the confines of his own country. He was critical of how absolute power had also become a god in Nicaragua, and said the Nicaraguan revolutions clearly demonstrated what happens when power is made an absolute. The archbishop asked in one of his homilies that the United States stop sending military aid to El Salvador, and then wrote personally to President Carter with the same plea, pointing out that such aid would only bring about more injustice and repression to his people. At the Catholic University of Louvain in Belgium, where Romero received an honorary degree, he delivered a marvelous address using the prophetic words of Jeremiah to chastise the corrupt rulers of his country for the expulsions, repression and persecution that they had brought upon his people. Romero was nominated for the Nobel Peace Prize by the British Parliament. As it turned out, Mother Teresa won the award that year, but nonetheless it was clear that Romero's prophetic voice was now being heard around the world. He was increasingly becoming a serious threat to the ruling powers in his country, to some leaders outside his country and even to some of the leaders of his own church.

Romero no longer saw God as "above history," but rather as "within history"—a God who worked with people to gain their liberation. He said: "God and human beings make history. God saves humanity in the history of one's own people. The history of salvation will be El Salvador's history when we Salvadorans seek in our history the presence of God the Savior."[33] This was a God ever-active in history, a God who lived within the hearts of his people, especially those struggling for their human rights. Romero said: "God saves in history. Each person's life, each person's history, is the meeting place God comes to. How satisfying to know one need not go to the desert to meet him, need not go to some particular spot in the world. God is in your own hearts."[34]

Romero discovered that listening to the poor helped him understand what the world was really like and what the mission of the church should be. He began to find God in the faces of farm workers without land or money, in mothers who had no medical assistance when they gave birth, in children without food or schools. He found God in the faces of factory workers who got fired when they stood up for their rights, in the mothers and wives grieving for their loved ones who had disappeared, and in the shanties of those who lived wretched and tortured lives. He believed that God works through his people to share and lighten the burdens of the poor. It is God's will that we work to better the lives of others. Romero put it this way: "We know that every effort to better society, especially when injustice and sin are so ingrained, is an effort that God blesses, that God wants, that God demands of us."[35] For him, God keeps on saving in the concrete events of history. Thus in the abduction, tortures and killings, Romero could point out: "That is where we are to find our God."[36] Religion no longer was a private matter for Romero.

Romero now embraced a radical interpretation of the Second Vatican Council's notion of the "signs of the times." The bishop became a "listener" and gave careful ear to the sufferings, hopes and dreams of his people. He once said, "The people are my prophet."[37] He also listened carefully and intently to what was going on in his government, his social surroundings and his church. Gradually, Romero discerned what God was calling him and his people to do in their own historical situation. He decided that he would truly accompany his Salvadoran people—in this time, in this place, and amid the present conflicts. That was God's true calling for Oscar Romero. Romero believed that he had much to learn from the people, and that in charisms which the Holy Spirit gave to the people, he could find "the touchstone of his authenticity."[38] It was in the demands of the moment that there is "much of God to be found...."[39]

Archbishop Romero had become a symbol for Vatican II's teachings on the church in the modern world. He told his people that he was learning along with them the "harsh truth" that following Jesus meant being immersed in the world, and not cut off from it. He had come to understand that the church is not a fortress set apart from the world, but a church who follows Jesus, "who lived, worked, struggled and died in the midst of the city."[40] He pointed out that there are political dimensions of the Christian faith, because this is God's world and God defends the rights of people. Those that trample the rights of God's people must find themselves in conflict with God's church. The church is concerned about life, about human rights, about those who are voiceless, about those who suffer. Romero did not see this as inappropriate meddling, because he maintained that once politics began "to touch the altar," it could expect the church to speak up. Romero could be quite blunt on this:

> Let this be clear: When the church preaches social justice, equality, and the dignity of people, defending those who suffer and those who are assaulted this is not subversion; this is not Marxism. This is the authentic teaching of the church.[41]

He said that he felt it was his mission to build a church "according to the heart of God."[42] If the church wishes to carry out its mission to save the world, then it would have to be concerned about the worldly issues of hunger, poverty and oppression. Its mission is indeed a difficult one, for it faces the sins of the political and economic orders.

Opposition

Romero began to receive the same resistance to his prophetic words as Jesus himself had experienced. When Jesus identified himself with Isaiah in the synagogue, his own townsfolk drove him out of town and even attempted to throw him off a hill. Jesus' lament over this has been quoted through the centuries: "Truly I tell you, no prophet is accepted in the prophet's hometown" (Luke 4:24). The same would be true for the archbishop. Once Romero took his stand for his people, he found himself marginalized and ultimately hunted down, just as Jesus had been.

The archbishop knew the risks but decided to take them. He noted that once you stand in solidarity with the poor and oppressed, you run the same risks they run—persecution or even death. Romero's preaching about new interpretation of the "God of history" and "God of the poor" and the social mission of the church became increasingly more threatening to the wealthy landowners and the military that worked for them. Romero was regularly attacked in the media and some newspapers began to run large ads criticizing the archbishop for not censuring his "bad priests," and described him as a shepherd more confused than his sheep. One headline stated that Romero was directing a terrorist group. An article declared that he had been seeking psychological counseling and had serious mental problems. (Dr. Rodolpho Semsch, his counselor, testified against these allegations and was later murdered.) There were constant efforts to humiliate and intimidate Romero. When he visited his people in the rural areas, Romero would be stopped and body-searched. At one point, the church radio transmitter that he used to broadcast his sermons was destroyed by a bomb. Death threats came more frequently, and were more ominous. Romero made special efforts to attend to his prayer life, so that he could "stay united with God" throughout this crisis. His homilies became stronger, and he told his people that he would not flee the cross, but would embrace it along with his people. His oft-quoted line goes to the heart of it: "I have frequently been threatened with death. As a Christian, I do not believe in death without resurrection. If they kill me, I will be resurrected in the Salvadoran people."[43]

While Romero did receive support from some church leaders, many aggressively opposed his positions. Pope Paul VI had been an inspiration to Romero with his writings on the development of peoples, and had personally given warm support to Romero's mission to his people. In a personal audience, the pontiff took Romero's hand, expressed confidence in him and told him to be a patient and courageous leader. Romero's relationship with John Paul II was not as encouraging. While John Paul gave him a sympathetic ear, it was extremely difficult for Romero to get personal audiences. In the conversations between the two men, Romero was conscious that the pontiff had heard a great deal of negative criticism, and the archbishop found himself on the defensive. John Paul was kind toward Romero, yet admonished him and informed him that a recommendation to replace him with an apostolic administrator was under consideration.

Many in the Vatican Curia were willing to believe the negative things they heard about Romero. He was from time to time summoned to Rome, receiving harsh criticism from curia officials, who were worried about his "conversion." When Romero was nominated for an honorary degree from Georgetown for his work in human rights, the Vatican worked hard behind the scenes to prevent the award from being given. Vatican officials also strongly opposed Romero's letter to President Carter, in which he protested U. S. military aid to his country. Romero knew that many powerful church leaders were lobbying to have him replaced.

Romero also faced strong opposition from the papal nuncio in El Salvador, Archbishop Gerada, who often seemed to side with the wealthy people, who strongly opposed the political work of Romero and sent a great deal of negative criticism back to Rome, actively working for Romero's removal.

The archbishop was also betrayed by many of his own fellow bishops. They sent reports to receptive ears in the Vatican that Romero was confusing the people and dividing the country. Some complained to Rome that Romero was both naive and wily, and that he had imposed a politicized and Marxist pastoral ministry on the church and the country. Some said that Romero was being influenced by liberation theologians, and that he was being led around by a group of radical priests who blessed terrorism and defamed the government. One Salvadoran bishop, Marco Revelo, publicly stated that many of the rural catechists and their priests were influenced by Marxism. Another bishop openly declared that the peasant organizations were Communists, and that Grande and the other priests who were killed were leftists. One of Romero's own priests told the press that the archbishop directed terrorist groups and was sympathetic toward agents of subversion.

Of course, such treacherous activities pained Romero deeply, not only because they undermined his own mission, but more importantly because such accusations rendered his priests all the more vulnerable to attacks from the government. He was beginning to see the high cost attached to speaking for a God who stood in judgment of the atrocious brutality that had been unleashed in El Salvador. His call to the church to oppose governmental abuses and defend the poor won the archbishop few friends among the hierarchy.

Though Romero was deeply hurt by these betrayals, he never struck out in revenge, but always reached out to his attackers, whether within the government or the church, with forgiveness and friendship. He humbly admitted his own deficiencies, but maintained that he was working out of goodwill, and was not guilty of the things of which he was accused. He told his accusers that he was serving the church with love. In one of his last homilies he pleaded for peace and reconciliation:

> And above all, there is God's word, which has cried to us today: reconciliation! God wills it—let us be reconciled, and we shall make of El Salvador a land of brothers and sisters, all children of one Father who awaits us all with outstretched arms.[44]

To bring about such reconciliation, Romero was always open to communication and collaboration, even with his most destructive enemies.

In spite of Romero's passionate preaching and confrontational attitude, he was always committed to nonviolence. When he spoke out against the brutality of his own government, he was no less vehement in this condemnation of the acts of revenge and terror from the leftist rebel groups. He constantly reminded his people that such violence only generated more bloodshed and suffering. In many sermons that were broadcast throughout the country, he repeatedly condemned the violence on both sides, and called for peace. He fought not only the daily violence in the streets and country-side, but also the structural violence within his gov-ernment. He said: "We must remove the structural violence, social injustice, exclusion of [c]itizens from the management of the country, repression."[45]

In one of his pastoral letters, Romero discussed the various forms of violence. He opposed violence when it was institutionalized, arose out of terrorism and the spontaneous violence connected with protests and demonstrations. While Romero allowed for legitimate violence in self-defense, he pleaded for the power of nonviolence. Jesus' advice to turn the other cheek was not passive or cowardly, he said, but showed "evidence of great moral strength that can leave an aggressor morally defeated and humiliated."[46] Romero mentions Paul VI's allowance for legitimate insurrection in ex-ceptional situations, but says that the church prefers nonviolence. He concludes: "We cannot place all our trust in violent methods if we are true Christians or even simply honorable persons."[47]

Eventually it became obvious to Romero that his days were numbered and that Calvary was just ahead. Before he left for the Latin American Bishops' Conference in Puebla, Mexico, Romero was warned by the nuncio for Costa Rica that his life was in danger. Romero's confessor points out that the archbishop's last retreat was "his prayer in the garden." By now, Romero was expressing his fear of death and was feeling vul-nerable in his tiny unguarded house next to the hospital. He feared that he would be kidnapped and tortured, that his house would be bombed. Understandably, he was having trouble sleeping.

In spite of these very normal fears, on another level Romero showed little concern for his own life. In one of his last sermons, he made a dangerous move and demanded that soldiers disobey when they were ordered to kill their own people. His words were broadcast throughout the country, as he spoke for a God deeply concerned with matters so worldly as military orders:

> God's law must prevail that says: Thou shalt not kill! No soldier is obliged to obey an order against the law of God. No one has to fulfill an immoral law. It is time to take back your consciences and to obey your conscience rather than the orders of sin.... I beg you, I beseech you, I order you in the name of God: Stop the repression![48]

In the eyes of his enemies, Romero had gone too far.

The readings at Romero's last Mass were strangely providential. The Pauline reading proclaimed the resurrection of the dead (1 Corinthians 15). The Psalm for the day read: "The Lord is my shepherd....Even though I walk through the valley, I fear no evil; for you are with me; your rod and your staff they comfort me.... And I shall dwell in the house of the Lord..." (Psalm 23). And the gospel could not have been more appropriate: "[U]nless a grain of wheat falls into the earth and dies, it remains just a single grain; but if it dies, it bears much fruit." (John 12:24 ff.) Romero spoke in his homily of the need to take risks for the kingdom, and he shared his vision of a new human family, and pointed out that to achieve this we must be willing to suffer for peace and justice.[49]

As Romero finished his homily and went to the altar,

a shot rang out from the back of the chapel. The archbishop lay at the foot of the altar, mortally wounded. He was rushed in the back of a panel truck to a hospital, but was soon pronounced dead—he had drowned in his own blood.

A chill went through the entire country that night. Few could believe that their own government would be so desperate that it would murder an archbishop as he celebrated Mass. There had not been a murder like this since that of Thomas á Becket in 1170.

The Salvadoran people knew that a great prophet had risen in their midst and was now taken from them. He had bravely spoken for a God who was offended by the oppression of the poor, for one who vigorously worked for the liberation of his people. This is not a "sky God" who watched from a distance. Nor was this a "pocket God" who could be manipulated to sanction the greed and savagery of those in power. This was a God deeply within the blood and guts of everyday life, a divinity within the people, whose reign of love, compassion and peace would ultimately prevail on earth as it does in heaven.

The prophet Oscar Romero has not been forgotten. As he predicted, he has risen in the lives of his people, and his message of hope and reconciliation continues to be spoken throughout the world. His tomb has now become the shrine of a saint, his humble home a place of pilgrimage, the chapel where he was gunned down a modern Calvary. Many pilgrims, even those who were not alive during his time, are deeply moved by his story and his words. Romero teaches them about a God of compassion, one who is in solidarity with the poor and downtrodden all over the world. His life and death bears witness to a God who abhors violence and who stands in solidarity with the outcasts of the world. The words of another prophet seem applicable to Oscar Romero:

> The Lord has given me
> a well-trained tongue,
> That I may know how to speak to the weary
> a word that will rouse them.
> Morning after morning
> he opens my ear that I may hear;
> And I have not rebelled,
> have not turned back.
> I gave my back to those who beat me...
> My face I did not shield
> from buffets and spitting....
> The Lord God is my help....
> Who will prove me wrong? (Isaiah 50, 5–9)

CHAPTER SIX

The God of the Cross

EDITH STEIN

On August 7, 1942, Johannes Wieners was on a prison train in the station in Breslau, Germany, when a freight train pulled up. Guards opened the doors of a cattle car, and Johannes could see people stacked in the car, some dead, others sitting dazed and lifeless in filth. Suddenly, a woman dressed as a Carmelite nun appeared in the doorway, her habit splattered with body fluids. The nun sadly looked into the distance and said to Herr Wieners: "This is my hometown, but I will never see it again. We are going to our death." At this, the door of the cattle car was closed and

191

the train went off to its final destination—a gas chamber and burning pit in Auschwitz. The woman was Sister Teresa Benedicta of the Cross, known before she entered the convent as Edith Stein, an accomplished philosopher, teacher and writer. A convert from Judaism, Stein had moved away from earlier views of the punishing warrior God that she had been taught as a child to atheism. From there she became attracted to the sacrificing and loving God she found in Jesus. Gradually, Stein became more determined throughout her life to follow her Lord to a Calvary of her own.

Jewish Roots

Stein was born in 1891 in Breslau on Yom Kippur, the Jewish Day of Atonement. Stein wrote that her mother always laid great emphasis on the fact that her youngest was born on the holy day commemorating the offering of sacrifices for the sins of the nation.

Stein's family was quite liberal in their religious practices. Though they went to synagogue on the Jewish high holy days, celebrated Passover and kept some of the dietary laws, the family business stayed open on the Sabbath, and prayers at home were said in German rather than Hebrew. Because Stein was a girl, she received only a superficial Jewish education, and seemed to know little of Jewish history. Her understanding of Jewish beliefs about salvation and the afterlife were quite limited, and perhaps contributed to her later moving away from Jewish religious practices. Still, she was always proud of her Jewish heritage, and even in times of danger never attempted to hide her religious roots. Her niece, Susan, once wrote of her: "She would always be part of the family and always part of the Jewish people, even as a nun."[1]

Edith Stein's mother, Auguste, was a tough-minded and determined woman. Her husband died suddenly when Edith was only two, and she had to take over the family lumber business and raise her seven children alone. She was known to be exceptionally kind and generous to her employees, and was viewed as the most capable merchant in town.[2] Auguste led her family in the worship of the God of Israel. She would light candles at the beginning of the Sabbath, with the traditional words: "Lord, do not burden us overmuch, but give us the burdens we are able to bear." She was devoted to the Jewish faith and expected the same from all her children. Edith dutifully accompanied her mother to synagogue, and though she had little appreciation for the ceremonies, was impressed with her mother's complete absorption with God.[3] Her mother advised her: "What one wants to do, one can do. As one strives, so will God help."[4]

Stein wrote that even as a four-year-old she loved learning and would memorize all the literature and songs that her older brother Paul taught her. She fought to go to school early and was outstanding in her studies until she was thirteen. It was then that she decided to drop out of school and give up praying and the practice of her Jewish faith. As a number of teens do, Stein simply decided that religion was irrelevant and declared herself an atheist.

Six months of domestic work and babysitting her sister's children was enough to persuade Stein to return to school. She finished the lower school in 1908 and moved on to high school at seventeen. In that same year, an Austrian teenager by the name of Adolf Hitler failed the entrance exam to the Vienna Academy of Arts. For some time he would wander the streets of Vienna as a drifter, an amateur patron of the arts and an ardent reader of anti-Semitic literature.

At age twenty, Edith enrolled in the University of Breslau to study psychology. While there, she fell into reading some of the fatalistic novels of the time, and experienced a severe depression. Even though she claimed to believe in God no longer, Stein says that she was brought out of this dark period by hearing Martin Luther's *A Mighty Fortress is Our God* at a Bach concert. Soon after this incident Stein decided that the psychology of the day was too superficial and spiritless for her, and she made up her mind to leave home and enroll in the school of philosophy at Göttingen University.

Göttingen attracted her because of its excellence in the field of phenomenology. Stein had read *Logical Investigations* by Edmund Husserl and was fascinated by his insights on the rediscovery of "spirit" in philosophy. He had moved beyond the dry philosophical conceptualizing and mechanical views of reality that bored Stein. In contrast, he was working theories of empathy and intuition and developing new first principles for finding the spiritual basis of phenomena.

This was a magical time in Stein's life. She was now on her own, away from family and religious ties, and was free to do her own search for the truth with youthful exuberance. The Göttingen school of phenomenology was flowering, and Edith was part of all the intellectual and social excitement. This would be one of the most formative times of her life as she studied intensely, made many enduring friendships, went on hiking trips and marched with the suffragettes of the

Democratic Party. Most importantly, she could follow "the master," Professor Husserl, and other teachers in their search for the spiritual center of reality. Stein had found what she thought was the path to truth. Ultimately, this path would lead her to Truth itself, the Creator of all reality.

Stein liked Husserl's realistic approach to philosophy. She wanted to take a rigorous and objective approach to reality and get to the heart of things. At Göttingen she met other professors who had gone beyond even Husserl. She was profoundly influenced by Max Scheler, who had converted from Judaism to Catholicism. She was taken with Scheler's creative genius, his deep feeling for human values and his empathetic heart. His strongly intuitive approach to reality opened up new worlds for Stein. His strong commitment to the spiritual beauty of Catholicism attracted her. She began to attend evening sessions on religious questions such as the nature of the holy and belief in the eternal. Stein began to see the human person as one who by nature searches for God. Faith began to stir within her. She wrote: "The bars of the rationalist prejudices I had unconsciously grown up with collapsed, and there, standing in front of me, was a world of faith."[5]

Adolf Reinach was another teacher who had a strong influence on Stein. Reinach was much more personable than Husserl, and taught Stein that education should be interpersonal and dialogical. He invited her into his home to meet his wife and family. At one point, as in the case with many graduate students, Stein began to despair that she did not have the makings of a scholar. Reinach gave her the support and encouragement she needed to continue toward her academic goals. With his help, she began her dissertation on the topic of empathy. Later, when Reinach and his wife converted to Christianity, Stein would once again be challenged with questions about religious faith.

When World War I broke out in 1914, Stein followed her friends and patriotically joined the war effort as a nurse in Austria. At the same time, the young drifter Adolf Hitler, who had left Austria to avoid military service there, volunteered for the German army in Munich, serving as a corporal. It is ironic that these two young people, whose lives would intersect tragically in the Final Solution of the Nazi regime, at one time were both serving the same side during World War I.

Stein served her country bravely and was awarded the Medal of Valor. She returned to the university, still interested in her studies, but now hoping for "a great love and happy marriage." She was for a while very close with Hans Lipps, a young man she had met at the university. However, Lipps fell out of favor with Husserl, and ultimately faded from Stein's life. In 1916, Stein received her doctoral degree *summa cum laude* and accepted an offer to follow Husserl to the University of Freiburg. There she would dutifully, and with little appreciation from Husserl, try to decipher and edit his shorthand manuscripts and teach introductory courses on phenomenology.

In 1917 a key event happened in Stein's search for meaning, an event that introduced her to the cross. She had received the tragic news that her mentor and friend Adolf Reinach had been killed in battle, and his family asked her to come to Göttingen to put his papers in order. Stein hesitated. Without any concept or belief in life after death, she did not know what comfort she could offer to his family.

Stein ultimately decided to go, and was much surprised at how Reinach's wife was able to deal with her suffering and sadness. Frau Reinach appeared to be filled with hope and was actually able to bring peace and consolation to the rest of the family and friends. Stein was deeply affected by such faith, and wrote that this was her "first encounter with the Cross and the divine power that it bestows on those who carry it. For the first time, I was seeing with my very eyes the church, born from its redeemer's sufferings triumphant over the sting of death. That was the moment my unbelief collapsed and Christ shone forth—in the mystery of the Cross."[6]

Edith began to read the New Testament and to reflect on the possibility of becoming a Christian. In the midst of the pessimism and depression following Germany's defeat in the war, Stein wrote that she was buoyed up by being able to "rest in God." By this she meant breaking from all intellectual activity, putting aside all plans and decisions, and putting her future in the hands of God. Stein was now beginning to have real faith in God. This was not the God of judgment and retribution of whom she had so often heard in her childhood, but a God of love and peaceful security. Stein now felt drawn to move toward this God, at least intellectually. As for her will, that was another matter; Stein was still not sure what future she would choose.

Edith followed her ambition to be a professor, and with Husserl's recommendation applied for a professorship at Göttingen in 1919. Much to her disappointment, she was turned down—women were rarely employed as professors at that time. During that period another renowned German philosopher, Martin Heidegger, began to work with Husserl at Freiburg, and published some of the manuscripts on which Stein had worked without giving her credit. Heidegger would eventually become an important influence on Karl Rahner, the famous Jesuit theologian who studied under him at Freiburg.

Meanwhile, Hitler had just written his first political manifesto, citing the crimes of the Jews against Germany as the cause of Germany's defeat in the war. He recommended that Jews should lose all their privileges and ultimately be "removed" from the fatherland. Hitler had abandoned his Catholic faith and was now an atheist. Stein had moved from atheism to a faith in God and would soon move toward Catholicism.

The Process of Conversion

On one trip to Frankfurt, Stein had an experience that touched her deeply. She stopped in the cathedral for a few moments and saw a woman with a shopping basket come in, kneel down and say a short prayer. She had never seen this in her synagogue or in Protestant churches—people coming in to talk to God as they would with any other friend.

On another occasion, Stein was visiting friends and sat up all night reading a book from their shelves—the autobiography of the Carmelite mystic Teresa of Avila. The next morning, as she put the book down, Stein reflected "This is the truth."[7] She had read the story of Christ drawing a person through prayer into union with the divine. She had learned how Christ had died for others and had proclaimed that he was the truth. In Christ she found how truth and love could be united.

Stein found many parallels between her life and that of Teresa of Avila. Teresa's grandfather was Jewish, but she had lost interest in that faith when she was young, and suffered parental opposition when she entered the convent. Throughout the rest of her life, Stein would identify with how Teresa was led along by prayer to union with God. She would experience the same mercy of God holding her up through times of darkness and painful renunciation of the world. She would identify with Teresa as she felt the special favor that God shows those who set aside the self and the world. Like Teresa, she would be transformed through love of the cross. Ultimately, she would identify with the persecution Teresa received because of her beliefs.[8]

After years of looking in the highways and byways, Stein had come to a significant point in her search for God. She had been led by Teresa to begin to let go of the things that kept her from God. Teresa had showed her how to begin to embrace the cross and open herself so that God could come to her in silence and solitude. Stein could no longer run from the light.

As soon as she could, Stein bought a catechism and a missal and began to search for the truth in Catholicism. Soon after that she was baptized into the church, a decision that broke her mother's heart. Auguste Stein saw this as an act of great disloyalty.[9] It is said that when she heard her daughter's decision, Auguste bowed and wept. Stein tried to be sensitive to her mother's pain, so on visits home would still observe the Sabbath and go with her mother to temple to pray, but then she would sneak out quietly to early morning Mass. Still, Auguste never got over her youngest child's conversion. Despite her protests, though, Auguste could not help but see that her daughter had new radiance. She once had to confess: "Never have I seen anyone pray as Edith did."[10]

Stein had to accept the harsh reality that there seemed to be no professorship in her future, and she took a position teaching German in a Dominican convent school in Speyer. She said: "What was not included in my plans lay in God's plans."[11] Stein's eight years there were nearly monastic. She worked hard at her teaching, lived simply and spent much time in prayer. Her students saw her as a kind yet demanding teacher who affected them more by who she was than by what she said. In the classroom, she was an excellent teacher; outside the classroom she was a friend who ate with the students, took walks with them and counseled them when they turned to her.

She also led her students in many projects for helping the poor and needy in the village nearby the convent school. She recognized the cross in these lives and wanted to help them with their burdens. She wrote: "There is a vocation to suffer with Christ and thereby cooperate with him in the work of salvation."[12] One student reported: "With her you sensed you were in the presence of something pure, sublime, and noble, something that elevated you and brought you to its own level."[13] At the same time, many of the sisters also turned to Stein for advice and spiritual direction. And she did all this, refusing to take any salary beyond what she needed for expenses. During this period, she also made long retreats at the famous Benedictine Abbey in Beuron.

In 1925 Stein's friend Erick Przywara, a well-known Jesuit philosopher-theologian who taught the Catholic theologian Hans Urs Von Balthasar, helped move Stein back into scholarly activity. Przywara was a scholar of John Henry Newman, a renowned nineteenth-century convert from Anglicanism, and suggested that Stein translate Newman's letters into German. Edith soon felt empathy with Newman, who also had to struggle with the decision to convert to Catholicism. From Newman's writings, she gained many new insights into the Catholic tradition.

Next Edith was invited to translate Thomas Aquinas's *Disputed Questions on Truth* into her native language. As with her work on Newman, this venture opened up a new world of philosophy and theology for Stein. Aquinas caught her interest and brought her keen mind back into the search for God. Aquinas taught her that she need not leave the world or give up her scholarship to find God, but that God indeed could be both served and discovered through the intellectual life. His work taught her the necessary connection between faith and reason, as well as showed her how philosophy and theology can go hand in hand in the search for God. At the same time, Aquinas confirmed Stein's belief that the experience of God transcends all that we can think or say about God. Stein began writing scholarly books and articles once again. She once said that God was "the master educator," and she was open to learn new insights into this God through her studies.[14] She was discovering that she could worship God by doing scholarly work, for those who are seeking truth are in fact seeking God. She wrote: "My desire for the truth was one sole prayer."[15]

Edith then launched a study of the feminine, perhaps moved in part by the way she and other women
had been kept out of university life and positions of
leadership. She was convinced that women were unique
by nature, and should therefore have educational systems designed to meet their particular needs. She was
strong in her conviction that women should be given
open opportunities to bring their special gifts to the
world of higher education. In her popular lectures, Stein
taught that women were made uniquely in the image of
God, and required a specific kind of nurturing of their
feminine nature. This contrasted with the Nazi doctrine
that women were for "church, kitchen and children,"
and that the best service a woman could provide for the
Fatherland was to propagate strong Aryan children to
build up the Germanic race.[16]

Stein was suddenly in great demand as a speaker to
women's groups. She encouraged women to enter all
the professions and insisted that there was no profession women could not occupy with competence.
Women have been given singular strengths by God, she
believed, and can therefore bring much needed help
and a fresh perspective to the professions. Maternal instincts, an enormous capacity for interpersonal relationships, and extraordinary capacities for empathy and
love were particular gifts that women could bring to
professional life.[17]

It was Stein's position that women are more emotionally centered than men, and therefore require intellectual training to keep them objective. She felt that
women needed special training in connecting with others and the world.

She strongly opposed the exclusion of women from

professional life and their lack of freedom in choosing a career as contrary to God's design. However, she did not ignore the crucial role that women play in the home and in the spiritual and moral development of children. She strongly advocated that these roles not be neglected by professional women, addressing an issue with which we still struggle today. She urged women not to be so caught up in materialism and greed that they have to work to the point where they neglect their families and their parental responsibilities. She counseled them to sustain a strong spirituality and life of prayer so that they could balance work and home life. Edith soon became so busy on the lecture circuit, with her research, and with philosophical conferences that she had to resign her teaching job at Speyer.

In her lectures throughout Europe, Stein was critical of the church's disregard of marriage, sexuality and women's issues. She was a strong advocate for feminine equality in both society and church. She pointed to the importance that women held in Jesus' ministry, stressed how important women were in the ministry of the early church, and pointed to the deaconesses in history as examples of positions that should be available to women. She even raised the question of women's ordination and, though she did not think it would ever come about, wanted to leave it an open question to be explored.[18] Cardinal Lustiger of Paris, himself a convert from Judaism, and whose mother also died in Auschwitz, said in a recent visit to the United States that Stein's work on feminism is an important contribution and was most influential on John Paul II's writings on women's issues.[19]

In 1931 Edith decided to attempt once again her

lifetime goal: becoming a university professor. She applied for a position at the University of Freiburg, hoping that her understanding of phenomenology as well as her connection with Martin Heidegger—now Husserl's successor—would open some doors for her. Stein was wrong. Her application for a position at Freiburg was not taken seriously, and she was abruptly told that there was no job for her.

In the past, Stein had faced job rejections because she was female. Now the doors were shut on her because she was Jewish. By this year, Adolf Hitler had become well-established as a leader in the new Nazi party. He was to be elected chancellor in 1933, and his anti-Semitic doctrine was spreading rapidly throughout Germany. Unfortunately for Stein, Martin Heidegger, whom she thought would support her application to Freiburg, was, at least early on, a strong supporter of the Nazi movement.

Edith accepted her rejection as somehow providential. She believed that there was a "great and merciful Providence behind all of it" and wrote that, "There is a state of resting in God, of a complete relaxation of all mental effort, when one no longer makes any plans or decisions, where one no longer acts, but abandons all the future to the Divine Will."[20]

In 1932 Stein accepted a position at the German Institute for Scientific Pedagogy in Munster. She continued to travel to philosophical conferences as a colleague to such notable philosophers as Jacques Maritain, Etienne Gilson and Nikolay Berdyayev. Anti-Semitism continued to escalate in Germany, and Stein looked on in dismay as university students attacked Jews. In 1933 the Institute decided to remove Stein from her teaching post. Any hopes of gaining an academic position were dashed. At forty-two and the peak of her powers, the cross of discrimination had been placed squarely on her shoulders.

There was still time for Stein to flee to Latin America or the United States, as many other academics (such as Protestant theologian Paul Tillich, renowned scientist Albert Einstein and father of psychology Sigmund Freud) had done. But she decided to stay, saying that she was willing to accept the destiny of her people as her own.[21] In one of her essays she wrote:

> I spoke to our Savior and told him that I knew it was his Cross which was now being laid on the Jewish people. Most of them did not understand it; but those who did understand must accept it willingly in the name of all.[22]

She perceived that her calling was to be an offering, a sacrifice for both the persecuted and the persecutor. She felt that perhaps God was asking her to give of herself in an act of loving sacrifice to bring forgiveness and healing into the chaos that was gathering around her. As a Jew, a Christian and a woman who loved her native land, Stein seemed to be called to a singular destiny.

During this same time, Edith was moved to prophetically write to Pope Pius XI and ask him to issue an encyclical against Nazi anti-Semitism. She had hoped to go to Rome and ask him personally, but when she was refused a private audience, she wrote an impassioned letter. Whether her plea reached the pope is not known. Stein received simply a papal blessing for herself and her family. She later reflected that all the things she predicted to the pope in 1933 had come true. She wondered if he received her letter, and if he ever thought about it.

Edith had wanted to enter religious life when she was baptized, but was told that she would have to wait some years before such a move. With that time having passed and her academic career over, she was finally free to answer God's call. She felt that she could best answer that call by living a life of self-sacrifice as a Carmelite.

Entering Carmel

In 1933 Stein applied to enter the Carmelite convent in Cologne and was accepted. Again, this was a serious blow to Stein's mother. Auguste said to her in frustration: "Why did you have to get to know [Jesus]? He was a good man—I'm not saying anything against him. But why did he have to go and make himself God?"[23] Her mother had also heard many horrible things about convents and was in despair over her daughter's decision. She felt that she was abandoning her people at a time when they needed her. Not only was Auguste losing her own people, she was now also losing her baby daughter. Where had she failed in raising this daughter to be a good Jew? After a painful last visit with her family, Stein left for the convent. She wrote: "I couldn't feel any violent upsurge of enthusiasm over it: I had just been through something too terrible for that. But I did feel a great sense of calm, knowing that I was coming into the harbor of God's will."[24]

Having led a disciplined life, Stein quickly adjusted to the austerities of the Carmelite convent. The Carmelite tradition was what she had been seeking. The order had been founded on Mt. Carmel in Palestine by crusaders in the Middle Ages. It had begun in the spirit of the great Jewish prophet, Elias, who was closely associated with Mt. Carmel and whose motto was taken up by the order: "With zeal am I zealous for the Lord God of Hosts." The Jewish-Christian context here was appropriate for Stein, who still treasured her Jewish background and saw it as an asset in her following of Jesus the Jew. Of course, the work of Teresa of Avila, a Carmelite, had inspired Stein to convert to Catholicism. Moreover, Stein had always been inspired by the "little way" of another Carmelite—Therese of Lisieux. She believed that Therese's life had been transformed by the love of God and had hopes that she would have the same experience in Carmel. She was never happier and commented that during her novitiate she had "never laughed so much during my whole life."[25]

In Carmel, Edith hoped to be led by her God, and to provide little resistance. She wanted to be free from all attachments and surrender to God. The rule of Carmel brings together both Jewish and Christian spirituality. It reads: "Put on the breastplate of justice that you may love the Lord your God with your whole heart, and your whole soul, and with your whole strength, and your neighbor as yourself."[26] Its ideal is to pray always, night and day, meditating on the law of the Lord. Stein would have to renounce attachments to her past enjoyments and her past fame. There would be times of darkness and abandonment. She wrote that all sufferings are nothing "compared with the dark night of the soul, when the Divine light no longer shines, and the voice of the Lord no longer speaks. God is there, but He is hidden and silent."[27] At the same time there were enormous gifts. "God kept something for me in Carmel which I had not found anywhere else."[28]

Edith's fellow sisters noted that she was at first distant and reserved, but soon became relaxed and even playful. She joined in with the youthful joking of her fellow novices. Members of the community have noted that she seemed to be filled with love and happiness. Though she was just a beginner, she impressed the other novices as a person already completely devoted to God. She later wrote that during this period, even though she was quite happy, she sensed that there were challenging times ahead. The spirit of anti-Semitism was now rampant in Germany, and she knew that a convent could not protect her from arrest, or worse. In her writings at that time, she reflected on her own death. She wrote about how the passion and death of Jesus continues in his followers and identified herself with Jesus as the Lamb of God. She wrote that the union of God with the soul "is purchased through the cross, perfected with the cross and sealed for all eternity with the cross."[29] She found herself consoling the many Jews she knew through letters and during visits from friends, many of whom were planning to emigrate.

In spite of the comfort she felt in her new life, there were difficulties. She quickly found the "cross" in having to submit to women of less intellect and education. This mature, accomplished professional had to accept that she was inept at the domestic chores expected of her. Stein, now Sister Teresa Benedicta of the Cross, also had to carry the unexpected burden that her superior wanted her to continue with her academic work in the convent. She was expected to continue her writing, but without the necessary scholarly resources available. The stress was twofold: She was frustrated by frequent interruptions from her scholarly work for community prayers, and yet distressed that the work took time from the prayer for which she had so longed and joined the convent in the first place. She attempted to reconcile these pursuits by recalling her early belief that by seeking the truth, one is seeking God. She often felt awkward, and yet said that she was grateful for God's call and hoped that they could soon make a "passable" nun out of her.

In 1936 Sister Teresa revised and finished her book *Finite and Eternal Being* in which she dealt with the human search for God. Beginning with simple human acts of perception, the book shows how human reflectivity comes from the Creator, and can be a path toward union with the Creator. Using what she had learned from Aquinas as well as from phenomenology, she describes her own unique views on how the human experience of *being* can be a path toward the divine. Unfortunately, she could not find a publisher who would accept a work by a Jewish woman.

Sister Teresa also wrote on spiritual themes. She studied the works of Teresa of Avila and John of the Cross and was particularly intrigued by the notion of human beings as temples of God, indeed having their very lives transformed into God. She began to write about mysticism, not as some esoteric activity for "the elect," but as a person's experience of God dwelling in the soul. Following the Carmelite tradition, she entered more deeply than ever into the life of prayer, "meditating day and night" on the Lord, believing that ultimately she could be one with God. She believed that prayer was actually God praying within us. She must, therefore, "let go," rest in God and allow herself to be transformed by the Spirit of God. In a poem, she expressed this conviction:

> What are you, kindly light, who fill me now,
> And brighten all the darkness of my heart?
> You guide me forward like a mother's hand,
> And if you let me go,
> I could not take a single step alone.
> You are the space embracing all my being...
> Nearer to me than I myself am,
> And more within me than my inmost self.[30]

By 1938 it was clear that Hitler was going to war and would continue to use the Jews as scapegoats for his actions. The eighth of November was the infamous *Kristallnacht* when Jews were driven from their homes, their businesses demolished and synagogues burned. Stein began to understand that God was calling her to use her life as an offering. She wrote about how she had chosen "of the Cross" in her name and that she would have to carry the cross of the Lord in the name of others. At times, she seriously wondered if she would survive. She wrote: "I have a great desire to see all of this sometime in the light of eternity."[31] She continued to listen for the Spirit of God, awaiting, as she said, "his least wink."[32] At one point, she thought of going to the Carmelite convent in Palestine, but when further immigration of Jews was banned there, her superiors decided to transfer her out of harm's way to the Dutch convent of Echt. Not wanting to endanger her sisters in Cologne, Stein agreed to leave the community she loved and move to a foreign country.

Sister Teresa was received in Echt with hospitality and kindness, although no permanent commitment was made for her to stay. She set herself to discover what God was now asking of her. She seemed intensely aware that somehow she was being uniquely drawn into the redemptive work of Christ, being asked to fill up what is lacking in the passion of Christ (Colossians 1:24). In 1939 she wrote of wanting to offer herself as a sacrifice of atonement for peace, for the breaking of the "reign of Antichrist," without a world war. In the same year, she wrote her final testament, saying that she accepts in advance the death that is to come to her, and wants to offer her life and death for her order, for the Jewish people, for the deliverance of Germany, for world peace and for her family.[33] Her poems at this time are moving. Here she wrote of the Nazi destruction:

> Furious the storms which rage across the lands.
> Oaks whose deep roots sank into earth's own heart,
> Whose crowns soared proudly up to hea'n
> Lie now uprooted, rent asunder—
> Horror, despoilment, round about,
> Does not the storm shake faith's foundations?[34]

And here she reflects on her feelings of being a refugee:

> When we must journey into foreign lands,
> And, door to door, our shelter seek,
> Walk then before us as our trusty guide.[35]

In 1940 Rosa, Stein's younger sister, escaped to Holland to join Edith, but when Germany invaded Holland soon afterward, the danger continued. In her new convent, Stein was asked to continue her scholarly work. She began a new book, *The Science of the Cross*. This is, in a sense, her last testament. Here the "science" of the cross is not so much a study or theology of the cross as it is a description of how to "live" the cross as a truth. As biographer Hilda Graef has written, this living truth is "placed in the soul like a seed, takes root in her and grows, gives the soul a certain character and forms her in all she does or leaves undone."[36] Stein wanted to be formed and shaped by the cross; she also wanted to "be formed into the image of the Cross-bearer and the Crucified."[37] Although that phrase is taken from Stein's study of the writings of John of the Cross, it is at the same time a description of her life. It is written with the serenity of one who follows Jesus to Calvary without fear of death, with forgiveness toward her oppressors, and with awareness that somehow this sacrifice is redemptive.

Stein's life was lived in the shadow of the cross. She lost her father when she was just two years old; she was not able to marry the man she loved; her professor and mentor Reinach was killed in the war; and her "master" Husserl did not recognize the devoted work she did for him. Stein's mother had rejected her conversion and her decision to enter the convent. She was never able to achieve her life's goal—to be a professor of theology in a university. And when she finally answered God's call to enter the convent, Stein was in time betrayed and executed by people from her own country. Truly she could identify with the Lord, whose young and promising life was also cut short by treacherous betrayal and execution.

In *The Science of the Cross,* Stein discussed John of the Cross's renunciation. It is curious how, as with Teresa of Avila, there are many parallels between the lives of John of the Cross and Edith Stein. Both lost their fathers in their childhood, and experienced a great deal of failure in their lives. They both nursed the sick and dying during wartime. Saint John and Stein were both kidnapped, imprisoned and beaten by their own people. Both had their writings suppressed, and were familiar with the darkness of God's apparent withdrawal from their lives. The two were also similar in how they were powerfully transformed by the love of God.

In this work, Stein explored John of the Cross's notion that Jesus asks souls to share his cross and redemption, but few are able to respond. She wrote: "God has created human souls for himself and given them even on earth the immeasurable fullness and ineffable bliss of his own divine life. This is the goal to which he directs them and to which they are meant to tend with all their might. But the road is narrow, the ascent steep and laborious, and most people fall by the way."[38]

Edith here commented on a central notion of John of the Cross's mystical writings, the dark night of the soul. She saw the night as invisible, formless, a darkness that can threaten and swallow up the searcher for God. It is a night that can deprive the searcher of the senses, and can condemn one to a shadowy and ghostlike existence. Instead of an experience of God, there is empty solitude and silence. It is the night of faith, where Stein's brilliant mind and extensive research were of little value. In this night one longs for God beyond all else. She wrote: "And since the soul is incapable of tasting God's essence in this life, no sweetness or delight that can be tasted, however sublime, can be God."[39]

Edith knew this dark night well in her times of tension with her family, and the frustrations with her academic career. In the future, she would no doubt know this in the desolation of a boxcar filled with terrified people and the horrors of a death camp. She came to realize that it is in the midst of this dark night that we are purified and prepared for loving union with God, here and hereafter.[40] Here we encounter a God beyond what we normally know and experience of God, a God beyond all images, a God who transforms our whole selves through an intense fire of love. This night and this cross are the path to resurrection.[41] It is only by surrendering to God that we can be one with God.

Stein discussed John's notion that Jesus saved the world through humiliation, desolation and annihilation. This would also be her way toward a God who could bring light and love to such chaos. She knew the cross, and would ultimately experience apparent annihilation by brutal enemies. Yet, in the midst of it all, she would find her saving God and experience the joyful exhilaration of being part of God's saving action. She wrote of how we pass "through the atoning fire to the blissful union of love.... It is death and resurrection. After the Dark Night there shines forth the Living Flame of Love."[42]

Her work also studies John's notion of prayer as communion with God. She wrote that true prayer is living with God.[43] Contemplation is the ladder that one ascends step by step to union with God.[44] It is an inward ascent to God who is at the center of one's soul. She wrote: "In its ascent to God the soul rises above itself or is raised above itself. Yet thus it actually reaches its own interior."[45] Here God is revealed as the very "mystery of our own being."[46]

Stein wrote that John gladly endured insults and brutalities for the sake of reforming his brothers in Carmel. She comments on the patience and resignation needed for the person seeking the experience of God in suffering. Little did she realize what demands would be put on her in this area at the end. She would face the same desolation as the Lord, would experience being forsaken by her people and her God. She would be asked to forgive and to commend her own spirit to God as Jesus had done.[47]

Sister Teresa never finished her book on *The Science of the Cross*. Instead, as someone has said, she lived out the rest of the book as she walked to martyrdom. "Before she could put the last touch on it, she was called to become, through her actions and as a victim to men, the complete model that shows forth the doctrine of the Cross."[48]

Ways of Knowing God

In 1941 Teresa finished a scholarly article and sent it to *The Thomist*, a prestigious philosophical magazine in the United States. The article, "Ways to Know God," was published posthumously in 1946. Behind the intricate scholarship, one finds additional commentary on her journey to God. She comments on the approach to God through negative theology, where one gradually discovers what God is "not." She had experienced this in her own life when she rejected the sometimes angry and punishing images of God in the Scriptures. She speaks of positive theology where one uses analogy between creator and creatures. Stein had explored this approach often in her love for nature and in her intense research. So often she had relied on "symbolic theology," seeing the divine in all of creation.[49] She had sought God in the world, and from her experiences in the war, in her studies and in teaching was filled with touches of the divine. She wrote:

> This world is our world, in which we experience love
> and joy, which we face enthralled or admiring, awed or
> horrified; it is a meaningful whole which speaks to us in
> a thousand voices, revealing its being as a whole and in
> every one of its parts, and nonetheless remaining a mys-
> tery forever. It is this same world which by all it mani-
> fests and conceals points beyond itself to Him Who
> through it reveals himself mysteriously. [50]

For Stein, the symbols were in themselves given by God,
not by us. She described God as "the original theologian," who speaks through nature and carves the divine
image within the created world. She recognized the
myriad of messengers through which God reveals:
"God speaks through his messengers: His words to be
received as his must be somehow distinct from ordinary
human words and those speaking the words must be
legitimated as God's messengers."[51] She had encountered such messengers; her mother, professors, students, spiritual advisors and religious superiors. Stein
insisted that faith is necessary to read all of this, and
faith itself is a gift.

She wrote of the prophet, who stands before God
and speaks for God. This is one "touched by the Divine
Presence in one's innermost being."[52] Here she also
pointed out that even though one experiences the light
of God, God remains a hidden God. No matter how personal the experience, it is an experience of mystery. "All
this is possible in the light of faith. Our knowledge of
God is thereby enriched, our relation to God deepened
or ordered in a better way, but we do not stand, nonetheless, before God's face."[53]

Ultimately, the searching must be open to God and
allow God to let himself be found. This God is found in

silence, openness and receptivity. God speaks to us in many ways: to hear, we must surrender in utter detachment from all.

The Beginning of the End

In the early 1940s Jews in growing numbers were being shipped east for extermination. Stein decided that once again she was putting her community in danger. She planned to move again, this time to a Carmelite convent in Switzerland, and she applied for a Swiss visa. Meanwhile she was called in regularly for interrogations by the SS (*Schutzstaffel*), the Nazi security police. Stein rankled the officials when she greeted them with "Praised be the Lord Jesus," instead of the expected "Heil Hitler." She was informed that her "conversion" and life as a nun did not change the fact that she was a Jew, and she was required to wear the yellow star on her Carmelite habit.

Matters came to a head when church officials protested the deportation of Jews from Holland. In retaliation, the Nazis decreed that all Jewish Catholics would be arrested and deported. Early in August 1942 the gestapo (Nazi secret police) banged on the convent door and gave Edith Stein and her sister Rosa five minutes to gather their things. It was devastating for all, but Stein calmly took her sister by the hand and said: "Come, Rosa. We're going for our people."[54] Stein saw more clearly now the cross to which she was called. The passion of Jesus the Jew for the salvation of the world called to her.

With hundreds of others, the two women were taken to a camp in Amersfoort in the middle of the night.

There they were shoved and clubbed into dormitories with thousands of other prisoners. Panic, despair and depression set in quickly. However, witnesses later pointed out that Stein seemed to have a cheerful calm about her as she went about caring for the children and soothing those who were distraught. Next she was shipped with twelve hundred Jews to another camp in Westerbork, Holland. There families were separated, prisoners were photographed with their prison ID numbers and then were herded into packed barracks. The air was filled with moaning, weeping and cries of despair. Stein again was noted for her calm composure, as she cared for the children, washed clothes and tried to make the barracks livable. She had once written: "It is an obvious truth that sympathy with one's neighbor grows in measure that the soul is united to God by love."[55]

Each day it was becoming more clear to her that she was coming face to face with her destiny—her sacrifice would not only be to offer herself in conversion to Christianity, or in accepting the challenges of religious life. Now it seemed that she was being called to endure a horrible execution at the hands of people who hated her. Teresa was being asked to offer her life and death for both the victims as well as the persecutors in this frightful holocaust of human life. At that point, she discovered that, although some of her family members had escaped to the United States, her brother, sister and sister-in-law had been sent to the camps. They would be executed within a year.

Stein found herself to be in a unique position. She was a Jew, who throughout her life had borne the cross of being a Jew, and who would now be killed for being one of her people. At the same time, she was a loyal German, who had demonstrated for democracy in her country and had won the Medal of Valor for her heroic work in the war. She was a Christian, who decided to follow in the footsteps of Jesus in her own love, forgiveness and crucifixion. And she was a Carmelite nun, vowed to a life of praying day and night, of being zealous for the Lord God of hosts, and of linking her contemplation with courageous action for others. In her person, Stein could singularly transform the horrors of the Holocaust into an act of love, forgiveness and atonement. Jacques Maritain had perceived this nobility in her when he wrote of "the total generosity which one felt in her and which was to bear fruit in her martyrdom."[56]

On August 9, 1942, cattle cars filled with 559 people pulled into the pretty village of Birkenau in Germany, just outside the Auschwitz concentration camp, where its gas chambers and crematoria were still under construction. Many had already died in transit or were broken psychologically. One guard noted that the Carmelite nun was one of the few who had maintained her sanity. The prisoners were divided into two groups: those who could work and those who could not. Edith and Rosa were classified as the latter, and were loaded into trucks and taken to two windowless cottages. With the others, they were shoved into the houses. The doors were bolted, and poisonous Zyklon B gas was discharged through the ceiling vents. In fifteen minutes, the screams and cries subsided and there was only the silence of the dead. The bodies were placed on wooden pyres and burned. The ashes were used for fertilizer or simply dumped into a nearby river. Stein, who had been born on the Day of Atonement, had offered her life and her death for others. Now it became clearer why she had added "of the Cross" to her name in religious life.

Canonization

On October 11, 1998, Pope John Paul II canonized Saint Teresa Benedicta of the Cross in St. Peter's Square in Rome. The canonization was not without controversy. Some Jews objected that this nun was called a Christian martyr since she was killed because she was Jewish. Others felt that the canonization was another example of Christians attempting to co-opt the Holocaust as their own. Those even more militant claimed that Stein had betrayed her Jewish roots by converting to Christianity. And there were those who resented her forgiveness of her Nazi persecutors, as well as some who thought that she had indeed been engaged implicitly in the old "Christ-killer" myth against the Jews. Others claimed she was attempting to bring about the conversion of the Jews to Christianity.

Nonetheless, John Paul II steadfastly proceeded with the canonization process, maintaining that Sister Teresa's glory was in the cross of Jesus Christ, who died for all. (Ultimately, she had been arrested because she was a Jewish-Christian, as part of a reprisal for the church's stand against the persecution of Jews in Holland.) The pope stressed the Jewishness of Stein and pointed out that though she could have at one point been rescued, she said: "Why should I be spared? Is it not right that I should gain no advantage from my Baptism? If I cannot share the lot of my brothers and sisters, my life, in a sense, is destroyed."[57] As a Christian, Teresa had led people to look with confidence to their sufferings, to the cross and "draw from its mystery of love, the confidence and strength to walk faithfully in the footsteps of the crucified and risen Christ."[58]

John Paul II pointed out that from the beginning Stein was a seeker of truth, a seeker of God, and that in time she found that truth had a name: Jesus Christ. He offered her as an example to young people today who live in a world where everything is permitted. He told them to imitate Edith Stein, to search the depths, and not be satisfied with the superficial. He mentioned that, for Stein, truth and love were interrelated and that, once she discovered the truth, she gave herself in loving sacrifice.

The pope spent some time on Sister Teresa's identification with the cross. He said that through the cross she was able to encounter the God of Abraham, Isaac and Jacob, as well as the God of Jesus Christ. She bridged the cross of the Jews with the cross of Jesus. As a Jew, she belonged to Jesus, not only spiritually, but in blood. Gradually, through her life she became aware of her unique vocation to ascend Calvary and to embrace the cross with serenity and trust, as did her Savior.

CHAPTER SEVEN

The God of Peace

DANIEL BERRIGAN

In 1968 a quiet, scholarly Jesuit committed an act of civil disobedience by burning draft files in Catonsville, Maryland. Daniel Berrigan, along with his brother Philip and other peace activists, would be tried and sentenced on what he describes as the greatest day of their lives. Berrigan would eventually be sent to prison for this act, and would become the voice for many who believe that the true God never supports war or the creation of weapons of destruction and death.

Daniel Berrigan described his life as a "pilgrim's progress through a fierce antihuman landscape."[1] His is the story of an extraordinary individual, who at first attempted to fit into the church and world of his day, until it eventually became clear to him that both accepted violence and war. Gradually this pilgrim became an outsider, a protester against the Vietnam War, a destroyer of government property, the voice of one crying in the wilderness. His was a prophetic voice, and he did all that he could to smash the idols of the god of war and hold up the one God of peace to the world. Along the way, Berrigan drew fire from officials of the church, his religious community and the American government. He was exiled, rejected and imprisoned, and yet refused to accept a God who would either permit or take part in war.

What path led this Jesuit priest to such a radical juncture? What made him willing to suffer all the dire consequences connected with following this God of Peace?

Early Years

Berrigan wrote that he began his religious pilgrimage as a "skinny agnostic," who memorized the Catholic catechism and went through the motions of a child's religion. He recalls that in his youth he experienced little freedom within himself and believed that somehow he was predestined to defeat. He recalls that for many years he was unable to free himself of a sense of failure, ill luck and blank destiny. This feeling followed him through his schooling and into the Jesuits. It touched on his friendships and his family life, and seemed to deny that either he or his God was free. He knew that God was supposed to cherish and care for people, yet

Berrigan felt that in his regard, "God was blind as a bat and indifferent as a grave."[2] Berrigan was the youngest of six boys, the "runt of the litter" who had a difficult time walking until he was nearly in school. He looked up to the brother closest to him in age, Philip, who would later influence his involvement in the peace movement.

Dan had the persistent feeling that faith was not so much a personal gift from God, as it was something that held him in its grip. Thus, his prevailing image of God as a child was of someone who had him in his clutches, much as his own dominating father. Berrigan describes his father as a man who was self-centered, a naive know-it-all, who moved from place to place seeking his fortune. He would blaze up "furious and dangerous," and was neither affectionate nor nurturing to his wife.[3] Berrigan seemed to prefer a God in the image of his mother, who was strong, compassionate and nonjudgmental. He says that she was strong in her spirit, a survivor with a deep faith and enough courage to prevent her husband from breaking the spirit of his sons. (It was his mother that would stand by him later, even through imprisonment, always loving him and maintaining that he was following God's law.) Unfortunately, the controlling image of God prevailed in Berrigan's young life.

Dan's initial experience with the will of this God came through the Catholic church, which he saw to be dominated by male clerics, who in turn had a strong influence on family life. He wrote that in this male church, the clerics and the husbands spoke as one, as though from Sinai, and demanded obedience of wives to their husbands. Berrigan wrote that as a child he found himself caught between the tides of fortune and faith in a

God, who governed life through priests, nuns, rituals and images of saints. It was through the priests and nuns that God seemed to dispense a kind of "generalized misery" in young Dan's life. This God seemed to dispose of all things in the manner of a Solomon or a pope.[4]

Early on, God's will concerning Dan's future came to him, in part, from the nuns. At the time, nuns did much of the teaching in Catholic schools and were extremely influential on the religious formation of their students. Among other promising candidates, Berrigan was led into the convent parlor one day so the nuns could help him determine the will of God regarding his vocation. Their suggestions for his future sounded attractive, and Berrigan joined the Jesuits immediately after high school.

The traditional notion of God as a distant, often angry figure continued to prevail during Berrigan's seminary years at St. Anthony on the Hudson. Though his Jesuit experience often gave him a sense of God's presence, taught him to pray and have a personal relationship with God, the early retreats reinforced his notion that God was "fearful and awful."[5] Always there was a striking irony surrounding this image, in that this ostensibly good God seemed to stand by indifferently while horrors and atrocities were being enacted on the world stage.

Soon after he entered the Jesuits, he was told that the divine will would now come to him through the commands of his religious superiors. He describes himself as now walking the long black line of anonymous Jesuits, led by a Jesuit priest. Berrigan describes his religious superiors as "the human expression of the law of the universe, and the Lawgiver; to pass the law along, that the body might move in unison with the stars in their course, and all together sing the glory of God."[6] Berrigan depicts the novice master as a "lion" who guarded the gate of the novitiate; a man who was extremely impressive, but as wild and willful as Berrigan's own father. This superior stood in the place of God, an icon and oracle of Christ, and demanded blind obedience. Berrigan was dedicated to his Jesuit brothers and conformed, but he would later comment on how far life in the long black line was from the original freedom of the gospel that had been announced and embodied in Christ.

In the early 1940s Berrigan moved on to Woodstock, Maryland, to study philosophy and Latin, a language as "dead as the jawbone of Aristotle." He wryly recalls how uneasily God must have been standing by, as the instructors attempted to prove his existence.

During his time at Woodstock, World War II ended. Dan's brother Philip returned from Europe a decorated veteran, and came to celebrate the victory with Berrigan and his fellow seminarians. Philip, who would become one of the most vocal peace demonstrators of his time, marched in uniform, and led a ragtag parade of seminarians, waving flags and singing jubilantly over their military victory!

Getting Born

Just months after that victory celebration, Berrigan was ill in the hospital. A nurse brought him a newspaper article about the U. S. bombing of Hiroshima, Japan, which horrified him. Soon after, he returned to the seminary. He later wrote that while he and his fellow seminarians were engrossed in Thomas Aquinas's five ways of proving God's existence, a new god was coming into existence: the atomic bomb. Berrigan and his classmates, shielded in the seminary, did not understand the implications of such a weapon.

In 1946 Berrigan accepted an assignment to St. Peter's Prep School in New Jersey, to teach high school Latin. He wrote that a dam was beginning to burst in his brain as he began to face his own humanity. Though he deeply loved the Jesuits, he was beginning to feel uncomfortable in the long black line, and often felt as though he was walking with a flock of church crows, or with a group of chanting Buddhist monks in their saffron robes. But the Jesuit view was that his religious superiors were oracles of the divine will and the plans they made for his life were of divine origin.[7]

As Berrigan taught, he began to realize that his views on God and war were out of balance with the views of his students. His criticism of the bombing of Hiroshima was not well received by his hawkish students. They vehemently opposed his views and were quite comfortable believing in a God who sanctioned the slaughtering of innocent people. He wrote: "The classroom of fifteen-year-olds! They suddenly became an aroused chorus, savage and loud. No moral doubts clouded these Americanettes. With considerable heat I was informed that I scarcely knew my arm from my elbow, a bomb from a berry. We did Good! We saved lives, didn't we! It was them or us, wasn't it!"[8]

At the high school, he observed that both the students and their parents had no difficulty going through the motions of Christianity. He was perplexed that his students could be baptized, follow the seasonal rhythms of Christian worship, receive the sacraments, be exposed year after year to elite Catholic education and still go off to war in good conscience. He concluded that most Catholics must have lax consciences, in order to believe in a God who condoned their participation in the mass murder of war.

In 1949 Berrigan began to study theology at Weston, Massachusetts. He called these his predawn years, for a new light was beginning to break through. Gradually his notion of the will of God moved from something handed down to him through others to something he discerned in his own heart and conscience. At Weston, he began to study theology, which purported to be the study of God, but which he said turned out to be a "hatful of nineteenth-century watch parts," focused on loyalty oaths and fighting adversaries. He observed that he and his fellow students were still cut off from the world, innocent as the unborn, and studying a theology which took little notice of such worldly events as war. He later wrote that they were living in an ecosphere, a self-justifying, self-sufficient world, where wars were simply distant rumors. As young Jesuits, they were expected to live the life of the mind, and ignore political matters. Berrigan felt that he and his classmates were "Stonehenge men," who were being trained to be unquestioning civil servants in church and government structures. They were protected from the signs of the times and were told to ignore the theological earthquakes that were going on in Europe.

In 1952 Berrigan was ordained to the priesthood, and the following year was sent to France for further studies and ministerial work. For the first time, Berrigan began to experience the exhilaration of personal freedom and the importance of becoming a human being through relating to and serving others. Berrigan continued to search for the will of God for himself. While he traveled around Europe, he encountered many people who had firsthand experience with the horrors of war and who were deeply committed to the God of peace. Such people would eventually have a profound influence on him. When he returned to the United States, he was assigned to teach at another Jesuit prep school, this time in Brooklyn. By now, he was distressed by the arms race and the proliferation of atomic weapons. He wrote that he felt the earth had been mined and could explode at any time. It was as though technology had replaced morality and God's creative process, and the world was now fully equipped to self-destruct.

During his assignment in Brooklyn, Berrigan became chaplain of some Young Christian Workers and worked with groups of laypeople, ministering to the Puerto Rican immigrants in the area. He said that his soul was now moving in a contrary wind. He began to separate from some of the conservative views in his community, went for long walks in the city at night, struggled with deep questions and wrote poetry. Eventually some of his poems were published, and he won a prestigious award and a measure of fame. Still, he had no sense of the cyclone that was beginning to gather around him.

In 1957 Berrigan was assigned to teach Scripture at LeMoyne College in Syracuse. In that same year, he stumbled over a "trip wire," which brought the wrath of the local bishop upon him. Berrigan had supported a controversial pacifist, and as a result was severely reprimanded by the prelate. He noted that this situation was a startling experience of the "disease of power," where church authorities claim to be interpreting the will of God while they hack off people's limbs and heads. Fortunately, he was saved this time from the bishop's wrath, but he knew that it would only be a matter of time before he would be shunted about in order to preserve divine order and the divine will and subjected to those who whisper as they kill: "God's will! God's will!"[9]

By now Berrigan was beginning to realize that the will of God was neither to be identified with some blind fate, as he had believed as a child, or even necessarily with the will of his superiors. Rather, he began to discern an invitation to freely follow God's way, an invitation that included the sustenance and provisions for the weariness and discouragement that would have to be endured.[10] Berrigan had learned that God could not be "immobilized" by superiors or distanced from life by those who believed in God, and yet supported violence. God had to be given the freedom to be God. As he expressed it: "This Christian is acutely conscious of God as God."[11]

During his years at LeMoyne, Berrigan maintained his high ideals about the church and its relation to God. He still saw the church as the place of truth and salvation. For him, the church was the adulthood of man, the climax of sacred history, and the locus where God and all reality could be found.[12]

In his youthful idealism, Berrigan still believed that the church was all knowing and that no one could possibly add to what the church knows about the divine realities. The church was, in fact, the "Mind of God."[13] He believed that the church had effortlessly gained knowledge of all of creation, and that it alone was able to bring about the exchange of the human and the Divine, and in time, the exchange between time and eternity. He wrote that the church knew the world, creates it anew, redeems and sanctifies it, and acts as the mediator of the Trinity. He waxed lyrical as he wrote: "What is not known by her, and still lives? What is named by her, and not saved? Hers is the only intelligence that can fall with splendor, power, with a sense of possession and redemption on the whole of creation, and the least members of it."[14] He gives the church such titles as: the vessel of truth, the total truth, the secret of the Trinity, the thought of God, the bride of God, and the very fullness of God. The members of the church have the intuition of God, and outside the church no one can really know or love anything in truth. It was Berrigan's conviction that every theologian and artist should strive to share in the self-consciousness of the church and attempt to know the world as the church knows it.

For Dan, the church was the center of history. The world, time, events, all remained peripheral, isolated phenomena outside the boundaries of the church. Here, only the Judeo-Christian view was capable of giving meaning to history and, in fact, without Christianity there was no history in the objective sense. It is the church that actually made history through her rites, sacrifices and organization, which, as they moved through time could not be ignored by people of good will.[15]

He wrote with a pre-Vatican II triumphalism as he described the glory of the church, and said that it was coextensive with the dream of God, a dream that embraced all of creation. The church was a divine thing, with unique powers that go far beyond the certitude of reason. The church used unique God-given powers to declare her own unchanging nature.

Berrigan's early attitudes toward those outside the church were also typical of the pre-Vatican II period. He wrote of "pagan man," who had been given over to an impersonal world that was owned by Satan.[16] He pointed out that the Christian is one who possesses himself in an infinitely larger universe than the natural man. The saints of the church, according to early Berrigan, were those who were utterly liberated, those who infallibly used creatures in relation to God. They were the supreme examples of the church's triumphant consciousness of her mission and power. They were the examples of the church's impulse toward full possession of human lives.

In these early ecclesial views, Berrigan saw the church as the one way to achieve salvation and eternal life. The church herself is immortal and her life circulates in the whole Body of the justified, a gift and instrument for achieving eternity. The church possesses and communicates the fullness and catholicity of the Word Incarnate to its members. Once a person is awakened to the reality of the church and turns to her, that person forms an act of love of God. Thus, loving the church is authentic obedience to the first and second commandments. The church here seems to be the only way to God.[17]

Berrigan's Christology at that time linked the church with Christ in such a way as to indicate that salvation is through Christ alone. He indicates that all reality finds place in the church in a hierarchical fashion, and that all things and all humans converge in the one man, Jesus Christ.[18] Berrigan stressed the divinity of Jesus, saying, "Human nature, united to this Divine Person; now able to express for the first time in a human body, the Divine Act from eternity; able to express how God would act, if He were man."[19]

Ironically, while Berrigan was writing so idealistically about Jesus and the church, he was at the same time beginning to feel alienated from church authorities. The castigation he had received from the bishop of Syracuse for supporting a pacifist began to turn him from church authorities, leaders who purported to be men of God, while at the same time accepting the violence of war. He later said that, during that period, the church accepted the lunacies of the Cold War as inevitable, and even as "God-given ingredients of our world."[20]

A Significant Sabbatical

Eventually, Dan's views on pacifism made his colleagues at LeMoyne nervous. He was given a sabbatical, which would in fact mark the end of any stable future academic career in Jesuit education. He wrote that from then on he became a wanderer of the earth, preaching an unwelcome message of nonviolence and a God of peace.

God seemed to have interesting times in mind for him. Inevitably, his sabbaticals and exiles would become periods of enlightenment. This time off (1963–1964) gave him the opportunity to travel throughout parts of Eastern Europe and South Africa. In both areas, he had the opportunity to visit deeply religious people who were struggling for peace. These contacts helped move him ever further toward radical positions against the god of war.

In Eastern Europe, Berrigan met people who cast a cold eye toward the myth that the kingdom of God was to be identified with the United States. Seeing the deprivation in these areas made the young Jesuit all the more cynical about notions of freedom in the United States that were too often false. He cynically concluded that this so-called freedom allowed the American people nothing more than the power to consume, vote in a moral void, amass wealth, attend superficial worship and pay for weapons of mass destruction.

In South Africa, Berrigan was shocked to find people who were resigned to see oppression as God's will, and he was scandalized at the silence in the churches toward apartheid, a rigid system of segregation. He said there here he found "a manipulated God created in our own image, a God in servitude, to our fear, our ego, our instincts of cruelty and violence."[21] He was disgusted by the denial of oppression that he heard from the pulpits. Instead of liturgy, he found himself witnessing a debased magic, wherein worshipers presumed that God, the true and truthful One, could be invoked by a people who were locked in cowardice. Berrigan believed that the God of the Bible, the God of Christ, abhorred such criminal silence. He was now convinced that the God of truth was on the side of the victimized and the outcast.

A 'Quiet' Editor

In 1965 Berrigan returned to the United States and was assigned to the quiet task of working on the Jesuit mission magazine. This did not mean, of course, that his life would be uneventful, for by now Berrigan realized that for him God would never be the "mayor of a heavenly Dullsville."[22] That same year, his brother Philip had been ejected from his position in the seminary because of his conviction that the war in Vietnam was not only bringing death to the young, but was also increasing poverty for minorities. As Berrigan wrote, his brother would not accept that the squalor people had to live in was to be seen as a "dark disaster buried in some human grotesquerie known as the Will of God—that great refuge of the status quo."[23]

Dan and Philip both began to realize that the Vietnam War had to some extent commandeered the church and claimed the conscience of bishops, priests and laypeople, young and old. The brothers vehemently opposed this war, which had begun for the United States in the early 1960s, until its bitter end in 1976. It seemed to them that everyone had pledged to abandon all things and follow the god of war: to kill and die and maim and bomb. For the Berrigans, Cardinal Spellman became an icon of the period, as he dressed in a military uniform and was flown in an air force jet to the war zone to "bless the war." They simply could not go along with the majority of Americans who supported the cardinal, and focused on their belief that the war was helping to stop the spread of "godless" Communism. Many Americans opposed the Berrigans as radicals who were disloyal to their country, and priests who were wrong to get involved in political matters.

Philip was eventually "exiled" to parish life and Dan's exile would be soon to follow. The occasion would be the death of a young former seminarian, Roger LaPorte, who set himself on fire in front of the

United Nations building in protest of the war. Cardinal Spellman spoke against the suicide, and Berrigan was warned by his Jesuit superiors to keep quiet about the incident. At a Eucharist celebrated for LaPorte, Berrigan was asked to speak. He questioned whether the harsh judgment of the chancery reflected the compassion of Christ, and suggested that the death did not so much come from despair but perhaps out of a spirit of self-sacrifice, albeit naive and mistaken. He suggested that such imponderables be left to God.

This interpretation was not acceptable to Cardinal Spellman, who immediately contacted Berrigan's superiors and told them to take action. Dan was treated as a deserter. There would be "silence, then ostracism, scorn—and finally exile."[24] He was ordered to leave New York immediately, without even being able to visit his ill and aging parents. He was to take an extended tour of South America. While awaiting the needed documents, he was provided with a Quonset shed in the remote corner of the campus of Georgetown University. The year was 1965.

Exile

During Berrigan's exile from his community and his church, he took a dizzying tour of ten Latin American countries. He notes that throughout this time a sea change was taking place inside him. It was as though he had eaten "the apple of Genesis," and while he would not lose his love for the Jesuits or the church, he was becoming a distanced outsider. The tour of Latin America brought him face to face with a colonized culture, where the church was solidly on the side of the powerful and the wealthy. At the same time, he encountered small healthy cells of biblically-attuned people, usually led by women, who were passionately working with the poor. It was from these people that Berrigan learned that authentic peace must include working for justice.

As suddenly as Berrigan's exile had been decreed, it came to an end. Pressure from his friends and supporters back in the States had been effective, and he was told that all was forgiven and he could come home. Berrigan, of course, was not the least repentant, and returned now more resolved than ever to confront the god of war. In his own puckish style, he wrote: "I came home, worse than ever."[25]

Soon after his return, he was offered a position to work in the peace movement at Cornell University. At the time, he was very involved in the peace movement in New York City, and to him Cornell seemed like a falsely idyllic scene, all charming and tweedy, where the two gods of money and property flourished. At the same time, there was a building antiwar feeling on campus, and Berrigan thought he might be able to make a contribution.

While at Cornell, Berrigan became more deeply given to the peace movement. At one point, his brother Philip turned up on the campus and told him that a group was going to pour blood on draft records in Baltimore. Dan did not participate in that action, but demonstrated his views in other ways. At the end of 1967, he was arrested for demonstration at the Pentagon and the following year he went to Vietnam to negotiate the release of some captured American pilots. That same year a sixteen-year-old boy immolated himself in front of the Syracuse Cathedral. Berrigan visited the boy in the hospital, and when he smelled the odor of burning flesh as he had in Vietnam, Berrigan was deeply affected. He wrote: "The boy died, but not before he brought something to birth in me."[26]

Soon after, Philip came to Cornell again and this time asked Dan to participate in burning draft files in Catonsville, Maryland. After his participation, Dan's life, as well as his approach to God, would never be the same. He was convicted of destroying government property and sentenced to three years in prison. Berrigan fled, and lived underground until he was caught and then had to spend eighteen months as inmate #23742–125 in Danbury federal prison. He was arrested numerous other times, and lived as a "holy outlaw," writing, teaching, giving retreats and demonstrating for peace. He spoke against the warmongers, regardless of their position in society. From then on Berrigan would feel that there was light on him: "the light of the adversary, light of the church, light of the eye of God."[27] A new fire, the fire of a new Pentecost burned in his heart and there was to be no turning back. In a poem, he wrote:

> I left Cornell
> with half a wit, six mismated socks
> ski underwear, a toothbrush...
> Later, dismay: no Testament.
> I must construct, out of oddments, abrasions,
> vapor trails, dust, pedicabs
> three crosshatch continents, Brooks Brothers embassies
> their male models dressed to kill—
> all He meant and means. I touch
> shrapnel and flesh, and risk my reason
> for the truth's sake, an ignorant hung head.
> Man of one book, stand me in stead.[28]

Berrigan's writing on God and theological issues began to reflect his strong commitment to nonviolence. He insisted that the sovereignty of God stood free of the destructive power of human pride. This was no longer the all-powerful "in charge" God, of his youth, but a God who came to the weak and asked them to have faith, a God who wanted to share in their helplessness. Berrigan wrote:

> What do we hope for from Him? We may not hope that he will take up arms against evil men of power, or that He will somehow equalize the lot of rich and poor. Or even, closer to our case, that He will spring the locks and bars of prisons; or that he will end the war, will restore exiles to their families. We are not allowed to hope for an act of God that would amount to nothing more than an act of magic.... In all such areas, God wills to remain helpless; to make no difference, to interfere at no point, to force no issue. He is literally as passive as an infant before our freedom.[29]

Berrigan's God was a God who suffers and dies, a God who lets us be hurt, and yet a God who challenged the imperial machine. This was a dissident God, a God of resistance, a God of life.[30] It was a God who, at times, seems to be more absent than present, a God whose kingdom often seems to be a speck, a tiny seed buried underground.

Dan maintained that this "true God" was often a casualty of life as we know it today, and had been buried by both church and state. Eventually, he found that the people now more in touch with God were the poor and suffering in places like Eastern Europe, Africa and Central America. Berrigan clung to the God who preferred the underdog, the reject, the deviant and the outcast. This was a God who appeared to be silent, but who alone could bring the future into being. If there was to be judgment at all from this God, it would be upon those who commit atrocities on innocent people.[31]

Berrigan's God would henceforth be a living God, a God of history, whose covenant is "a nuclear free zone," one whose kingdom forbids bloodshed. This was a God of love, the disarmed God of Jesus Christ. Yet, this God was at times described by Berrigan as "victim." He wrote:

> I believe that God dies a little with every murder, every twist of cruelty, every lie, every concession offered to death. God dies in us, God dies in nature, God dies in innocent blood, God dies in a dying universe. God's voice is stifled, God's holy will is mocked, God's tenderness set to naught. Vast armaments declare God impotent, but military budgets prove God insolvent. Pretentious, absurd, sinister beyond belief, modern dictators declare God's rule ended.[32]

Already, Berrigan had learned that the mysteries of God are "hard—hard as nails, hard as wood, hard as fire, hard as jail, hard as isolation, hard as death."[33] God is a Holy One, who comes to us as justice, and who empowers us to rebel for peace and fight those who crush people in the name of God. Echoing the Jesuit poet Gerard Manley Hopkins, Berrigan wrote that the world and its people are charged with the grandeur of God.

Revisions on the Will of God

As Berrigan became more involved with the peace movement, ambiguity increasingly surrounded his notion of the will of God. He realized that the will of God could not be discovered as easily as his religious

superiors had once told him. He was quick to understand that the "fast food" of instant salvation and the
trashy magic of religion are often mistaken for the will
of God. He now saw that people have to painfully
search for the will of God, and that the search may even
lead them into such unlikely places as prison.

Dan's own difficult prison experience in the early
seventies helped him discover the will of God among
the ranks of those imprisoned for peace-protesting. He
came to believe that God was working through such
people to bring a new perception of compassion, and to
challenge the tired and mediocre understandings of the
past.[34] At the same time, he encountered in those who
ran the prison systems more of an identification with
"Caesar's" will, and a rejection of the God who wills
compassion, hope, joy and freedom. He was appalled at
those who think that they are living for God, and at the
same time serve as "wardens for the wretched" in pris-
ons and concentration camps.[35]

Berrigan was convinced that the evil in the world
was not in any way the will of God. Such evil, he believed, must therefore receive our more vehement
protests. He was dismayed that so many people thought
that they were obeying God's will by participating in
oppression and violence, when in fact they were mis-
taking the commands of "Caesar" for God's will.
Berrigan insisted slavery, the attack upon Hiroshima
and the victimization of people in El Salvador could
never be seen as God's will.[36] For him, there were no just
wars. God's will was abundantly clear—we must always walk away from bloodshed and war.

Dan often had harsh words for what he considered
to be "false gods." He attacked the "papier-mâché" God

constructions of theologians and the deadly god talk that can bury people in confusion.[37] He condemned the "gods of the state," where inflated egos, the drive for power, technology and money are held up to us for worship. Such gods could only drag us into the abyss, and so Berrigan exposed false gods, where the divine had been debased, had lost savor. He pointed out that when the false gods of violence do not exist, we create them. These were the gods of citizenship, of order, of war, of imperialism, of the edges of expanding empire, of domination and power, of colonials.[38]

Dan rejected talk of a God who wills wars, or who sanctions the destruction of countless lives. He cried out against the way the state played God with its "pseudo-divine charade," setting rules that decide who lives and who dies. He was critical of those who play god by their complicity in the "nuclear crucifixion of the world," or in the deliberate refusal to love certain people.[39]

At times, Berrigan suggested that we call off much of our god talk until we get in better touch with the true God. He wrote:

> I had rather a hundred times spend my life's energies working to heal the injustice around me, and never once speak of God...than spend life converting others to God, while I gave not a snap for prisoners, slave camps, wars, starving peoples, the sins of the mighty. To what God would I be converting others, in such a demented case? In what God would I believe?[40]

He once commented that many have lost touch with the true God, and in his own poetic style once proclaimed: "We must offer Him a blood transfusion."[41]

Berrigan was steadfastly critical of those who take up arms for the love of the kingdom of God.[42] He pointed out that in every Christian crusade, murder and violence was invariably baptized in religious ideology and in a theology of the kingdom of God.

He persistently struck out against the U.S.'s penchant for war. During the Vietnam War, he described the American government as the beast of the apocalypse which, like the Roman government of old, was self-sustaining and arrogant. The activity of this beast was war, generating spectacular human advances in every field, where man appears less as a collaborator of God than the supplanter of God. Berrigan wrote: "God is my hope—I have little hope in armies, in the powerful, in dogmas or absolute truth."[43] He would see war as the end of the world, the day of the Lord, the holocaust where children are massively sacrificed to the gods of war. He often lamented the loss of gospel for forgiveness and love of enemy. He pointed out that, for many, there is only a God who punishes. Such people are at a peace only with a God of war and thus turn to the "killing weapons of the God of weapons."[44]

Berrigan would have to pay a steep price for his pacifism, especially during the Vietnam War. Dan watched as this war seeped into many lives. He says that the war reached perilously into his own life, destroyed its former shape, drained his energy, disrupted his friendships, and made his life one of division rather than unity. This war, he says, became his cross. At times in his life underground and in prison, Berrigan seems to have experienced the dark night of the soul, where even God seemed to shun him.[45]

The many hardships connected with peacemaking never brought Dan to give up his efforts. He continued his struggle for peace with compassion and hope, and seldom lost his unique sense of humor. One striking story of the latter was an occasion when he was taking his students to demonstrate against the war in El Salvador. The protest was stopped by the police and the students were arrested. As they were being put in the police van, Berrigan shouted after them, "Everyone gets an A."[46]

For Dan, the Spirit of God was always nonviolent, so he chastised those who played god by taking part in the arms race, or by deciding who lives and who dies. Such decisions are not godly at all, but rather are participants in the mystery of evil. Berrigan lamented that we so often know our enemies more than we know our neighbors, and that so often presenting a "disarmed God" is seen as a scandal. It was his view that the real scandal was that the mainline churches had either joined in the killing of war or stood by in silence.[47]

Berrigan maintained that we simply could not go on destroying human beings thinking that this is for the greater honor and glory of God.

> How is a man to live today? How is he to live; how is it possible for a man to do something other than kill his brother—the practically universal demand laid upon him by the state, approved by a silent church? Is there another way, which will allow men to live here and now, will allow the unborn to get born, and to live their lives in a way different from the way sanctioned today?[48]

Nor did Dan believe that we should continue to make profit out of the death of our fellow human beings. He maintained that we would never achieve the peace of Christ through complicity with people who destroy. The Christian pacifist, therefore, has a clear option in a world where "the great powers and lackey churches have reached agreements," and that is for complete non-violence.[49] For violence, according to Berrigan, was nothing other than a betrayal of God. In its place, we must choose love rather than hate, bread rather than bullets, the preservation of life rather than "allowable murder."[50]

For Berrigan, the true God was a casualty of our wars and had been buried by both church and state. Through a tortuous route, the United States came to Hiroshima and the arms race, and Dan called for a return to the Sermon on the Mount and a renewal of consciences. He called all to love their enemies and develop a spirituality of nonviolence, lest we all perish through our own arms race. He called for the spirit of God, the spirit which can free from retaliation and thirst for revenge, and liberate from the tragic irony where the nonviolent hero often ends up dead. He called for an end of the mentality where the disarmed God in Christ is a scandal in history. For him, the weapons of faith, the weapons of Jesus, had to be nonviolent: truth, integrity, the gospel, salvation and the word of God.[51]

Berrigan maintained that those who resisted death and worked hard for social change were the ones who could truly overcome death and be fulfilled in resurrection—people who would have nothing to do with death, whether by death by napalm, carpet bombing, starvation, military sorties, imprisonment or disappearance. He repeatedly said that he categorically refused to climb aboard the death train, and would always maintain his stand with life and resurrection. In his play *The Trial of the Catonsville Nine*, he wrote:

> But I was trying to be concrete
> about death because death
> is a concrete fact
> as I have throughout my life
> tried to be concrete
> about the existence of God
> Who is not an abstraction
> but is someone before me
> for Whom I am responsible.[52]

Jesus as Role Model

Jesus Christ was Berrigan's ultimate role model for pacifism. He pointed out that it was Jesus' courageous stand for the God of peace that brought his own suffering and death. He was crucified for the crime of representing a God of peace in a community of citizens who, like many today, were "silent, enlisted, taxpaying, acquiescent, lock-stepping citizens."[53] Jesus stood for a dissident God who raised questions to the imperialistic machine. He once pointed out: "If you want to follow Jesus, you better look good on wood."[54]

Berrigan saw Jesus as the "baring of the heart of God," the full revelation of the warmth, human commingling, servanthood, friendship, tenderness, majesty and personalism in God.[55] He was convinced that the mystery of the cross is tied up in the mystery of war, which destroys so many lives, including the moral lives of those who do violence to others. When he and his friends poured blood on the draft records in the town of King of Prussia, Dan saw this as a symbol of the outpouring of the blood of Christ, and a witness that there should be no shedding of blood by anyone, under any circumstances. Later, when he saw the suffering of so many in El Salvador, he said that those being tortured and killed were limbs of the body of Christ. He quoted a poem by the Jesuit Rutilio Grande, a close friend of Archbishop Romero:

> And if Jesus were to cross the border they would arrest him. They would crucify him again because they prefer a Christ of sacristy or cemetery, a silent Christ, a Christ according to our image and our selfish interests.[56]

At one point, Berrigan wrote to young Jesuits that we dishonor Christ when we participate in war, racism and poverty. He told them that the peace of Christ was not won in complicity with the destruction wrought by governments. Rather, the peace of Christ requires that we face change, confront our fears and resolve to renew ourselves daily in terms of the gospel. One of his most touching lines in this regard was written in prison: "I believe in Jesus Christ. He sustains my spirit, he speaks to me in my brothers and sisters." He came to see Jesus vividly in the face of his brother Philip and in the faces of his other fellow prisoners.[57]

A Modern Prophet

Berrigan stood resolutely before the church and the nation as a prophet of peace and nonviolence. He put before his people the Word of God, which put acts of violence and war under the scrutiny of God. As a representative of this Word, Berrigan worked to liberate the world from the desire to have power over the life and death of others. He bore witness to the truth that we must not kill, but must love our enemies. He stood for a God who wants to liberate humanity from its self-destruction.

Dan was well aware that prophets suffer persecution, even execution. Yet, it was his conviction that to banish the prophets is to banish God from history. [58] The prophets take the side of the poor and the oppressed and, in this, stand for God. He believed that the living God is on the side of all humanity, but especially loves the lowliest. No ideology, whether of the state or church could convince him otherwise. His prophetic voice continued his protest to American oppression in El Salvador, Nicaragua and Iraq. He declared his solidarity with the homeless, AIDS patients and prison inmates. As Jean Vanier points out:

> Berrigan is a rebel for peace, giving support and friendship to every person and initiative that can reveal the heart of God and the yearnings of the Spirit. Berrigan is a rebel for peace, gently fighting against the weight of spiritual power that crushes people in the name of God. [59]

A Church for the Oppressed

The Second Vatican Council solidified Berrigan's notions that the church should not retreat from life and should give special honor to the poor. Looking back, he realized that the church of his seminary training accented mercy rather than justice and had stressed the life of the mind, while leaving conscience in a state of sorry neglect. In contrast to his earlier idealism concerning the church, he now became its harshest critic.

He said that the church was unfaithful to its God-given mission to the poor and defenseless. The church had become too rich, and would have to return to its poor beginnings if it wished to be one with God and

God's people. In order to be faithful of God, the church would have to become more relevant to today's problems and not "disappear into the shrine."[60] And he cautioned that if the church were incapable of reading the signs of the times, it, too, would become obscure as a sign.

Berrigan came to believe that the churches were among the institutions which no longer promote the best interests of the people. Berrigan wrote from prison: "Churches and synagogues fear the Scriptures, and fear living them...."[61] He criticized the church for its silence toward violence and its anger against those who protest against it. It was his conviction that when churches embrace war, they betray the God of history.[62]

Berrigan was strident in his criticism of those who honor a God who approves of destruction, and he sharply chastised many of the American church leaders who seemed to be "inoculated against Christ and his Spirit."[63] He rebuked them for spending their lives in oiling the ecclesiastical machinery, and for conducting charades that went by the name of worship, even in the White House. Berrigan believed such church leaders suffocate the Word of God and are acting as Grand Inquisitors who forget Jesus.

Berrigan at times wrote isolated from his country and church. At one point, he became so depressed that he thought he and his brother were "dead men," in the minds of many in the United States.[64] He even wondered whether or not God was shortchanged in having to settle for such as Berrigan and his brother to bring enlightenment to a state and church that had become so locked in a tired and rigid mediocrity.[65]

His sharpest criticism of the church was aimed at its

indifference and silence while people were killing each other. Berrigan hoped to bring the church to identify with God's concern for those who are trying to survive such tragic violence. In an interview with Robert Coles, he speaks of this as a mission:

> My brother and I feel that there's an important chapter of history to be written in our own time, and we would like to help write it. It is a chapter of history which, we hope, will see the center of the church's concerns located at the edge of society—where human lives are involved in a really tragic struggle for survival and human dignity.[66]

An Open Church

Berrigan came to reject the otherworldly approach to Christianity that had been so integral to his Jesuit training. He bluntly declares that many Christians were "out of it," and thus created a God who was also "out of it." Berrigan found it ironic that many people had moved beyond the church's indifference to worldly matters and had taken up action for peace and justice outside the church. The church, according to Berrigan, must reenter the world through action, for it is through action that the God of history is revealed. He observed that while such action will bring much suffering to the church, it will at the same time help the church rediscover its authentic being before God, and the world.[67] In the early 1970s he wrote:

> I would say that by the grace of God I am able to draw upon something quite important and healthy in a long tradition, and I found around me constant manifestations of that "something" in the lives of other people— no matter what tradition and what background they

happen to draw upon for spiritual strength. For all the bad and evil to be found on this planet, I find much goodness struggling for birth and struggling for expression.[68]

In time Berrigan acquired a solidarity with people of all faiths and backgrounds. He was encouraged that at least a minority of Catholics were able to do what they thought right in the peace movement and were doing this peace work with their brothers and sisters from other faiths. His perspective expanded and he could agree with Simone Weil, a modern French philosopher, who wrote of the notion of "putting on the universe for God," and embracing both the reality of God and the reality of human suffering as one.[69]

As Dan grew older, his hope became grounded, not so exclusively in the church, as in something "God inspired" that lives on in the majority of good people. He firmly believed that "something" is human dignity. He wrote: "When faith in God is alive, there are no alternatives to the human; neither state, nor ideology, nor cultural idolatries—nor, indeed, Church."[70] For Berrigan, this "soul-force" to protect the innocent lived through the Hindu Gandhi, the German Protestant theologian Dietrich Bonhoeffer, in religious communities everywhere and indeed with the entire human community. He faced the fact that, like it or not, we inhabit the globe in company with other humans who vary greatly in outlook and who are accustomed to name their God in various ways. And he concluded, "Most are capable of great goodness, many of heroism."[71]

Though Berrigan's relationship with the church and the Jesuits during his senior years has not been as stormy as it once was, he has not lost his critical edge.

In his 1999 commentary on the Book of Job, he wrote: "Firm lines are drawn; law and order is in the ascendancy; expulsions and exclusions are thunderous in the air; women and gays and the divorced are put down or put to the door."[72] Dan Berrigan has remained realistically faithful to his prophetic calling. He is still a strong advocate for peace, and now ministers to those living with AIDS in New York City.

Daniel Berrigan has always sat attentively at the game of life, insisting that the cards be dealt truthfully and honestly. He has demanded that the game be played nonviolently, and has been willing to stake his freedom, and even his life. To vehemently resist arms making, killing and war, Berrigan has toiled as a teacher, poet, preacher, counselor, inmate, priest and friend, but his story is first and foremost of one who, no matter what the consequences, has remained a servant of the God of peace. He now says that his only regret is that he did not start his peace activism earlier so that perhaps more lives could have been saved.

In Berrigan's poem "There Must Be a God," he says:

Let there be a God
is man's big news; let Him sow as much heart
as a good man musters;
leave us alone
to make do, fumble about, fret through;
He must leave us our sins to learn and ravel;
sweat, start false, feint, dissimulate.[73]

Dan Berrigan sees no evidence that holiness will conquer the wolves of the world, but for him in the end what matters is that each of us does our best and leaves the rest to God.

CHAPTER EIGHT

The God of the Abandoned

MOTHER TERESA

The tiny, middle-aged Lady of Loreto nun set aside her voluminous black habit, long veil and starched coif and put on the simple cotton sari of the poor. She then walked away forever from her congregation and the stately school where she had taught for almost twenty years. After a brief medical training, she moved into the filthy, stench-filled slums of Calcutta with just a few coins in her pocket, walked amid the squalor, the sick, the abandoned and the dying. She gathered several children around her and began to teach them their alphabet by writing in the mud: a humble beginning indeed for the person who would become one of the most outstanding religious figures of our time—Mother Teresa of Calcutta. This is the story of a child who first found her God amid a traditional Catholic Albanian family; it is the tale of a woman who would go on to discover and then reveal to the world God's unique presence in the poorest of the poor.

Family Foundations

Mother Teresa's given name was Agnes Bojaxhiu, and she was born in 1910 to Albanian parents in Skopje, Yugoslavia. (At that time, Skopje was still part of the Ottoman Empire. At present, it is part of Macedonia.) Drana, her mother, was a strong-minded and deeply religious woman. From her, Agnes learned to center her life on the church and to be generous to the poor. Drana often invited poor neighbors to the family table, and would take Agnes with her when she went to care for the sick and the poor. She showed Agnes how to wash ailing people and tend to their wounds, and she urged her daughter to treat each person as a child of God.

Agnes's father Nicola was a shrewd entrepreneur who was quite successful as a merchant and owner of a construction company. Nicola was also an ardent political activist for Albanian independence. He seems to have passed onto his daughter a shrewd business sense, as well as a strong loyalty to her Albanian heritage. Even though Mother Teresa took Indian citizenship, she was always emphatic that she was "all Albanian."[1] Nicola, along with his wife, also taught Agnes to offer food, shelter and care to the poor. He once told his daughter: "Never take a morsel of food that you are not prepared to share with others."[2] Tragically, Nicola died suddenly following a political meeting. His son Lazar maintains that his father was poisoned by his political enemies. Agnes, who was called Gonxha ("Rosebud") by her father, was only eight when he died, and throughout her life had a special empathy for children who had lost a parent.

Agnes was brought up among a stalwart Catholic minority in a largely Muslim area. Her home was a key gathering place for the local parishioners, often visited by the bishop and the clergy. Early on, she became familiar with dealing with people from another faith, as well as with church leaders. She was active in her parish, adding her rich and talented voice to the choir, and working with the sodality. Her parish was served by Jesuits, and she grew intensely interested in their mission work, especially in India. By the time she was eighteen, Agnes had decided that she, too, would become a missionary. She told her mother Drana of this decision, and hard as it was to lose her daughter, Drana responded: "Put your hand in His hand—and walk all the way with Him."[3]

Lazar was not so impressed. He was now a lieutenant in the Albanian army and found it strange that his bright and lovely young sister would give up her good life and family to become a nun. Agnes wrote him in the feisty and idealistic style of a teenager: "You will serve a king of two million people. I shall serve the king of the world."[4]

Agnes, convinced that joining the convent and becoming a missionary in India was a calling from God, signed up for the Loreto Sisters, who ran mission schools in India. She later wrote of this decision: "When

I was eighteen, I decided to leave my home and become a nun. Since then, I never doubted even for a second that I did the right thing. It was the will of God, his choice."[5] Oddly, the Loreto Sisters' postulancy was in Ireland. So, Agnes, who did not know a word of English, would have to travel from Yugoslavia to Ireland, so that she could be a missionary in India! In 1928 the *Catholic Mission* magazine, which had greatly influenced her decision, gave a charming account of her departure:

> Gonxha Bojaxhiu is an Albanian born in Skopje, to whom God's call came while she was still in school. Just as St. Peter immediately left his nets behind him, so Gonxha set off in the name of God. Everyone was surprised, because she was top of her class and much admired. She was the life and soul of the Catholic girls activities and the church choir, and it was generally acknowledged that her departure would leave an enormous gap. When she left Skopje, about a hundred people were at the station to see her off. They were all in tears and greatly moved.[6]

Agnes remained only two months in Ireland, and was then sent to the Loreto novitiate in Darjeeling, India, a beautiful resort area at the foot of the Himalayan Mountains. During her early years, Agnes is remembered as shy and quite ordinary. This is, no doubt, because she was still learning the English, Hindi and Bengali languages.

In 1931 she made her vows as a Loreto nun, and took the new name of Teresa, after Saint Thérèse of Lisieux, a French nun who practiced the "little way," and who was named patron of the missions.

Teresa was sent to teach in St. Mary's School, in Entally, Calcutta—not a particularly prestigious assignment. Entally was the least exclusive of the order's girls' academies in Calcutta. It was divided into two schools: the main school, which served wealthy families, and St. Mary's, which served poor and middle class children for free. At St. Mary's, Teresa taught alongside the Daughters of St. Anne, a diocesan order of nuns who wore the Indian sari and, besides teaching, worked outside the walls with the poor. Teresa was impressed by the dress and work of these nuns. In time, Teresa was made headmistress of the school and was also put in charge of the Daughters of St. Anne.

Teresa was beloved by her students, who called her "Ma." She taught them religion and also geography, which she later saw as a good preparation for her world travels. One of her students gave this report on her teaching: "Mother taught us religion, and she did so in such a way that everything became vividly clear before our eyes. Through her words, the love of Jesus and the remembrance of his sacrifice were branded on the soul. We understood the beauty of sacrificing ourselves in turn for him."[7]

A Call within a Call

Throughout her nineteen years at St. Mary's, Teresa was regularly reminded that her God was uniquely a God of the poor, and that she was called to serve the poor as a missionary. There were many instances when glimpses of the poor brought her attention to her early call from God. When Teresa first arrived in Calcutta by boat, she was disturbed by the depth of the poverty, the overcrowding, the multitudes of beggars and half-dressed refugees. But she was soon whisked off to the beautiful mountain retreat in Darjeeling. For a brief period, she had the opportunity to serve at a small medical station, and wrote ecstatically about the experience: "The tiny veranda is always full of the sick, the wretched, and the miserable. All eyes are fixed, full of hope, on me.... My heart beats in happiness: I can continue your work, dear Jesus."[8] The poor and suffering were deeply touching her spirit, and Teresa was beginning to meet her God intimately in them.

At St. Mary's, Teresa was surrounded by walls, which shut out the destitution and suffering. She encouraged the girls in her Sodality to work with the poor, but she could not leave the cloister and accompany them. She listened intently to the stories of the Daughters of St. Anne, who worked in the slums, but she could not participate with them. Teresa's mother would not let her forget her commitment to the poor. When Teresa proudly reported to her mother that she was doing well as a teacher and had become the headmistress of the whole school, Drana answered: "Dear child, do not forget that you went out to India for the sake of the poor."[9]

Then two events brought the poor starkly into Teresa's life. In 1943 a great drought hit the area, and at the same time the Japanese in nearby Burma were bombing the city. The girls of the wealthy families returned home and the school was opened as a transit camp for refugees and the poor of the area. Teresa found herself face to face with desperate people, with the diseased and dying. She held children whose stomachs were bloated from hunger, and who had been orphaned. Sister Rosario of Loreto maintains that this experience made a deep impression on Teresa.[10]

In 1946 there was another frenzy of violence in Calcutta, as Muslims and Hindus slaughtered each other by the thousands. Food was cut off from the school, and although Teresa knew that she was not supposed to go out, she went out anyway, and amidst the peril and carnage talked some soldiers into bringing some rice back to her starving students. As Teresa returned to the convent through the blood-drenched streets and looked at the horrors of dying and dead bodies, Teresa realized that she had been staying behind "safe walls" while people were suffering and dying. The God of the abandoned was calling her beyond the cloister.

Shortly after Teresa's foray into the streets of Calcutta, she came down with tuberculosis and was sent off to Darjeeling for rest and a retreat. It was on the train ride that Teresa had her well-known inspiration. Here is her own account of the event: "It was on a train that I heard the call to give up all and follow Him into the slums—to serve Him in the poorest of the poor. I knew it was His will and that I had to follow Him. There was no doubt that it was to be His work."[11] It became clear to her that she should leave the convent, move to the slums, and seek out God among the abandoned. She says: "I knew where I belonged, but I did not know how to get there."[12]

Even though Teresa was sure what God wanted of her, she was an institutional person. Her God worked through channels, and it would take her two years before she could get permission to answer her new call. She was a vowed religious, and the move would require considerable paperwork and permission from her religious superiors as well as from church officials.

In 1947 Gandhi finally succeeded in gaining freedom for India. Before the British left, they partitioned
Pakistan from India, causing huge migrations and a
bloody feud between Hindus and Muslims. Over a million people were killed. Teresa was transferred out of
Calcutta to a safer convent, and she continued to await
permission to follow her calling. Teresa knew she had to
await the will of God through her superiors, but at times
she tried to hurry it. She wrote her archbishop, who had
been quite ill: "Your recovery will be a sign that I can
begin my work with the poor. Please, your Grace, get
well soon."

Finally, in 1948 Teresa received "exclaustration,"
which meant that she remained a nun but was now
under the authority of the local archbishop and would
be free to begin establishing a group of her own. Had
she been "secularized," as her own archbishop had requested, Teresa would have gone off on her own as a lay
person, and perhaps would never have been heard of
again. For years, Teresa, as well as her archbishop,
thought that the exclaustration had come from the pope,
but years later it was learned that the Archbishop of
Delhi had never forwarded her request to Rome lest it
be lost in the labyrinth of Vatican bureaucracy. He simply changed her archbishop's request for "seculariza-
tion" to "exclaustration."[13]

Teresa prepared to move out of her convent. She
said that leaving her community was the hardest thing
she ever did, even more difficult than leaving her country and family to join the convent. At first, she says she
experienced a great deal of anxiety and loneliness.

The sight of a nun dressed like the poor and head-
ing out alone to face the overwhelming hopelessness in

the slums of Calcutta drew skeptical, even cynical reactions from many. One Jesuit thought that Teresa was giving in "to the wiles of the devil." Another remarked: "We thought she was cracked." Many of the older clergy thought that this young nun had gone mad. The archbishop later said: "I gave her a year."[14]

Meeting the Poorest of the Poor

Few realized the toughness and determination of this tiny Albanian nun. She had come to the conclusion that she could uniquely find her God in the poor and she was determined to follow her calling. She wrote: "Where is God? We believe he is everywhere—he is the creator, he is everything. But where is he to my human eyes? To make it possible for me to see the face of God with my human eyes, he has made himself the hungry one, the naked one, the homeless one, the lonely one..."[15] At the same time, she was now convinced that to know the poor it was not enough to read about them or to take a walk in the slums. For her, it was necessary to become one with the poor in their need. She said, "We have to dive into it, live it, share it."[16]

Convinced that "God was going with me. This is his work," Teresa dove in. She walked, her feet bare inside her new sandals, through the mud paths of the slums, amidst the starving, the diseased, the abandoned and the dying. She had to somehow learn the experience of the poor. Teresa had little experience with the poor, and now she was to live among them as one of them, available to their overwhelming needs. Often she felt helpless and lonely. In her early journal she wrote about her first inkling of what the poor endure:

> I learned a difficult lesson. Poverty must be so hard for
> the poor. When I was looking for a house for my settle-
> ment, I walked around and around until my arms and
> legs ached. I thought how much pain they have to en-
> dure in soul and body when they're out looking for a
> place to sleep, for something to eat, and security.[17]

On one occasion, she stopped at a convent and asked if she could eat her lunch inside. She was directed to the back of the convent and had to eat the few morsels she had under the back stairs. Becoming one of the poorest of the poor, and then finding God in them, would not be easy.

Teresa knew that the love of God was in her heart and was somehow in those around her. The challenge was to make the connection, to show them her love and through that rekindle in the poor their own awareness that they were loveable, that they were loved by God. She would start with one person at a time, an abandoned child, a dying person, a leper. For Teresa, these were the outcasts, the least of the brethren of whom Jesus had spoken.

Initially Teresa was given a room with the Little Sisters of the Poor, and would spend the day seeking out the abandoned. Once Teresa entered the slums, she began to do what she knew best—teach. She gathered a small group of urchins, began teaching them reading and basic hygiene, and passed out bars of soap for rewards.

Teresa would not be alone for long. Quickly some of her former students began to join with her in her service of the poor. In 1949 she wrote to her close friend Jacqueline De Decker: "You will be glad to hear at present I have got three companions, great zealous workers.

We have five different slums where we go for a few hours. What suffering, what want of God...."[18]

Together with her new companions, Teresa began with the poor children in the street and set up small free schools for them. To support her cause, she would go about soliciting money and empty buildings. Few could pass up her charming offer: "I am going to give you a chance to do something beautiful for God."[19]

Each day the nuns gathered the disabled, abandoned and malnourished infants and children from the streets and brought them to a place were they would receive affection and care. Mother Teresa staunchly believed that each child was "created in the image of God to love and be loved." She not only recited but lived Jesus' instruction: "Let the little children come to me, and do not stop them, for it is to such as these that the kingdom of God belongs" (Luke 18:16). Her mission would be to bring the love and kindness of God to these little ones, and thus help them realize their dignity and their preciousness in the sight of God. She wanted her sisters to be the "carriers of God's love" for these children.[20] Their simple acts to love and care for the children would keep the light of God burning in the lives of these little ones. She believed that God loved these children through her and through her sisters. To those who would abort, she would later plead: "Please don't kill the child. I want the child. I am willing to accept any child who would be aborted."[21]

Eileen Egan, a leading American lay advocate of the poor, gives a moving account of one of her visits to a school for leprous children set up by Mother Teresa:

> It was a nightmare in broad daylight. The cruelty of their fate possessed my imagination. And yet, I thought, here where life was at its cruelest, mercy was nearest. Mother Teresa looked on the faces of these scourged children and saw the face of God.[22]

Teresa next sought out those who were dying alone in the streets. This was commonplace at the time, largely because death is seen by many Hindus as unclean. They often hired untouchables to deal with death and handle corpses so as to avoid contamination. The poor themselves were often put out into the street and left to die abandoned, uncared for in their last hours.

Shocked at the sight of people dying in the streets, Teresa commented that many people seemed to be taking care of their pets better than they care for people, who are children of God. She began hailing reluctant cab or rickshaw drivers to bring these people to the hospital, but was often turned away. She complained to the police, and when they did not respond, she rented a small apartment and began to carry the dying there. The neighbors were not at all impressed with the horrible sights and smells to which this little nun subjected them, and they had her shut down.

Teresa then went to the health department and was given an abandoned Temple of Kali, the goddess of death. The place had become a hangout for vagrants and thugs, and was filthy with garbage and human waste. Teresa and her companions cleared the space, rolled up their sleeves and in one day had the place clean, outfitted with cots and ready to receive the dying with loving care.

The local Hindu priests were outraged at the nuns taking over the area. Though the temple had been closed for some time, it had been a place of pilgrimage, and the priests thought that the nuns would defile it and convert the dying Hindu patients into Christians. The local Hindu neighbors became hostile and gangs of hoodlums threatened Teresa and her companions. Undeterred, Teresa stepped out and faced them down with a challenge: "Come on, just kill me, if you want. But stop disturbing our work."[23] On another occasion, a Hindu man threatened to kill Teresa and the others. She simply smiled at him and told him that if he killed her and the others, they would only hope to reach God sooner.

Mother Teresa's tender care to the dying and her deep respect for the rituals of all faiths soon won over her opponents. A dying Hindu would have his or her lips moistened with water from the Ganges and would hear readings from the *Gita*; a Muslim would hear the Koran; and Catholics would be anointed with oil. Moreover, she would not baptize anyone, even a child, unless the person requested it.

Given Mother Teresa's upbringing in a traditional church where a rather exclusive notion of God and a doctrine of "outside the church there was no salvation" were taught, her openness to other faiths is remarkable. Her God was the God of all people. In an appeal to the Indian government for religious freedom, she once wrote, "You can call him Ishwar, some call him Allah, some simply God, but we all have to acknowledge that it is HE who made us for greater things: to love and to be loved. Who are we to prevent our people to find this God who made them—who loves them and to whom they have to return."[24]

Actually, Mother Teresa was known for her strong

and incisive interfaith statements long before the Second Vatican Council's openness to other religions. Her views must have, and no doubt still do, give pause to some Vatican officials. She once said of the religious situation at her home for the dying: "God is here. Castes and creeds mean nothing. It does not matter that they are not of my faith."[25] She believed that all people were equal in the sight of God. It was her position that religion was a matter of conscience; it was not her mission to convert, but to "help a Hindu become a better Hindu, a Muslim a better Muslim, and a Catholic become a better Catholic."[26] To her, how one lived one's life was the proof that one belonged to God, not religious affiliation. She said: "Whether one is a Hindu, Muslim or a Christian, how you live your life is proof that you are or are not fully his."[27]

Eventually, Teresa became quite comfortable worshipping in Hindu, Muslim and Buddhist temples. That comfort zone must have been strained at that time, however. On one occasion she had to sit next to some Jain monks who, by custom, sat stark naked during their ceremonial worship.[28] As she became more international in her experience, Mother Teresa's interfaith perspective would take on a global dimension. She once said: "People throughout the world may look different or have a different religion or position, but they are all the same. They are people to be loved. They are all hungry for love."[29] She said that she and her sisters had no difficulty working in countries with many faiths, and were able to "treat all people as children of God. They are all brothers and sisters."[30] Teresa's God was now the God of all people.

Tending the Dying

As we have seen, those who were left to die in the street were viewed by Mother Teresa as Jesus himself before them in "the distressing disguise of the poorest of the poor."[31] She would often quote Gandhi, whose presence and work in India had a deep influence on her: "He who serves the poor, serves God."[32]

Once they had a suitable place, each day the sisters would gather these ghostly figures with their festering sores and feeble bodies and bring them to a place of refuge. Teresa often told the story of the man, half-eaten by worms, whom she picked up from the gutter and took to her home for the dying. The sisters removed the worms from his body, washed and fed him, and tried to make him comfortable. He said: "I have lived like an animal in the street, but I am going to die as an angel, loved and cared for.... I am going home to God."[33] This story epitomizes what Mother Teresa set out to accomplish in her new calling—to bring God's love to the poorest of the poor.

At first most of the unfortunates whom Teresa gathered up did die. But eventually, as medicines improved and the Sisters became more skilled in care for the dying, many survived. In time, more than half of the dying who were gathered from the street by the Sisters were cured and sent home.

Caring for Lepers

In 1950 Mother Teresa received approval for her new congregation of the Missionaries of Charity, and continued to establish a number of free schools and homes for abandoned children, as well as a home for the dying. She then turned her attention to the tens of thousands of lepers in Calcutta. The city's hospital for lepers had been shut down, and the lepers in Calcutta were rejected and shunned by their families. They lived in impoverished "bustees" on the outskirts of the city, begging for food.

Teresa was first approached by five lepers who had lost their jobs and homes and turned to her in despair. She could not bring lepers to her places because of the fear of contagion, so she would travel out to their tents and huts, visit them, and bring them food and medical attention. Eventually, she was able to set up first class medical mobile units and local clinics that could treat leprosy and a host of other diseases. Teresa would not accept the common belief that leprosy was a curse from God. Instead she saw it as an infectious disease that could be treated with the latest antibiotics, and if caught in time was curable within two years. Teresa would set up many leprosy clinics and rehabilitation centers. She gave lepers access to baths and massages, taught them occupational skills, and even secured a printing press so that they could have their own newspaper.

Again, the lepers were part of Teresa's poorest of the poor and she believed that though leprous in their bodies they were not leprous in their hearts. Her gift was that she could see beyond the twisted limbs and open sores and find the vivid presence of God in each person. She helped the lepers regain their self-respect, dignity and awareness that they were children of God. And she constantly taught her sisters: "When you handle the sores and wounds of the poor, you must never forget that they are the wounds of Christ."[34] For her, there was something sacramental in this experience with the lepers and other outcasts, and she often linked it with Eucharist: "If we can see Jesus in the form of bread, we can also see him in the broken bodies of the poor."[35]

In just a few short years, Mother Teresa had made deep inroads into the slums of Calcutta and had gradually ferreted out the poorest of the poor among children, the dying, the leprous and the destitute. She was learning to live as one of them, serve them, and bring them the love of God, as she felt she had been called by God. She tells a humorous story of those early days, when she had come down with a high fever and went into delirium. In her dream she died and went to St. Peter's gate, but was not allowed in because "there are no slums in heaven." In the dream, Teresa grew angry with Peter and said: "Very well, I will fill heaven with slum people; then you will be forced to let me in."[36]

The Blessedness of the Poor

Teresa, who until now had led a rather sheltered life, with only glimpses of the poor, was now learning much about the suffering and difficulties of the destitute. She was also discovering the unique dignity, strength and goodness that often exists in them. She tells the story of how she once brought some rice to a starving Hindu family, and was deeply impressed when the mother of the family gave half of the rice to a hungry neighboring family. Teresa learned that the poor could have a greatness about them, and a power of endurance that the rich often do not possess. She later wrote about this amazing insight: "I can tell you I have never yet in these twenty-five years heard a poor person grumble or curse for feeling miserable."[37]

Teresa often observed that the people whom she served, whether they were destitute, addicted, or diseased, were beautiful people with wonderful personalities.[38] She often pointed out that the uniqueness of the poor often lies in their courage, wisdom, insight into self and their detachment from material things. She learned that their greatness lies in their enormous power to endure in spite of all their hardship. She came to realize that often the poor are stripped of all things, and are therefore free. They can often die with joy, because they are free of all attachments. Moreover, their struggle to survive can give them a strength and a sense of sharing with their fellow poor. Often all the poor really have to give other people is love.[39] Mother Teresa's unique calling was to help the people rediscover this beauty and dignity within themselves. They had to be brought to realize that they were indeed children of a loving God.

Later Teresa would learn that poverty took other forms, among them the hunger for love and human dignity. She would discover that the greatest poverty was lack of love, and that such poverty could be found among the rich as well. She came to understand that the poverty of the heart was even more difficult to relieve.

The Power of God's Love

Mother Teresa was learning some unique lessons about the love of God as she extended her experience with the most needy in Calcutta. First, she learned the importance of the "now" in bringing love to people. She was quite practical in her day-to-day, person-to-person service to each of the needy she met. She said: "Our work is today. Yesterday has gone; tomorrow has not yet come. We have only today."[40] It is in this "now" that Teresa would show through her compassion and love that God truly "is," and may not be relegated to the archaic traditions of the past. She was, therefore, quite practical in her spirituality, and often stressed that love has no meaning unless it is put into action. It was in the concrete actions of service to others, whether it be caring for the sick and dying, teaching a disabled child, giving medicine to a leper, or simply smiling at one's own child at home that make up "God's love in the world today."[41]

Mother Teresa taught that God's love is the most powerful force in the world, certainly much more powerful than sin, hatred, poverty or the weapons of war. She believed that universally people have a hunger for this love and that it is the only real answer to loneliness and hunger. For her it was simple: "God has created us to love and be loved."[42]

Teresa taught her Sisters that if they want to radiate this love of God, they must have a clean heart that is open and forgiving. Then they must seek out the lonely, the unwanted, the unloved, and extend love to them. Once asked by a man why she had picked him up out of the filth of the gutter and bathed his open festering sores, she simply answered: "Because I love you."[43]

Teresa came to live, as it were, in a zone of God's love, keenly aware that she lived, moved and had her being in God, that she was encompassed by God, indeed "swimming in God." It was her mission to extend this experience to others through her great kindness and care. She remarked that what mattered was not how much we do, or how much we give, but the amount of love that we put into the doing and giving. The heart of Teresa's mission was to extend God's love to others, and thereby help them recognize and revive the image of God in themselves. In the early documents of her new congregation, Teresa's goals are clear: take care of the poorest of the poor, "show them the love of Christ and awaken their response to his great love."[44] As she once told the distinguished audience, which gathered at Cambridge University to honor her: "He sends you and me to prove that he loves the world.... We have to be his love today."[45]

Teresa had already done some travel on speaking engagements. Her first trip out of India was to Las Vegas in 1960. Haltingly, she began a speaking career that would be worldwide for over three decades: "I have never spoken in public before. This is the first time, and to be here with you and to be able to tell you the love story of God's mercy for the poorest of the poor— it is the grace of God."[46] On this trip, she visited other areas of the United States and Europe. She then proceeded to Rome to gain permission for her missionaries to be answerable directly to the Vatican.

By 1965 Mother Teresa was able to send her Missionaries of Charity worldwide in their search for the poorest of the poor. In the past, missionaries had come from all over the world to bring the gospel message to India. Now, this nun and her followers set out to bring a new gospel message concerning service to the poor from India to the world. She began by opening a home for the dying in a remote village in Venezuela in the summer of 1966. From there she began her historic expansion of houses to 125 countries throughout the Americas, Europe, Asia and Africa. There would be times when leaders would not be aware of such extremely needy people in their midst. "I will find them," she would say, as she headed off to the worst areas to ferret out "her people," God's poorest of the poor. With her wry sense of humor, she once quipped: "If there are poor on the moon, we shall go there too."[47]

Mother Teresa had a deep sense of God's providence. It was her compass, and she often said that her goal was not to be successful, but to be faithful to God's plan. We have seen how meticulously she followed her call to the convent and then to serve the poor of Calcutta. Her God was a God of the "now," the present, who gradually led her to fulfill the divine will. For her, the past was gone, the future unknown, and so her commitment was "for today." She therefore saw each person placed before her and her followers as "a sign that God wants us to do something for him or her. It is not chance; it has been planned by God."[48] With a deep commitment to prayer and with careful discernment, Teresa would respond to the poor and suffering as they called out to her. She would say simply: "God showed us what to do."[49]

At the same, time Teresa always realized that God's providence remained a mystery. She accepted that divine providence was beyond our understanding, and yet she firmly believed God never lets us down. She would point out that she does not pretend to know what God is doing, and yet she always remained sure of one thing—"He doesn't make mistakes."[50] She pointed out that we are the ones who make mistakes, and that even then, God is able to draw good out of these mistakes.

Teresa always knew that she would have to do her

part. She was tireless in her efforts, meticulous in her planning, and most dedicated to details. One young man who met her at a convention rather brazenly said that she was "one shrewd cookie."[51] Another tough retired British major who worked with the homeless with Mother Teresa described her as a "plain little nun who bullies me.... Yes, she bullies me. Not unkindly, I hasten to add, but when she wants something badly she insists and one feels that one is arguing with God himself. It's an unequal struggle. I always capitulate."[52]

Mother Teresa believed that you have to work as though everything depends on you and then leave the rest to God. For her, holiness was a combination of God's grace and our free choices. It involved tremendous effort, while at the same time abandoning oneself to God.

Amazing things happened once Teresa set to work. "Everyday" miracles happened, as food and money showed up just in time. She relied on God to provide, and usually God did. Once Cardinal Cooke offered to give her a grant of five hundred dollars a month for each of her Sisters serving in New York City. The Cardinal was rather taken back when Mother Teresa refused the money and said: "Do you think, Your Eminence, that God is going to become bankrupt in New York?"[53]

But Mother Teresa also had her failures. She had to watch children and adults die before her eyes after great efforts to save them. Some of her houses were not successful, like her house in Northern Ireland, which had to be closed. When Teresa failed, she could be confused, lonely and feel like "an empty shell," but ultimately she would accept that what she set out to do was simply not God's will.

In God's Hands

She thus saw herself as an instrument in God's hands, "a pencil in the hand of God" with which God wrote what God wants; a power line through which the current of God's power could pass. She wrote: "That's the beautiful part of God, eh? That he can stoop down and make you feel that he depends on you."[54] At the same time, she believed that God would not force self on anyone.

It must have been difficult for Teresa to sustain such a humble perspective once she became a celebrity. By the late 1960s, especially through the efforts of Malcolm Muggeridge, who made several videos and wrote a celebrated book on her, Teresa was to become a world-renowned figure. She attracted enormous crowds and large contributions everywhere she spoke. She was hosted by popes, many heads of state and famous people. Also, she was presented with countless awards, including the Vatican's John XXIII Peace Prize in 1971, an Honorary Doctorate of Divinity from Cambridge University in 1977, the Nobel Peace Prize in 1979, the Bharat Ratna Award (India's highest honor) in 1980, and the Congressional Medal of Honor from the U.S. Congress in 1997.

Teresa always showed up dressed in her simple sari and sandals, and carrying her few belongings in a cloth bag. Though she bore all the constant press of the media patiently and responsively, it was never easy for her. She used to joke that all the publicity was her "purgatory." She once commented: "I have said that if I don't go to heaven for anything else, I will be going to heaven for all the publicity because it has purified me and sacrificed me."[55]

Teresa was always able to see things in the light of faith. She saw her accomplishments, and they were extraordinary indeed, as less than a drop in the ocean, and yet she saw that the ocean would be lacking something without them. She saw her work as valuable because it was God's work, and she continued through many years of physical ailments. After her first heart surgery a reporter asked her if this meant the end for her work. Her answer was simply: "I work for God. He'll tell me when it's time to stop."[56] And on another occasion when asked what would happen to all her work when she died, she replied that if the Order is God's work, it will survive.

Suffering and the Will of God

Teresa, more than most, witnessed tremendous human suffering and degradation. Her theology of suffering was quite traditional. She did not see suffering as a punishment from God, but rather as a "gift from God" to help people be more Christlike by experiencing his passion. She would tell the lepers she worked with that God must have trusted them a great deal in order to give them this terrible disease. Of course, not everyone could relate to her views of suffering. There is the amusing story of a woman suffering with cancer who was told by Mother Teresa that her cancer was a kiss from Jesus. The woman answered with the plea: "Mother Teresa, please tell Jesus to stop kissing me."[57]

Her view on suffering came from her understanding of the Incarnation. Her God came to share our suffering, and now our suffering is a way of sharing in the passion of Jesus. Such shared suffering for her was the way to salvation. This in part was what brought her to live in solidarity with suffering people. She wrote: "only by being one of them can we redeem them by bringing God into their lives and bringing them to God."[58]

When asked about the terrible suffering from AIDS, Teresa would never see this disease as a punishment from God, nor would she stand in judgment of its victims. Still, when asked what can be done about the horrific situation with AIDS, she answered, "Nothing. It's God's will."[59]

As for poverty, Teresa never claimed that to be a gift from God. She maintained that poverty was human creation, a result of greed, and the refusal to share the goods of God's creation with others. Poverty could only be solved if people gave up their selfishness, their drive to accumulate and cling to material things. So suffering is a gift from God, but poverty is not. What is difficult to ascertain is how Mother Teresa distinguished between poverty and the suffering that so often goes along with it.

In spite of Teresa's modesty and her description of herself as a mere instrument in God's hands, others felt that her presence gave them a profound experience of the divine. The Hindus have a concept called *darshan*, which means that the very sight of a holy person brings blessing. Many in India and then throughout the world felt that Mother Teresa could evoke such an experience. Jean Vanier, the well-known minister to people with mental disabilities tells the story of a teenager who saw Mother Teresa in Toronto. The girl had been having serious doubts about her religion, and when she saw how full of God and love Teresa was, her doubts vanished.

Mairead Corrigan McGuire, herself a Nobel laureate

for her peacemaking in Northern Ireland, was also notably impressed when she saw Teresa. She observed that Mother Teresa said nothing she had not heard before or read from the gospels, but that she somehow brought the gospel to life by her presence. She wrote:

> I think what makes Mother Teresa's words so effective is that she is living out her words in her life. When she tells you that she loves people and she is loved by God, one cannot for a moment doubt that fact. Standing on the hill outside the tent with the gentle rain refreshing me, looking out over the sea, and listening to Mother Teresa saying, "God loves you," I felt a deep peace and, though tired, felt the desire to rededicate myself and redouble my efforts for peace.[60]

Archbishop Helder Camara, the great champion for the poor in Brazil, also comments on the power of Teresa's presence. He met her only once, but says that the encounter was unforgettable. The archbishop noted that it was not a matter of her words, but what she *was* that made a difference. And he remarked the church should learn from her that the young today look not to nice speeches and resolutions, but to those who have the courage to bring these to life and action.[61]

Teresa was aware of the power of her presence. She often liked to quote Newman's prayer: "Help me, wherever I go, to spread thy fragrance, let me preach without preaching, wordlessly...by my example, by the force of attraction, the very imitation of my acts, the obvious fullness of love that my heart feels for thee."[62]

Even hardened prisoners could experience that blessing in her presence. When she visited San Quentin, a prisoner on death row said that he would not go out of his way to see anyone no matter how famous. But when Mother Teresa came, he hustled to the front to see her and said later that she had incredible vitality and warmth. When she left, Mother Teresa wrote the governor and asked for clemency for the prisoner.

Prayer

Teresa taught that prayer was needed in order to understand God's love for us. She explained that it was through constant prayer that she came to see the preciousness of all people in the eyes of God. She wrote: "Everything starts with prayer. Without asking God for love, we cannot possess love, and still less be able to give it to others."[63] Prayer helps us to have a clean heart, and with a clean heart, Teresa believed we are able to see God and others and radiate God's love to them.

But for Teresa, prayer was more than asking, it was listening and being intimately united with God. She often told her Sisters that without such intimacy it would be impossible for her or any of them to make the sacrifices to live among and serve the poor.

To those who said that they had difficulty praying, Teresa would say to let Jesus speak in your heart for you. Moreover, she would urge them to see their every action for others as a prayer. With great power she wrote: "He prays in me, He thinks in me, He works with me and through me. He uses my tongue to speak; He uses my brain to think. He uses my hands to touch Him in the broken body."[64]

Teresa taught her Sisters that prayer should be the heart of their spiritual lives. She established schedules in all her convents when there would be time for silence, solitude and prayer. Though her Sisters would be committed to serving the poor and destitute in the streets around them, their personal lives would be cloistered from "worldly affairs." She taught them that such solitude and silence would give them the opportunity to "be alone with God, to speak to Him, to listen to Him, to ponder His words deep in our hearts."[65] She taught them that prayer would give them the energy and the strength they needed to handle the trying situations they faced among the destitute. She insisted that prayer together would help them "stay together and love each other as Jesus loves...each one of you."[66]

Nonviolence

Living for so many years in the land of Gandhi had its effects on Teresa. She often quoted his teaching on the poor, the untouchables, and on the importance of living in solidarity with them. Teresa also seemed to have been influenced by his teachings on nonviolence. Throughout her life she opposed violence in all forms. Being witness to slaughter in her own streets, she learned the futility of war. Her view was that only love and compassion will bring true peace, not bombs and guns.

For Mother Teresa, human life was precious for it was "God's beautiful presence in the world."[67] It was therefore evil to destroy human life, whether it is in war or in abortion. She was absolute in her belief that human life belongs to God and that we therefore have no right to destroy any life. Her letter to George H. Bush and Saddam Hussein just before Desert Storm in 1991 captures her convictions. She told both of them that she was writing with tears in her eyes and the love of God in her heart as she pleaded with them for the poor and those who will become poor if the war should come about.

She begged them to be reconciled and to work for God's peace.[68]

Critics

Like all public figures, Mother Teresa had her critics. The most vociferous was Christopher Hitchens, an American journalist who produced a highly critical documentary on Teresa, objecting to her taking donations from dictators like Baby Doc Duvalier of Haiti and controversial figures like Charles Keating. He also attacked her views on abortion and birth control, especially since she lived in one of the most populated countries of the world. Hitchens's bombast got very little exposure in the United States, and where it did appear in Europe, it caused much indignation and a rush to Teresa's defense.

To such attacks Teresa merely reiterated her non-judgmental attitude and her firm commitment to the dignity of all human life. Teresa admitted that attacks on her, especially false ones, brought her suffering. With her usual good humor and honesty she said that it was one thing for her to call herself a sinner, but when someone else said it she felt upset.[69]

Others criticized Teresa for remaining too neutral in political matters. To them she merely reiterated her resolve not to mix into politics. She had little use for political matters, believing that they often led to conflict and war. She felt that if she got embroiled in politics, it would deeply affect her mission to bring love to the poor. She maintained that the poor needed deeds, not words, and she reminded her critics that it was not her task to evaluate political, economic or social systems.

She said those who feel called to change structures should follow their consciences. She pointed out that each of us must serve in whatever way we are called. As for her, she felt called to help poor individuals, and not to deal with institutions.[70]

Teresa also received broadsides from those who thought she was interested in charity but not justice. One critic used the old bromide on her that she should give the poor a rod to fish instead of simply handing them free fish. She calmly answered that the people she served were not able to stand with a fishing rod, so she gives them the fish. Then with a glint in her eye she said: "I will give them fish, and when they are able to stand, then I shall send them to you and you can give them a rod."[71]

The end of Mother Teresa's journey came on September 5, 1997. As fate would have it, her death occurred on the day of Princess Diana's funeral in London. The two women, though so very different in background and appearance had somewhat become soul sisters. Teresa had been Diana's mentor during the difficult times during her marriage and subsequent divorce. Teresa recognized the beautiful princess's hunger for love and advised her that she would receive much love if she began to serve the poor. Such influence may have prompted Diana's mission to poor children, AIDS patients and victims of land mines. When Diana was killed in a car accident, there was indeed an amazing outpouring of love for her throughout the world. This was testimony not only to her celebrity, but also to the love she had given to the poor.

On September 13, Mother Teresa's body was borne through the streets of Calcutta on the same gun carriage

CONCLUSION

that had carried Gandhi. As the carriage moved along, the countless poor she had served lined the streets to bid a sad farewell to their Mother. She was given a state funeral, attended by dignitaries from all over the world, as well as by her beloved poor.

Teresa had come quietly from Eastern Europe to convents in Ireland and then Calcutta, where she worked for almost twenty years as a teacher of girls. Then, she enigmatically left her convent to show God's love to the poorest of the poor. Eventually her life and work burst forth on the world—an explosive phenomenon of gospel living. When she died, Teresa left behind 4,000 followers and 600 houses for the poor in 125 countries. But most importantly Teresa bequeathed a shining legacy. The poorest of the poor had been brought to center stage as precious children of God, worthy of the world's love and care. And Jesus' words rang through the world with new clarity and meaning: "Whatever you do for the least of these, you do for me."

Beatification

Pope John Paul II shortened the time required for canonization in Mother Teresa's case and opened her cause of canonization less than two years after her death. In view of Mother Teresa's widespread reputation of holiness and the many favors being reported, the pope approved the decrees of her heroic virtues and miracles on December 20, 2002.

In his homily on the occasion of Mother Teresa's beatification on October 19, 2003, John Paul II proclaimed how greatly she walked the way of Jesus in love and service to all. He pointed to her as a role model for being always steeped in prayer, serving the poorest of the poor, saving countless children, and extending welcome and love to the unwanted. The pope closed by proclaiming to the world: "Let us praise the Lord for this diminutive woman in love with God, a humble Gospel messenger and a tireless benefactor of humanity. In her we honor one of the most important figures of our time."

CONCLUSION

Working on these heroes' lives and writings has been extremely inspirational and instructional for me. The whole experience has given me new insights into the mysterious and varied ways in which God moves in the lives of individuals. When I was finished, I sat down and read the manuscript through to look for patterns, common ground, themes that emerged throughout the stories of these eight lives. These are some of the things I observed.

The Influence of Parents. It should be encouraging to parents to observe the key role that parents played in the formation of these religious heroes. Parents were important early religious influences on all of these figures. The Jainism of Gandhi's mother gave him his foundation for nonviolence; Mother Teresa was taught by her own mother to serve the poor; "Daddy" King, Sr., was a role model for his son Martin; and Chardin's father inspired his son's love of nature.

Key Events in the Search. Each of these searches for God was as unique as the seeker. Some began in atheism or agnosticism and moved from truth to truth toward the Absolute. Others moved from the innocent faith of their youth to a more mature faith in the later years. Some, like Oscar Romero and Daniel Berrigan, experienced profound conversions within their own religious traditions.

But in each of these lives there were significant formative events which brought these heroes closer to an authentic God. For Oscar Romero, it was the brutal murder of his best friend, Rutilio Grande. For Gandhi it came when he was a thrown off a train. The birth of Dorothy Day's baby put her in touch with the magnificence of life and the power of creation.

At the same time, there were smaller occurrences, special impulses which moved them from truth to truth. Chardin was moved by the power within the very stones he picked up as a child. Mother Teresa was stunned by the poverty she saw in the streets of Calcutta, and Martin Luther King was stirred by the courage of Rosa Parks.

The God Within. Most of these heroes came to appreciate a God who is present within, and found this God in most unlikely places. Gandhi found his God in the untouchables, King in his humble foot soldiers as they were beaten, blasted with fire hoses and attacked by dogs. Mother Teresa found the divine in those abandoned to die in the gutter.

Providence. In one way or another, each of these individuals had a sense of God's providence working in their lives. Chardin believed that a cosmic God was the source of, goal of, and power within all creation. King firmly believed that his people were destined for freedom from segregation and oppression. Day fervently trusted that God would provide her with the food, shelter and clothing she needed to aid the poor and homeless, while Mother Teresa described herself as merely a pencil in God's hands.

False Gods. Often our heroes struggled to unveil the false gods of the world. Berrigan saw the nuclear bomb as an emerging and detestable new god, and he vehemently exposed the false gods of power, technology and money. Romero denounced the gods of privilege and profit that were worshiped by many of the wealthy in his country. And Stein recognized the frightening reemergence of ancient pagan gods in Nazism, and denounced the anti-Christian message of Hitler.

Jesus. Jesus, in one way of another, represented the presence of God for all of these heroes, even for the Hindu Gandhi. Day saw God assuming humanity in Jesus, so that God could now be found within her own neighborhood, especially among the destitute. Jesus' teachings on the God coming as the least of the brethren and in the outcasts deeply moved most of our heroes. Chardin recognized the impact of the Incarnation on material reality, and experienced the cosmic Christ as the driving force within the evolution of all creation. Stein shouldered the cross of Jesus for those suffering persecution.

Children of God. So many of our heroes were driven to protect the poor and the oppressed because they saw them all as the children of God. Mother Teresa saved countless infants, the abandoned dying, lepers and homeless people. Romero gave his life to stop the disappearance and killing of his people. King taught his people that each person is "somebody" and that, regardless of color or national or religious differences, everyone is a child of God.

Critical of Their Churches. A strong theme running through these pages is that love of one's church can drive a loyal disciple to be critical of the church's shortcomings and to call the church to fidelity toward its mission. Day chastised her church for its riches, its identification with the wealthy class and its scandalous support of war. She called her church to be faithful to its mission of peace and justice. Romero criticized his church for being a fortress, cut off from its mission to the suffering of the world. Berrigan denounced church leaders who supported war, and harshly criticized the church for its silence toward violence.

All of these heroes were faithful to their churches and yet fully realized that the church is not God, and must be constantly challenged to carry out its mission more faithfully. Many had to pay a costly personal price for this loyal criticism. Often they were isolated, ostracized or silenced by their church.

The Importance of Prayer. Prayer was a central power in the lives of all these individuals. For Mother Teresa, prayer was like breathing, essential for the life of the spirit and the way to come to understand God's love.

There is Chardin's magnificent eucharistic prayer, where he uses the world as his altar and the human struggle as his oblation. Prayer helped King overcome his fears and enabled him to forgive those who oppressed him.

The Absence of God. All of these individuals experienced the darkness, the absence of God's presence as they moved on their journey. Day often felt loneliness and isolation as the destitute hopelessly crowded around her with their endless needs. Stein felt the invisible, formless darkness enveloping her as she searched in vain for a professorship, and at times, no doubt, as she headed for the nightmare at Auschwitz. Both Romero and Berrigan dealt with bouts of depression and uncertainty as they experienced rejection from both church and government.

Nonviolence. All of these religious heroes were committed to nonviolence. Gandhi, of course, was the master, and had a profound influence on many of the others. Day stubbornly protested the many wars through which she lived. King's civil disobedience used nonviolence to gain freedom and justice for his people. One wonders how Saddam Hussein and George H. Bush felt when they opened their letters from Mother Teresa, asking them to reconcile and avoid killing innocent people.

The Many Faces of God

It is evident after exploring these heroes' lives and writings that God remains a Mystery—a reality beyond images, descriptions, dogmas and creeds. Yet, for all of these people God was often close at hand, deeply felt in the events of their lives, glimpsed in the people they met, pursuing them in their minds and hearts. God came to them with many intriguing faces: as a God of truth, of the homeless, of the mountain. God came in the cosmos, as one beckoning to prophecy, and as a fellow sufferer sharing the cross. Divinity appeared as the power of peace and in the poverty of the abandoned. Each one of us might now ask: What face has my God shown to me?

Notes

CHAPTER ONE

1. Ignatius Jesudasan, s.j., *A Gandhian Theology of Liberation* (Maryknoll, N.Y.: Orbis Books, 1984), p. 78.
2. Jesudasan, pp. 77–78.
3. Louis Fischer, *The Life of Mahatma Gandhi* (New York: Harper and Row, 1950), p. 35.
4. Fischer, p. 333.
5. Raghavan Iyer, ed., *The Moral and Political Writings of Mahatma Gandhi*. Three vols. (Oxford: Clarendon Press, 1987), vol. 1, p. 8.
6. Iyer, vol. 1, p. 451.
7. William L. Shirer, *Gandhi: A Memoir* (New York: Simon and Schuster, 1979), p. 240.
8. Dennis Dalton, *Mahatma Gandhi* (New York: Columbia University Press, 2000), p. 44.
9. Dalton, p. 45.
10. Bhikhu Parekh, *Gandhi* (New York: Oxford University Press, 1997), p. 32.
11. Parekh, p. 32.
12. Jesudasan, p. 74.
13. Iyer, vol. 2, p. 132.
14. Iyer, vol. 2, p. 82.
15. Mohandas K. Gandhi. *Autobiography* (Washington, D.C.: Public Affairs Press, 1948), p. 413.
16. Eknath Easwaran, *Gandhi: The Man* (Tomales, Calif.: Nilgiri Press, 1977) p. 122.
17. Iyer, vol. 1, 387.
18. Iyer, vol. 3, p. 1.
19. Easwaran, p. 105.

20. Fischer, p. 118.
21. Fischer, p. 117.
22. Iyer, vol. 3, p. 468.
23. Iyer, vol. 2, p. 23.
24. Fischer, p. 302.
25. Fischer, p. 576.
26. Fischer, p. 294.
27. Iyer, vol. 2, p. 159.
28. Fischer, pp. 302–303.
29. Erikson, p. 412.
30. Erikson, pp. 280–281.
31. Easwaran, p. 116.
32. Iyer, vol. 3, p. 373.
33. Iyer, vol. 3, p. 186.
34. Shirer, p. 100.
35. Shirer, p. 9.
36. Easwaran, p. 112.
37. Iyer, vol. II, p. 7.
38. Fischer, p. 304.
39. Fischer, p. 324.
40. Erikson, p. 410.
41. Iyer, vol. 3, p. 273.
42. Ibid., vol. 2, p. 10.
43. Iyer, vol. 2, p. 361.
44. Fischer, p. 277.
45. Fischer, p. 266.
46. Fischer, p. 203.
47. Easwaran, p. 101.

CHAPTER TWO

1. Dorothy Day, *The Long Loneliness* (New York: Harper and Row, 1952. Reprinted by HarperCollins, New York, 1997), p. 12.

2. Dorothy Day, *From Union Square to Rome* (Silver Spring, Md.: The Preservation of the Faith, 1938), p. 1.

3. Day, *The Long Loneliness*, p. 20.

4. James Forest, *Love is the Measure: A Biography of Dorothy Day* (New York: Paulist Press, 1986), p. 7.

5. Bridgid O'Shea Merriman, *Searching for Christ: The Spirituality of Dorothy Day* (Notre Dame, Ind.: University of Notre Dame Press, 1994), p. 19.

6. Day, *The Long Loneliness*, p. 23.

7. William Miller, *Dorothy Day: A Biography* (San Francisco: Harper and Row, 1982), p. 22.

8. Day, *The Long Loneliness*, p. 38.

9. Merriman, pp. 31–34.

10. Miller, *Dorothy Day*, p. 34.

11. Day, *The Long Loneliness*, p. 80.

12. Ibid., p. 80.

13. Ibid., p. 81.

14. Ibid., p. 85.

15. Ibid., p. 84.

16. Forest, p. 59.

17. Ibid., p. 63.

18. Ibid., p. 64.

19. Day, *Union Square*, p. 142.

20. Day, *Meditations*, p. 14.

21. Coles, Robert. *Dorothy Day: A Radical Devotion* (Boston: Addison Wesley Longman, 1987), p. 109.

22. Ibid.

23. Dorothy Day, *House of Hospitality* (New York: Sheed and Ward, 1939), p. xiii.
24. Ibid.
25. Ibid., p. 111.
26. Day, *Meditations*, p. 61.
27. Dorothy Day, *Dorothy Day, Selected Writings: By Little and by Little* (Maryknoll, N.Y.: Orbis Books, 1994), p. 235.
28. Ibid., p. 230.
29. Ibid., p. 231.
30. Forest, p. 142.
31. Dorothy Day, *Loaves and Fishes* (New York: Harper and Row, 1967), p. 10.
32. Day, *Selected Writings*, p. 61.
33. Day, *Selected Writings*, p. 72.
34. William Miller, *All is Grace: The Spirituality of Dorothy Day* (Garden City, N.Y.: Doubleday, 1987), p. 62.
35. Forest, p. 17.
36. Miller, *All is Grace*, p. 62.
37. Merriman, p. 36.
38. Miller, *All Is Grace*, p. 31.
39. Ibid., p. 99.
40. Day, *Selected Writings*, p. xli.
41. Merriman, p. 224.
42. Ibid., p. 182.
43. Day, *Selected Writings*, p. 17.
44. Day, *Meditations*, p. 13.
45. Ibid., p. 76.
46. Day, *Meditations*, p. 88.
47. Miller, *Dorothy Day*, pp. 512–513.
48. Miller, *Dorothy Day*, p. 326.
49. Miller, *All Is Grace*, p. 36.
50. Day, *Union Square*, p. 155.

51. Day, *Selected Writings*, p. 213.
52. Ibid., p. 293.
53. Day, *House of Hospitality*, p. 255.
54. Coles, p. 67.
55. Miller, *Dorothy Day*, p. 198.
56. Day, *Meditations*, p. 30.
57. Ibid., pp. 314–315.
58. Day, *Union Square*, p. 13.
59. Day, *Meditations*, p. 52.
60. Day, *Selected Writings*, p. 172.
61. Ibid., p. 263.
62. Ibid., p. 272.
63. Forest, p. 103.
64. Ibid., p. 118.
65. Ibid., p. 117.
66. Ibid.
67. Coles, p. 101.
68. Forest, p. 164.
69. Miller, *Dorothy Day*, p. 487.
70. Forest, pp. 168–169.
71. Day, *Selected Writings*, p. 363.
72. Coles, p. 158.
73. Miller, *All Is Grace*, p. 159.
74. Merriman, p. 18.
75. Ibid., p. 189.
76. Forest, p. 154.
77. Coles, p. 28.
78. Day, *Meditations*, p. 106.
79. Miller, *Dorothy Day*, p. 517.
80. Forest, p. 206.

CHAPTER THREE

1. Martin Luther King, Jr., *The Autobiography of Martin Luther King, Jr.* (New York: Warner Books, 1998), p. 45.
2. Ibid., p. 2.
3. Stephen B Oates, *Let the Trumpet Sound: A Life of Martin Luther King, Jr.* (New York: Harper and Row, 1982). p. 11.
4. Oates, p. 18.
5. King, *Autobiography*, p. 20.
6. Ibid., p. 28.
7. King, *The Papers of Martin Luther King, Jr.*, 4 vols. (Los Angeles: University of California Press, 1992), vol. 2, p. 102.
8. King, *Papers*, vol. 2, p. 188.
9. Ibid.
10. Ibid., vol. 2, p. 512.
11. Ibid.
12. King worked on his dissertation while serving as pastor. Careless and misleading uses of references, perhaps done in haste, unfortunately left him open later to charges of plagiarism.
13. Oates, p. 47.
14. King, *Autobiography*, p. 128.
15. Ibid., p. 58.
16. King, *Autobiography*, p. 60.
17. Oates, p. 67.
18. Martin Luther King, Jr., *A Testament of Hope: The Essential Writings of Martin Luther King, Jr.* (New York: Harper and Row, 1980), p. 490.
19. King, *Testament of Hope*, p. 10.
20. King, *Papers*, vol. 4, p. 191.
21. King, *Testament of Hope*, p. 509.
22. King, *Autobiography*, p. 286.

23. Oates, p. 92.
24. Oates, p. 85.
25. King, *Autobiography*, p. 105.
26. Oates, p. 127.
27. Oates, p. 442.
28. King, *Testament of Hope*, p. 111.
29. Ibid., p. 215.
30. Ibid., p. 297.
31. King, *Papers*, vol. 4, p. 166.
32. King, *Autobiography*, p. 186.
33. King, *Testament of Hope*, p. 503.
34. Ibid., p. 496.
35. King, *Papers*, vol. 4, p. 298.
36. King, *Testament of Hope*, p. 46.
37. Ibid., p. 632.
38. Ibid., p. 141.
39. King, *Autobiography*, p. 286.
40. Ibid., p. 285.
41. King, *Testament of Hope*, p. 632.
42. Ibid., p. 258.
43. Ibid., p. 6.
44. Ibid., p. 119.
45. King, *Papers*, vol. 4, p. 770.
46. Ibid., p. 151.
47. Oates, p. 246.
48. Oates, p. 221.
49. Oates, p. 410–411.
50. King, *Testament of Hope*, p. 9.
51. King, *Papers*, vol. 3, p. 478.
52. King, *Testament of Hope*, p. 215.
53. Ibid., p. 257.
54. Ibid., p. 9.
55. Ibid., p. 42.

56. Ibid., p. 485.
57. Oates, p. 229.
58. King, *Papers*, vol. 3, p. 496.
59. King, *Testament of Hope,* p. 490.
60. Ibid., p. 248.
61. Ibid., p. 251.
62. King, *Autobiography,* p. 260.
63. Oates, p. 332 ff.
64. King, *Autobiography,* pp. 358–359.
65. King, *Autobiography,* p. 366.

CHAPTER FOUR

1. Pierre Teilhard de Chardin, *The Heart of Matter.* Rene Hague, trans. (New York: Harcourt Brace Jovanovich, 1978), p. 198.
2. Teilhard, *The Heart of Matter,* p. 198.
3. Ursula King, *Spirit of Fire: The Life and Vision of Teilhard de Chardin* (Maryknoll, N.Y.: Orbis Books, 1996), p. 12.
4. King, *Spirit of Fire,* p. 14.
5. Teilhard, *The Heart of Matter,* p. 200.
6. Ibid.
7. Pierre Teilhard de Chardin, *Hymn of the Universe.* Simon Bartholomew, trans. (New York: Harper and Row 1965), p. 62.
8. Ibid., p. 64.
9. Teilhard, *Christ in World of Matter,* p. 4.
10. Teilhard, *Hymn of the Universe,* p. 43.
11. Teilhard, *The Heart of Matter,* p. 26.
12. Ibid., p. 25.
13. Teilhard, *Hymn of the Universe,* p. 54.

14. Teilhard, *The Heart of Matter*, p. 167.
15. Quoted in King, *Spirit of Fire*, p. 51.
16. Teilhard, *The Heart of Matter*, p. 179.
17. Ibid.
18. Teilhard, *Hymn of the Universe*, p. 46.
19. Ibid, p. 55.
20. Pierre Teilhard de Chardin, *Writings in Time of War*. Rene Hague, trans. (London: Collins, 1968), p. 81.
21. Ibid., p. 188.
22. Teilhard, *The Heart of Matter*, p. 66.
23. Ibid., p. 74.
24. Ibid., p. 75.
25. Pierre Teilhard de Chardin, *The Future of Man*. Norman Denny, trans. (New York: Harper and Row, 1964), p. 11 ff.
26. Ibid., p. 16.
27. Ibid., p. 19.
28. Ibid., p. 23.
29. Pierre Teilhard de Chardin, *The Vision of the Past*. J. M. Cohen, trans. (New York: Harper and Row, 1966), p. 23.
30. Ibid.
31. Ibid., p. 25.
32. Pierre Teilhard de Chardin, *Science and Christianity*. Rene Hague, trans. (London: Collins, 1968), p. 14.
33. Ibid., p. 19.
34. Pierre Teilhard de Chardin, *Let Me Explain*. Jean-Pierre Demoulin, ed. Rene Hague et al., trans. (London: Collins, 1970), p. 126.
35. Teilhard, *Science and Christianity*, p. 22.
36. Ibid., p. 32.
37. Teilhard, *Hymn of the Universe*, p. 19 ff.
38. Mary Lukas and Ellen Lukas. *Teilhard* (Garden City, N.Y.: Doubleday, 1977), p. 92.

39. Pierre Teilhard de Chardin, *The Divine Milieu* (New York: Harper and Row, 1968), p. 47.
40. Ibid., p. 114.
41. Teilhard, *The Divine Milieu*, p. 35.
42. Ibid., p. 97.
43. Ibid., p. 150.
44. Ibid., p. 33.
45. Ibid., p. 110–111.
46. Lucas, p. 109.
47. Pierre Teilhard de Chardin, *Toward the Future*. Rene Hague, trans. (New York: Harcourt Brace Jovanovich, 1975), p. 26–27.
48. Ibid., pp. 30 ff.
49. Ibid., p. 36.
50. Chardin, *Science and Christianity*, p. 89.
51. Ibid., p. 93.
52. Pierre Teilhard de Chardin, *Human Energy*, J. M. Cohen, trans. (New York: Harcourt Brace Jovanovich, 1969), p. 67–68; See also Chardin, *Toward the Future*, p. 36.
53. Pierre Teilhard de Chardin, *Activation of Energy*. Rene Hague, trans. (New York: Harcourt Brace Jovanovich, 1971), p. 381.
54. Pierre Teilhard de Chardin, *Man's Place in Nature: The Human Zoological Group*. Rene Hague, trans. (New York: Harper and Row 1966), p. 120; See also Chardin, *Science and Christianity*, p. 103.
55. Teilhard, *Human Energy*, p. 109.
56. Teilhard, *The Vision of the Past*, p. 64.
57. Teilhard, *Man's Place in Nature*, pp. 61–62.
58. Teilhard, *The Future of Man*, p. 120.
59. Teilhard, *Activation of Energy*, p. 224.

60. Pierre Teilhard de Chardin, *How I Believe*, Rene Hague, trans. (New York: Harper and Row, 1969), p. 90.

61. Ibid., p. 19.

62. Ibid., p. 70.

63. Pierre Teilhard de Chardin, *Building the Earth*. Noel Lindsay, trans. (Wilkes-Barre, Pa.: Dimension Books, 1965), p. 63.

64. Pierre Teilhard de Chardin, *Christianity and Evolution*. Rene Hague, trans. (New York: Harcourt Brace Jovanovich, 1971), p. 89.

65. Teilhard, *Activation of Energy*, p. 240.

66. Teilhard, *The Future of Man*, p. 304; Teilhard, *Human Energy*, p. 92, p. 178.

67. Teilhard, *Christianity and Evolution*, 88 ff.; 135.

68. Teilhard, *How I Believe*, p. 81.

69. Ibid., p. 4.

70. King, *Spirit of Fire*, p. 207.

71. Teilhard, *Christianity and Evolution*, p. 136–137; 218.

72. Teilhard, *The Heart of Matter*, pp. 90–95.

73. Teilhard, *Christianity and Evolution*, p. 115.

74. Teilhard, *Let Me Explain*, p. 141.

75. See Brennan Hill, "On Monkey Trials And Teilhard," *Keeping Pace*, Padraic O'Hare, ed. (Dubuque, Ia.: Brown Roa, 1996), p. 25.

CHAPTER FIVE

1. Oscar Romero, *A Martyr's Message of Hope: Six Homilies of Archbishop Oscar Romero.* (Kansas City: Celebration Books, 1981), p. 167–168.
2. James R. Brockman, *The Word Remains: A Life of Oscar Romero* (Maryknoll, N.Y.: Orbis Books, 1982), p. 31.
3. James R. Brockman, *Romero: A Life* (Maryknoll, N.Y.: Orbis Books, 1989), p. 37.
4. Ibid., p. 38.
5. Oscar Romero, *The Church Is in All of You* (Minneapolis: Winston Press, 1984). p. 830
6. Brockman, *Romero: A Life,* p. 48.
7. Ibid., p. 56 ff.
8. Romero, *The Church Is in All of You,* p. 2.
9. Ibid., p. 5.
10. Romero, *The Church Is in All of You,* pp. 6–7.
11. Ibid., p. 107.
12. Oscar Romero, *A Shepherd's Diary.* Irene B. Hodgson, trans. (Cincinnati: St. Anthony Messenger Press, 1993), p. 125.
13. Romero, *The Church Is in All of You,* p. 11.
14. Brockman, *Romero: A Life,* p. 160.
15. Oscar Romero, *Voice of the Voiceless: The Four Pastoral Letters and Other Statements* (Maryknoll, N.Y.: Orbis Books, 1985), p. 173.
16. Brockman, *Romero: A Life,* p. 145.
17. Jon Sobrino, S.J., *Archbishop Romero: Memories and Reflections* (Maryknoll, N.Y.: Orbis, 1990), p. 16.
18. Oscar Romero, *The Violence of Love* (New York: Harper and Row, 1988), p. 9.
19. Marie Dennis, et al. *Oscar Romero* (Maryknoll, N.Y.: Orbis Books, 2000), p. 9.

20. Romero, *The Violence of Love*, p. 20.
21. Ibid., p. 104.
22. Ibid., p. 108.
23. Romero, *The Church Is in All of You*, p. 14.
24. Romero, *Voice of the Voiceless*, p. 138.
25. Romero, *The Church Is in All of You*, p. 38.
26. Ibid., pp. 34–45.
27. Brockman, *Romero: A Life*, p. 187.
28. Romero, *Voice of the Voiceless*, p. 173.
29. Romero, *The Violence of Love*, pp. 146, 163.
30. Brockman, *Romero: A Life*, p. 156.
31. Brockman, p. 176.
32. Romero, *The Violence of Love*, p. 153.
33. Ibid., p. 207.
34. Dennis, p. 73.
35. Romero, *The Church Is in All of You*, p. 110.
36. Romero, *The Violence of Love*, p. 133.
37. Dennis, p. 46.
38. Romero, *The Church Is in All of You*, p. 98.
39. Dennis, p. 46.
40. Dennis, p. 17.
41. Dennis, p. 39.
42. Ibid., p. 45.
43. Ibid., p. 90.
44. Brockman, *The Word Remains*, p. 239.
45. Dennis, p. 118.
46. Romero, *Voice of the Voiceless*, pp. 107–108.
47. Ibid., p. 109.
48. Dennis, p. 95.
49. Brockman, *Romero: A Life*, p. 24.

CHAPTER SIX

1. Freda Mary Oben, *Edith Stein* (New York: Alba House, 1988), p. 29.
2. Edith Stein, L. Gelber, ed., *The Collected Works of Edith Stein. Vol. One: Life In a Jewish Family* (Washington, D.C.: ICS Publications, 1986), p. 610.
3. Waltraud Herbstrith, *Edith Stein: A Biography* (San Francisco: Harper and Row, 1985), p. 122.
4. Stein, *Life in a Jewish Family*, p. 277.
5. Herbstrith, p. 20.
6. Ibid., p. 25.
7. Hilda C. Graef, *The Scholar and the Cross: The Life and Work of Edith Stein* (Westminster, Md.: The Newman Press, 1955), p. 33.
8. See *The Collected Works of St. Teresa Avila Vol. One, The Book of Her Life.* (Washington, D.C.: ICS Publications, 1976), pp. 5–6; 24–25, pp. 3–41.
9. Stein, *Life in a Jewish Family*, p. 18.
10. Herbstrith, p. 36.
11. Stein, *Life in a Jewish Family*, p. 1.
12. Edith Stein, L. Gelber, ed., *The Collected Works of Edith Stein. Vol. 5: Self-Portrait in Letters 1916–1942* (Washington, D.C.: ICS Publications, 1993), p. 21.
13. Herbstrith, p. 38.
14. Freda Mary Oben, "Edith Stein the Woman," *Carmelite Studies*, p. 16.
15. Stein, *Life in a Jewish Family*, p. 2; *Self-Portrait in Letters*, p. 54.
16. Oben, "Edith Stein the Woman," p. 18.
17. Ibid., p. 1.
18. Ibid., p. 17 ff.
19. See Graef, p. 82 ff.
20. Ibid., p. 30.

21. Oben, "Edith Stein the Woman," p. 20.

22. Ibid.

23. Herbstrith, p. 66.

24. Ibid., p. 67.

25. Oben, "Edith Stein the Woman," p. 23.

26. Josephine Koeppel, O.C.D., *Edith Stein* (Collegeville, Minn.: Liturgical Press, 1990), p. 96.

27. Graef, p. 131.

28. Koeppel, p. 27.

29. Harry James Corgas, ed., *The Unnecessary Problem of Edith Stein* (New York: University Press of America, 1994), p. 6.

30. Herbstrith, p. 91.

31. Stein, *Self-Portrait in Letters*, p. 315.

32. Koeppel, p. 155.

33. Herbstrith, p. 95.

34. Koeppel, p. 161.

35. Ibid.

36. Graef, p. 298.

37. Ibid., p. 209.

38. Edith Stein, *The Science of the Cross* (unpublished ms.), p. 23.

39. Ibid., p. 65.

40. Ibid., p. 30 ff.

41. Ibid., p. 41.

42. Ibid., p. 139.

43. Ibid., p. 85.

44. Ibid., p. 106.

45. Ibid., p. 114.

46. Ibid., p. 115.

47. Ibid., p. 329.

48. Ibid., p. xix.

49. Edith Stein, "Ways to Know God," *The Thomist*, p. 394.

50. Ibid., p. 399.
51. Ibid., p. 403.
52. Ibid.
53. Ibid., p. 411.
54. Herbstrith, p. 103.
55. Oben, *Edith Stein*, p. 70.
56. Ibid., p. 18.
57. *L'Osservatore Romano*, October 14, 1998, p.1.
58. Ibid.

CHAPTER SEVEN

1. Daniel Berrigan, *To Dwell In Peace: An Autobiography* (San Francisco: Harper and Row, 1987), p. 3.
2. Ibid., p. 48.
3. Ibid., p. 8.
4. Ibid., pp. 48, 81.
5. Ibid., p. 92.
6. Ibid., p. 102.
7. Ibid., p. 110.
8. Ibid., p. 108.
9. Ibid., p. 143.
10. Daniel Berrigan, *The Bow in the Clouds: Man's Covenant with God* (New York: Coward-McCann, 1961), p. 152.
11. Ibid., p. 130.
12. Ibid., p. 70.
13. Daniel Berrigan, *The Bride: Essays in the Church* (New York: Macmillan, 1959), p. 36.
14. Ibid., p. 37.
15. Ibid., pp. 35, 139.

16. Daniel Berrigan, *They Call Us Dead Men: Reflections on Life and Conscience* (New York: Macmillan, 1966), p. 12.
17. Berrigan, *The Bride*, pp. 26, 53, 104.
18. Berrigan, *They Call Us Dead Men*, p. 19.
19. Berrigan, *The Bride*, p. 77.
20. Berrigan, *To Dwell In Peace*, p. 137.
21. Ibid., p. 159.
22. Ibid., p. 151.
23. Ibid., p. 174.
24. Ibid., p. 181.
25. Ibid., p. 185.
26. Berrigan, *No Bars To Manhood*, 1970, p. 26.
27. Berrigan, *To Dwell In Peace*, p. 21.
28. Michael True, *Daniel Berrigan: Poetry, Drama, Prose* (Maryknoll , N.Y.: Orbis Books, 1988), p. 118.
29. Daniel Berrigan, *Lights on in the House of the Dead: A Prison Diary* (Garden City, N.Y.: Doubleday, 1974), p. 295.
30. Daniel Berrigan, *The Words Our Savior Gave Us* (Springfield, Ill.: Templegate, 1978), p. 61 ff.
31. Daniel Berrigan, *Steadfastness of the Saints: A Journal of Peace and War in Central and North America* (Maryknoll, N.Y.: Orbis Books, 1985), p. 49.
32. John Dear, ed., *Apostle of Peace* (Maryknoll, N.Y.: Orbis Books, 1996), p. 78.
33. Ibid., p. 96.
34. Daniel Berrigan, *America Is Hard to Find* (Garden City, N.Y.: Doubleday, 1972). p. 101.
35. Berrigan, *Lights on in the House of the Dead*, pp. 17, 166.
36. Berrigan, *Steadfastness of the Saints*, p. 22.
37. Berrigan, *Lights on in the House of the Dead*, p. 92.

38. Daniel Berrigan, *The Dark Night of Resistance* (Garden City, N.Y.: Doubleday, 1971), p. 26.
39. Daniel Berrigan, *Whereon to Stand: The Acts of the Apostles and Ourselves* (Baltimore: Fortkamp, 1991), pp. 7, 36.
40. Dear, p. 7.
41. Berrigan, *Lights on in the House of the Dead*, p. 232.
42. True, p. 168.
43. Daniel Berrigan, *Jeremiah: The World, The Wound of God* (Minneapolis: Fortress Press, 1999), p. 21.
44. Berrigan, *The Words Our Savior Gave Us*, p. 105.
45. Dear, p. 17.
46. Ibid., p. 175.
47. Ibid., p. 51.
48. Berrigan, *The Dark Night of Resistance*, p. 5.
49. Berrigan, *Lights on in the House of the Dead*, p. 51.
50. Berrigan, *Steadfastness of the Saints*, p. 39.
51. Berrigan, *Whereon to Stand*, p. 112.
52. Daniel Berrigan, *The Trial of the Catonsville Nine* (Boston: Beacon Press, 1970), p. 85.
53. Berrigan, *The Words Our Savior Gave Us*, p. 18.
54. Dear, p. 11.
55. True, p. 182.
56. Berrigan, *Steadfastness of the Saints*, p. 105.
57. Berrigan, *America Is Hard to Find*, p. 135.
58. Daniel Berrigan, *Consequences: Truth and...* (New York: Macmillan, 1967), p. 32.
59. Dear, p. 132.
60. Berrigan, *They Call Us Dead Men*, p. 181.
61. Berrigan, *America Is Hard to Find*, p. 104.
62. Berrigan, *Lights on in the House of the Dead*, p. 230.
63. Berrigan, *America Is Hard to Find*, p. 36.

64. Daniel Berrigan, *The Geography of Faith: Conversations Between Daniel Berrigan, When Underground, and Robert Coles* (Boston: Beacon Press, 1971), p. 71.
65. Berrigan, *America Is Hard to Find*, p. 101.
66. Berrigan, *The Geography of Faith*, p. 129.
67. Berrigan, *Consequences: Truth and...*, pp. 9, 28.
68. Berrigan, *The Geography of Faith*, p. 115.
69. Ibid., 141.
70. Berrigan, *Consequences: Truth and...*, p. 87.
71. Berrigan, *To Dwell In Peace*, p. 156.
72. Berrigan, *Jeremiah*, p. 19.
73. Daniel Berrigan, *False Gods, Real Men: New Poems* (New York: Macmillan, 1969), p. 27.

CHAPTER EIGHT

1. Eileen Egan, *Such a Vision of the Street* (Garden City, N.Y.: Doubleday, 1985), p. 357.
2. David Porter, *Mother Teresa: The Early Years* (Grand Rapids, Mich.: Eerdmans, 1986). p. 4.
3. Egan, p. 13.
4. Ibid., p. 15.
5. Ibid., p. 21.
6. Porter, p. 32.
7. Franca Zambonini, *Teresa of Calcutta* (New York: Alba House, 1982), p. 45.
8. Porter, p. 40.
9. Kathryn Spink, *I Need Souls Like You: Sharing in the Work of Mother Teresa Through Prayer and Suffering* (San Francisco: Harper and Row, 1984), p. 19.
10. Zambonini, p. 17.

11. Egan, p. 25.
12. Ibid.
13. Ibid., p. 30 ff.
14. Egan, pp. 38, 41, 95.
15. Mother Teresa, Jaya Chaliha and Edward Le Joly, eds., *The Joy in Loving: A Guide to Daily Living with Mother Teresa* (New York: Viking, 1997), p. 307.
16. Ibid.
17. Christian Feldman, *Mother Teresa: Love Stays* (New York: Crossroad, 1998), p. 29.
18. Joanna Hurley, *Mother Teresa: A Pictorial Biography* (Philadelphia: Courage Books, 1997), p. 61.
19. Egan, p. 59.
20. Mother Teresa, *The Joy in Loving*, p. 46.
21. Ibid., p. 61.
22. Ibid., p. 60.
23. Feldman, p. 32.
24. Egan, p. 149.
25. Mother Teresa, *The Joy in Loving*, p. 142.
26. Feldman, p. 97.
27. Mother Teresa, *The Joy in Loving*, p. 391.
28. Egan, p. 345.
29. Mother Teresa, *The Joy in Loving*, p. 151.
30. Ibid., p. 141.
31. Egan, p. 111.
32. Ibid., p. 419.
33. Mother Teresa, *The Joy in Loving*, p. 75.
34. Feldman, p. 56.
35. Ibid.
36. Mother Teresa, *A Gift from God* (New York: Harper and Row, 1975), pp. 8–9.
37. Ibid., p. 60.

38. Mother Teresa, *Words to Live By* (Notre Dame, Ind.: Ave Maria Press, 1983), p. 425.
39. Sunita Kumar, *Mother Teresa of Calcutta* (San Francisco: Ignatius Press, 1998), p. 58.
40. Mother Teresa, *The Joy in Loving,* p. 41.
41. Ibid., p. 50.
42. Ibid., p. 101.
43. Zambonini, p. x.
44. Egan, p. 42.
45. Feldman, p. 75.
46. Egan, p. 118.
47. Spink, p. 102.
48. Mother Teresa, *The Joy in Loving,* p. 63.
49. Egan, p. 44.
50. Mother Teresa, *The Joy in Loving,* p. 419.
51. Hurley, *Mother Teresa: A Pictorial Biography,* p. 78.
52. Anne Sebba, *Mother Teresa, Beyond the Image* (Garden City, N.Y.: Doubleday, 1997), p. 65.
53. Egan, p. 241.
54. Robert Serrou, *Teresa of Calcutta: A Pictorial Biography* (New York: McGraw-Hill, 1980), p. 73.
55. Serrou, p. 87.
56. Hurley, *Mother Teresa: A Pictorial Biography,* p. 114.
57. Mother Teresa, *Words to Live By,* p. 64.
58. Mother Teresa, *A Gift from God.*
59. Sebba, p. 155.
60. Egan, p. 392.
61. Serrou, p. 116.
62. Ibid., p. 97.
63. Mother Teresa, *The Joy in Loving,* p. 41.
64. Egan, p. 427.

65. Mother Teresa, *A Fruitful Branch on the Vine, Jesus* (Cincinnati: St. Anthony Messenger Press, 1998), p. 69.
66. Ibid., p. 51.
67. Mother Teresa, *The Joy in Loving*, p. 3.
68. Hurley, *Mother Teresa: A Pictorial Biography*, p. 110.
69. Mother Teresa, *Words to Live By*, p. 178.
70. Mother Teresa, *A Gift from God*, p. 46.
71. Mother Teresa, *Words to Live By*, p. 388.

Bibliography

MOHANDAS GANDHI

Dalton, Dennis. *Mahatma Gandhi* (New York: Columbia University Press, 2000).

Easwaran, Eknath. *Gandhi, the Man: The Story of His Transformation* (Tomales, Calif.: Nilgiri Press, 1997).

Erikson, Erik H. *Gandhi's Truth: On the Origins of Militant Nonviolence* (New York: W.W. Norton, 1969).

Fischer, Louis. *The Life of Mahatma Gandhi* (New York: Harper and Row, 1950).

Gandhi, M. K. *Autobiography* (Washington, D.C.: Public Affairs Press, 1948).

Iyer, Raghavan, ed. *The Moral and Political Writings of Mahatma Gandhi*. Three vols. (Oxford: Clarendon Press, 1987).

Jesudasan, Ignatius, S.J. *A Gandhian Theology of Liberation* (Maryknoll, N.Y.: Orbis Books, 1984).

Parekh, Bhikhu. *Gandhi* (New York: Oxford University Press, 1997).

Shirer, William L. *Gandhi: A Memoir* (New York: Simon and Schuster, 1979).

DOROTHY DAY

Coles, Robert. *Dorothy Day: A Radical Devotion* (Boston: Addison Wesley Longman, 1987).

Day, Dorothy. *From Union Square to Rome* (Silver Spring, Md.: The Preservation of the Faith, 1938).

_____. *House of Hospitality* (New York: Sheed and Ward, 1939).

_____. *Loaves and Fishes* (New York: Harper and Row, 1967).

_____. *The Long Loneliness* (New York: Harper and Row, 1952. Reprinted by HarperCollins, New York, 1997).

_____. *Meditations* (New York: Paulist, 1970).

Ellsberg, Robert, ed. *Dorothy Day, Selected Writings: By Little and by Little* (Maryknoll, N.Y.: Orbis Books, 1994).

Forest, James. *Love is the Measure: A Biography of Dorothy Day* (New York: Paulist Press, 1986).

Merriman, Bridgid O'Shea. *Searching for Christ: The Spirituality of Dorothy Day* (Notre Dame, Ind.: University of Notre Dame Press, 1994).

Miller, William. *All is Grace: The Spirituality of Dorothy Day* (Garden City, N.Y.: Doubleday, 1987).

_____. *Dorothy Day: A Biography* (San Francisco: Harper and Row, 1982).

MARTIN LUTHER KING, JR.

King, Coretta Scott. *My Life with Martin Luther King, Jr.* (New York: Holt Rinehart and Winston, 1969).

King, Martin Luther, Jr., Carson Clayborne, ed. *The Autobiography of Martin Luther King, Jr.* (New York: Warner Books, 1998).

_____. *The Measure of a Man* (Philadelphia: Christian Education Press, 1959).

————, Carson Clayborne, ed. *The Papers of Martin Luther King, Jr.*, 4 vols. (Los Angeles: University of California Press, 1992).

———. *Strength to Love* (New York: Harper and Row, 1963).

————, James Melvin Washington, ed., *A Testament of Hope: The Essential Writings of Martin Luther King, Jr.* (New York: Harper and Row, 1980).

———. *The Trumpet of Conscience* (New York: Harper and Row, 1967).

———. *Where Do We Go from Here?* (New York: Harper and Row, 1967).

———. *Why We Can't Wait* (New York: Harper and Row, 1963).

Oates, Stephen B. *Let the Trumpet Sound: A Life of Martin Luther King, Jr.* (New York: Harper and Row, 1982).

PIERRE TEILHARD DE CHARDIN

Cuenot, Claude. *Teilhard de Chardin: A Biographical Study.* Vincent Colimore, trans. Rene Hague, ed. (Baltimore: Helicon, 1965).

Francoeur, Robert T. *The World of Teilhard* (Baltimore: Helicon Press, 1961).

King, Ursula. *Spirit of Fire: The Life and Vision of Teilhard de Chardin* (Maryknoll, N.Y.: Orbis Books, 1996).

———. *Towards a New Mysticism: Teilhard de Chardin and Eastern Religions* (New York: Seabury Press, 1980).

Lubac, Henri de. *Teilhard de Chardin: The Man and his Meaning* (New York: New American Library, 1965).

Lukas, Mary and Ellen Lukas. *Teilhard* (Garden City, N.Y.: Doubleday, 1977).

Mooney, Christopher F. *Teilhard de Chardin and the Mystery of Christ* (New York: Harper and Row, 1966).

North, Robert Grady. *Teilhard and the Creation of the Soul* (Milwaukee: Bruce, 1967).

Teilhard de Chardin, Pierre. *Activation of Energy.* Rene Hague, trans. (New York: Harcourt Brace Jovanovich, 1971).

_____. *The Appearance of Man.* J. M. Cohen, trans. (New York: Harper and Row, 1965).

_____. *Building the Earth.* Noel Lindsay, trans. (Wilkes-Barre, Pa.: Dimension Books, 1965).

_____. *Christianity and Evolution.* Rene Hague, trans. (New York: Harcourt Brace Jovanovich, 1971).

_____. *The Divine Milieu* (New York: Harper and Row, 1968).

_____. *The Future of Man.* Norman Denny, trans. (New York: Harper and Row, 1964).

_____. *The Heart of Matter.* Rene Hague, trans. (New York: Harcourt Brace Jovanovich, 1978).

_____. *How I Believe.* Rene Hague, trans. (New York: Harper and Row, 1969).

_____. *Human Energy.* J. M. Cohen, trans. (New York: Harcourt Brace Jovanovich, 1969).

_____. *The Human Phenomenon* (Portland, Ore.: Sussex Academic Press, 1999).

_____. *Hymn of the Universe.* Simon Bartholomew, trans. (New York: Harper and Row 1965).

_____. *Let Me Explain.* Jean-Pierre Demoulin, ed. Rene Hague et al., trans. (London: Collins, 1970).

_____. *Letters from a Traveller* (New York: Harper 1962).

_____. *The Making of a Mind: Letters from a Soldier-Priest, 1914–1919.* Rene Hague, trans. (New York: Harper

_____. *Man's Place in Nature: The Human Zoological Group.* Rene Hague, trans. (New York: Harper and Row 1966).

_____. *On Love and Happiness* (San Francisco: Harper and Row, 1984).

_____. *The Phenomenon of Man.* Bernard Wall, trans. (New York: Harper, 1959).

_____. *Science and Christianity.* Rene Hague, trans. (London: Collins, 1968).

_____. *Toward the Future.* Rene Hague, trans. (New York: Harcourt Brace Jovanovich, 1975).

_____. *The Vision of the Past.* J. M. Cohen, trans. (New York: Harper and Row, 1966).

_____. *Writings in Time of War.* Rene Hague, trans. (London: Collins, 1968).

OSCAR ROMERO

Brockman, James R. *Romero: A Life* (Maryknoll, N.Y.: Orbis Books, 1989).

_____. *The Word Remains: A Life of Oscar Romero* (Maryknoll, N.Y.: Orbis Books, 1982).

Dennis, Marie, et al. *Oscar Romero* (Maryknoll, N.Y.: Orbis Books, 2000).

Romero, Oscar. *The Church Is in All of You* (Minneapolis: Winston Press, 1984).

_____. *A Martyr's Message of Hope: Six Homilies of Archbishop Oscar Romero* (Kansas City: Celebration Books, 1981).

_____. *A Shepherd's Diary*. Irene B. Hodgson, trans. (Cincinnati: St. Anthony Messenger Press, 1993).

_____. *The Violence of Love* (New York: Harper and Row, 1988).

_____. *Voice of the Voiceless: The Four Pastoral Letters and Other Statements* (Maryknoll, N.Y.: Orbis Books, 1985).

Sobrino, Jon. *Archbishop Romero: Memories and Reflections* (New York: Orbis, 1990).

EDITH STEIN

Batzdorff, Suzanne M. *Edith Stein: The Jewish Heritage of a Catholic Saint* (Springfield, Ill.: Templegate Publishers, 1990).

Bordeaux, Henry. *Edith Stein: Thoughts on Her Life and Times* (Milwaukee: Bruce, 1959).

Corgas, Harry James, ed. *The Unnecessary Problem of Edith Stein* (New York: University Press of America, 1994).

Graef, Hilda C. *The Scholar and the Cross: The Life and Work of Edith Stein* (Westminster, Md.: The Newman Press 1955).

Herbstrith, Waltraud. *Edith Stein: A Biography* (San Francisco: Harper and Row, 1985).

Koeppel, Josephine, O.C.D., *Edith Stein* (Collegeville, Minn.: Liturgical Press, 1990).

Oben, Freda Mary. *Edith Stein* (New York: Alba House, 1988).

Sawicki, Marianne. *Body, Text and Science* (Dordrecht: Kluwer, 1997).

Stein, Edith (Sister Teresia Benedicta á Cruce). "Ways of Knowing God," *The Thomist*, vol. IX, 1946, 379–420.

_____. L. Gelber, ed. *The Collected Works of Edith Stein. Vol. One: Life In a Jewish Family* (Washington, D.C.: ICS Publications, 1986).

_____. L. Gelber, ed. *The Collected Works of Edith Stein. Vol. 5: Self-Portrait in Letters 1916–1942* (Washington, D.C.: ICS Publications, 1993).

Sullivan, John, O.C.D., ed. *Carmelite Studies* (Washington D.C.: ICS Publications, 1987).

DANIEL BERRIGAN

Berrigan, Daniel. *The Trial of the Catonsville Nine* (Boston: Beacon Press, 1970).

_____. *America Is Hard to Find* (Garden City, N.Y.: Doubleday, 1972).

_____. *The Bow in the Clouds: Man's Covenant with God* (New York: Coward-McCann, 1961).

_____. *The Bride: Essays in the Church* (New York: Macmillan, 1959).

_____. *Consequences: Truth and...* (New York: Macmillan, 1967).

_____. *The Dark Night of Resistance* (Garden City, N.Y.: Doubleday, 1971).

_____. *To Dwell In Peace: An Autobiography* (San Francisco: Harper and Row, 1987).

_____. *False Gods, Real Men: New Poems* (New York: Macmillan, 1969).

_____. *The Geography of Faith: Conversations Between Daniel Berrigan, When Underground, and Robert Coles* (Boston: Beacon Press, 1971).

_____. *Jeremiah: The World, The Wound of God* (Minneapolis: Fortress Press, 1999).

_____. *Lights on in the House of the Dead: A Prison Diary* (Garden City, N.Y.: Doubleday, 1974).

_____. *Selected and New Poems* (Garden City, N.Y.: Doubleday, 1973).

_____. *Steadfastness of the Saints: A Journal of Peace and War in Central and North America* (Maryknoll, N.Y.: Orbis Books, 1985).

_____. *They Call Us Dead Men: Reflections on Life and Conscience* (New York: Macmillan, 1966).

———.*Whereon to Stand: The Acts of the Apostles and Ourselves* (Baltimore: Fortkamp, 1991).

_____. *The Words Our Savior Gave Us* (Springfield, Ill.: Templegate, 1978).

Dear, John, ed. *Apostle of Peace* (Maryknoll, N.Y.: Orbis Books, 1996).

True, Michael. *Daniel Berrigan: Poetry, Drama, Prose* (Maryknoll , N.Y.: Orbis Books, 1988).

MOTHER TERESA

Egan, Eileen. *Such a Vision of the Street* (Garden City, N.Y.: Doubleday, 1985).

Feldman, Christian. *Mother Teresa: Love Stays* (New York: Crossroad, 1998).

Hurley, Joanna. *Mother Teresa: A Pictorial Biography* (Philadelphia: Courage Books, 1997).

Kumar, Sunita. Mother Teresa of Calcutta (San Francisco: Ignatius Press, 1998).

Mother Teresa. *A Fruitful Branch on the Vine, Jesus* (Cincinnati: St. Anthony Messenger Press, 1998).

_____. *Words to Live By* (Notre Dame, Ind.: Ave Maria Press, 1983).

_____. *A Gift from God* (New York: Harper and Row, 1975).

_____. Chaliha, Jaya and Edward Le Joly, eds. *The Joy in Loving: A Guide to Daily Living with Mother Teresa* (New York: Viking, 1997).

Porter, David. *Mother Teresa: The Early Years* (Grand Rapids, Mich.: Eerdmans, 1986).

Sebba, Anne. *Mother Teresa, Beyond the Image* (Garden City, N.Y.: Doubleday, 1997).

Serrou, Robert. *Teresa of Calcutta: A Pictorial Biography* (New York: McGraw-Hill, 1980).

Spink, Kathryn. *I Need Souls Like You: Sharing in the Work of Mother Teresa Through Prayer and Suffering* (San Francisco: Harper and Row, 1984).

Zambonini, Franca. *Teresa of Calcutta* (New York: Alba House, 1982).

H

Heidegger, Martin, 198, 204
heroism, meaning of, 1–4, 12
Hinduism, 7, 8, 13, 26–27, 30,
 261, 262, 266–268, 271,
 279, 289
Hitchens, Christopher, 283
Hitler, Adolf, 32, 68, 72, 108,
 158–159, 193–194, 196,
 198, 204, 210, 289. *See also*
 Nazism
Holland, 210–211, 217–218, 220
Holocaust, 75, 191–192,
 217–220. *See also* anti-
 Semitism
Hoover, J. Edgar, 49
Hopkins, Gerard Manley, 241
Hound of Heaven (Francis
 Thompson), 48
Hussein, Saddam, 282–283,
 291
Husserl, Edmund, 194–198,
 204

I

Imitation of Christ (Thomas á
 Kempis), 45, 51
imprisonment, experience of,
 19, 27, 37, 47, 49–50,
 74–75, 223, 239–240, 242,
 244, 249
India, 6, 9–10, 14–16, 18–20, 24,
 25–30, 35–39, 103, 139,
 255–256, 257–285

Indian National Congress,
 11, 36
Iraq, 249, 282–283
Islam, 13, 38, 124, 127, 257,
 261, 262, 267
Ithaca (NY), 238–239

J

Jainism, 7, 268, 287
James, William, 51
Jesuits. *See* Society of Jesus
Jesus Christ
 influence of on spiritual
 heroes, 9, 13, 17, 30,
 56–59, 64, 71, 96, 97,
 106–107, 118, 159–160,
 174–175, 182, 183, 187,
 198–199, 207, 208, 217,
 219, 220, 221, 233–234,
 247–248, 265, 289
 as prophet, 155, 174–175,
 183
 role of in human affairs,
 97, 134–135, 141, 147–148,
 150
John XIII, Pope, 76
John of the Cross, Saint, 67,
 209, 212–215
John Paul II, Pope, 151,
 171–172, 184–185, 203,
 220–221
Johnson, Lyndon, 114
Johnson, Mordecai, 88
John the Baptist, Saint, 155